TERTULLIAN

THE TREATISE
AGAINST HERMOGENES

ADVERSUS HERMOGENEM

ANCIENT CHRISTIAN WRITERS

THE WORKS OF THE FATHERS IN TRANSLATION

EDITED BY

JOHANNES QUASTEN, S. T. D.
Catholic University of America
Washington, D.C.

JOSEPH C. PLUMPE, Ph.D.
Pontifical College Josephinum
Worthington, O.

No. 24

TERTULLIAN

THE TREATISE
AGAINST HERMOGENES

TRANSLATED AND ANNOTATED
BY

J. H. WASZINK
Professor of Latin
University of Leyden

NEWMAN PRESS

New York, N.Y./Ramsey, N.J.

Nihil Obstat:
    J. Quasten
      Cens. Dep.

Imprimatur:
    Patricius A. O'Boyle, D.D.
      Archiep. Washingtonen.
      die 19 Martii 1956

Library of Congress
Catalog Card Number: 56-13257

ISBN: 0-8091-0148-3

PUBLISHED BY PAULIST PRESS
Editorial Office: 1865 Broadway, New York, N.Y. 10023
Business Office: 545 Island Road, Ramsey, N.J. 07446

PRINTED AND BOUND IN THE UNITED STATES OF AMERICA

CONTENTS

PAGE

INTRODUCTION

1. THE DOCTRINE OF HERMOGENES AND ITS REFUTATION
   BY TERTULLIAN 3

2. ANALYSIS 13

3. MANUSCRIPTS, EDITIONS, AND TRANSLATIONS . . 17

TEXT

FOREWORD: WHO IS HERMOGENES? 26

THE BASIC ARGUMENTS OF HERMOGENES . . . 27

REFUTATION OF HERMOGENES' CONCEPTION OF MATTER . 31

HIS NOTION OF THE *EXISTENCE* OF MATTER IS UNTEN-
ABLE ON LOGICAL GROUNDS 31

a) MATTER AS EQUAL WITH GOD . . . 31

b) MATTER AND EVIL 39

POSITIVE PROOF FROM SCRIPTURE FOR A CREATION
OUT OF NOTHING 48

HERMOGENES' MISINTERPRETATION OF SCRIPTURE IN
SUPPORT OF HIS NOTION OF MATTER . . . 51

a) GENESIS 1.1 51

EXCURSUS: THE ASSUMPTION THAT SCRIPTURE SHOULD
HAVE MADE EXPLICIT MENTION OF A CREATION
OUT OF NOTHING IS GRATUITOUS . . . 55

b) GENESIS 1.2a 57

c) GENESIS 1.2b 66

FURTHER POSITIVE PROOF FOR A CREATION OUT OF
NOTHING 71

HERMOGENES' NOTION OF THE *CONDITION* OF MATTER IS
CONTRADICTORY AND ABSURD 73

CONTENTS

HERMOGENES FURTHER CONTRADICTS HIMSELF REGARDING
MOTION IN MATTER 79

HERMOGENES' THEORY ON *THE ACT OF CREATION*
REFUTED 82

EPILOGUE 85

NOTES

TO THE INTRODUCTION 89

TO THE TEXT 101

INDEX 173

TERTULLIAN

THE TREATISE AGAINST HERMOGENES

INTRODUCTION

1. The Doctrine of Hermogenes and its Refutation by Tertullian

Hermogenes had first lived in the eastern part of the Empire, perhaps at Antioch: this supposition derives from the fact that Theophilus of Antioch had composed a special refutation of his doctrine in which, according to Eusebius,[1] this apologist 'had made use of quotations from the Apocalypse of St. John.' Later[2] Hermogenes settled in Carthage, where he exercised the profession of painter.[3] He was still living when Tertullian wrote the *Adversus Hermogenem*;[4] a second treatise directed against him, the *De censu animæ adversus Hermogenem*,[5] was probably written a few years later.[6]

For our knowledge of the doctrine of Hermogenes the chief sources are Hippolytus, *Elenchos* 8.17 and 10.28, the present treatise, and the quotations from, and allusions to, the *De censu animae* which occur in the *De anima*.[7] Less important are three passages in other works of Tertullian (*Adv. Valent.* 16 and *De praescr. haer.* 30.12 ff. and 33.9), Theodoret, *Haer. fab. comp.* 1.19, Filastrius, *De haer.* 44, and St. Augustine, *De haer.* 41.

With regard to the data furnished by the present treatise, it should be kept in mind that Tertullian is by no means always a reliable authority for the doctrines of his opponents: frequently he records their arguments in a distorted form which makes it easier either to refute or to ridicule them;[8] moreover, for the sake of his argument he now and then makes them say things which at the best they

3

might have said.[9] Fortunately, in the present case it is comparatively easy to discern Hermogenes' actual statements, since as a rule literal quotations and records of his assertions are clearly marked as such and are also often repeated in essentially or even exactly the same form; further, a not inconsiderable part of the information given by Tertullian is corroborated by Hippolytus. In the notes on the following description of Hermogenes' doctrine I have included all the testimonies which I consider to be trustworthy.

Apart from one curious assertion concerning Christ which will be discussed at the end of this chapter, everything known about this doctrine is intimately concerned with the fundamental conviction that God must have created the universe out of pre-existent matter.

Hermogenes opened [10] the discussion of his subject by saying that God must have created all things either out of Himself, or out of nothing, or out of something. The impossibility of the first case was proved by him on purely logical grounds.[11] The second proposition was eliminated on the ground that if God had created the universe out of nothing, He must of necessity have created evil of His own will.[12] Tertullian states so often that Hermogenes wished to remove God from the creation of evil [13] as to justify our inference that primarily for this reason he came to assert a creation out of something, and, therefore, out of matter.[14] It was probably in this connection that he observed that a creation from nothing should have been explicitly mentioned in Scripture.[15]

As a second proof for this thesis, Hermogenes adduced the argument that God, as He was always God, must also always have been Lord, which implied that He must always have been Lord of something—Lord of matter. Matter, then must always have existed,[16] and for this reason it must have been without an origin, and also eternal.[17] In order to preclude the conclusion that matter, being unborn and eternal, should be accorded equality with God, Hermogenes pointed out that God retains undiminished His essence and His authority, since He possesses several predicates which matter does not have: He alone is the only and first Creator of all things, the Lord of the universe, and comparable to no other being.[18] Further, Tertullian's statement that 'Hermogenes refutes the argument of some people who say that evil things were necessary to shed light upon the essence of the good things,'[19] shows that he did not limit himself to setting forth his own convictions, but also refuted divergent solutions of the problem of the origin of evil.

In accordance with this doctrine Hermogenes asserted matter to be designated by the words 'beginning' in Gen. 1.1[20] and 'earth' in Gen. 1.2, while in the latter passage the past tense of the verb ('was'), in his conviction, denoted its eternal existence in the past, and the adjectives 'invisible' and 'unfinished' of the Alexandrine version referred to its chaotic condition.[21] For the point last mentioned he found further confirmation in the mentioning of four 'elements' in Gen. 1.2,[22] which elements he considered to have been the constituent parts of matter,[23] inasmuch as Scripture does not say that they were created by God.

As to the condition of matter, it may be regarded as certain that he asserted it to be without any quality. In the first place, he declared it to be neither corporeal nor incorporeal.[24] According to Tertullian,[25] this contradicts his statement that bodies were created out of its corporeal part, while its unordered motion was its incorporeal element;[26] we may be sure, however, that this division into a corporeal and an incorporeal 'part' was invented by Tertullian.

The argument probably ran as follows: 'If matter were actually corporeal, its incorporeal motion would not be understandable, and if it were actually incorporeal, it would be impossible that corporeal things were created out of it; therefore it must have been neither corporeal as such nor truly incorporeal.' Going on in the same trend, he explicitly asserted matter to be neither good nor evil,[27] thus explaining in the same way that both good[28] and evil things could be made out of it. Finally, he declared that matter was infinite—probably both in space and in time.[29]

It is *a priori* plausible that after asserting matter to have always existed together with God, he did not say that first matter had existed on its own in a chaotic condition and that then God created the universe out of it, but that he considered God's action on matter to have taken place from eternity. This supposition is confirmed by the fact that he said that God, as He was always Lord, was also always Creator. Of this activity of God he gave the following description: God, seeing the chaotic motion of matter—which motion may be compared to that of boiling water[30]—set a part of matter in order, thereby creating a cosmos[31] out of chaos, and did so by merely appearing and approaching it, just as beauty exercises an influence by its mere appearance and a magnet by its mere proximity.[32] Such action of God on matter was possible because God and matter have something in common, namely, an eternal motion which they owe to themselves.[33] Since matter is infinite,[34] God did not 'regulate' the whole of it but only a part. Everything that matter contained is present in all those parts of it which have been converted by God into the cosmos, so that 'the whole (that is, of matter as it was originally) can be known from its parts (that is, its modeled parts)';[35] therefore, matter may be called the model of the world, and the world 'the image of matter.'[36]

From the fact that matter could thus be modeled by God, Hermogenes deduced that it was subject to change and for that reason divisible.[37] Tertullian points out a striking contradiction between two assertions about its motion: it is described as very swift, and again as extremely slow;[38] probably Hermogenes had said that, like matter itself, the motion of matter was deprived of any quality.

From these data it does not yet become clear just how Hermogenes explained the origin of evil. We only know that he taught that it drew its origin from matter; on the other hand, he asserted that matter was in point of fact neither good nor evil. Since it is unthinkable that he should have contended that evil resulted from God's *fabricatio* of matter, its origin must be sought in matter itself. The most plausible solution is that given by Uhlhorn,[39] that evil consisted in the chaotic condition of matter, which condition did not disappear entirely in consequence of the creation, since a part of infinite matter was not modeled at all and, secondly, God's contact with the other part was of such a kind (cf. n. 32) that there, too, something of the original chaos remained.

As to Hermogenes' psychology, I may refer to the detailed discussion of this subject in my edition of the *De anima*, pp. 7*–14*. Hermogenes declared the soul to have sprung from matter, not from the breath of God, as we read in Gen. 2.7; he even substituted 'spirit' (πνεῦμα) for 'breath' in this text, arguing, in all probability, as follows (I repeat my reconstruction of this argument, *op. cit.* p. 12*):

It is certain that the soul has fallen into sin. Now Holy Scripture mentions 'the breath of God' in its description of the creation of man, whence it may be concluded that this 'breath,' too, if it formed part of the soul, would have fallen into sin; but then we would have to suppose a relation between God and sin, which is a blasphemous supposition and which must, there-fore, be rejected. Hence it must be demonstrated that the sub-stance breathed by God into Adam's face could not fall into sin; if we adhere to the reading 'breath of life,' this is not im-mediately evident, but if the text has 'spirit of life,' everybody will reject the possibility that this substance could have fallen into sin. This being established, we are obliged to conclude that this 'spirit of life' did not belong to the nature of the sinful soul. And so the nature of the soul did not spring from God, and for that reason must have originated from matter; the 'spirit of life,' breathed by God into Adam's face, was no more than an *accidens* of the soul.

Since, as is evident from further statements by Tertullian, this accidental 'spirit of life' was considered by Hermo-genes to comprise all the higher faculties of the soul, these faculties—including immortality— were, in his conviction, also *accidentia,* and so could be lost. It is thus that we can explain a curious sentence in the treatise *De origine animae* (C. P. Caspari, *Kirchenhistorische Anecdota* [Christiania 1883] 229): *Cesset Ermogenis qui dicit nihil post mortem hominem futurum;* this, as Uhlhorn has observed,[40] must refer to the loss of immortality in consequence of sin.

Hermogenes' Christology was, as it seems, generally in accordance with the doctrine of the New Testament,[41] but from Ps. 18.6 he inferred that after His Resurrection and before ascending to the Father, Christ left His body in the sun.[42] Filastrius[43] and St. Augustine[44] know of him only as a Patripassian; it is impossible for us to check the correct-ness of this statement.

As I have set forth in a paper, 'Observations on Tertul-lian's Treatise against Hermogenes,' *Vigiliae Christianae* 9

(1955) 129–47, there can be no doubt about the fact that
Hermogenes' doctrine on matter was primarily influenced
by Platonism, as was also observed by Hippolytus (*Elench.*
8.17). Indeed his description of unborn matter tallies completely with the interpretation of the 'secondary' [45] matter
of the *Timaeus* which we can fix for the first time in
Aristotle's *De caelo,* [46] and to which the Middle Platonists
added the statement that this matter is without an origin.
In this context we may refer to Plutarch, *De an. procr. in
Timaeo* 5 (1014 B), to Atticus—cf. Eusebius, *Praep. evang.*
15.6.4.—and the Platonists mentioned by Proclus in his
commentary on the *Timaeus* 84F. [47] Special attention
should be given to Albinus, since this author was much
read in the latter half of the second century and was also
well known to Tertullian [48] (perhaps also to Hermogenes).
For further details, see the paper just referred to.

We now come to the question whether Tertullian's
refutation of this doctrine was all his own elaboration, or
whether he also drew upon an authority. On account of a
similarity between the record given by Hippolytus and
Adv. Herm. 1, Harnack [49] has already expressed the supposition that the lost treatise *Against the Heresy of Hermogenes*
by Theophilus of Antioch must have been a source of the
Adversus Hermogenem; this supposition is confirmed by
the circumstance that, as Professor Quispel has demonstrated, [50] several arguments occurring in the second book
of Tertullian's refutation of Marcion have been taken from
the refutation of this same heretic by Theophilus.

The only thing which we know about this treatise
Against the Heresy of Hermogenes is that the author frequently quoted the Apocalypse of St. John, and, as we
have already seen, [51] Tertullian's quotations from the
Apocalypse in the *Adversus Hermogenem* are indeed fairly

frequent.[52] Apart from this, we have an opportunity in-
directly to fix a possible dependence of Tertullian on
Theophilus. Since early Christian authors—Tertullian in
the very first place—not infrequently discuss the same topic
in more than one of their works, striking similarities between the *Adversus Hermogenem* and the only work of
Theophilus which we still have, the three books *To Autolycus*, may hark back to Theophilus' own refutation of
Hermogenes: in such case the conclusion seems to be admissible that Tertullian borrowed the relevant topic from
this latter treatise, and that Theophilus either repeated it in
the books *To Autolycus*, or first discussed it in the last
treatise and afterwards dealt with it again in the *To Autolycus*. The following similarities deserve to be mentioned:

a) The thesis that God created the universe out of nothing
is defended by Tertullian throughout the present treatise
and so maintained by Theophilus, *Ad Autol.* 2.10: 'And in
the first place they (the prophets) have taught us unani-
mously that He made the universe out of nothing. For
nothing was equal in time to God, but, being His own
space,[53] and free of want, and existing before all time, He
willed to create man that He might be known by him';[54]
again, writing more in detail, *ibid.* 2.4: 'How can it be
surprising, if God made the cosmos out of underlying (the
term of Hermogenes!) matter? For when a craftsman[55]
has received his material from someone, he makes out of it
whatever he wants; but the power of God is shown by
this, that He makes whatever He wants out of nothing.'
Now it may be observed of course that the fact that
Hermogenes denied the possibility of a creation out of
nothing was already of itself a reason for Tertullian to up-
hold the contrary thesis, so that in regard to this point he

need not have been dependent on Theophilus. It should be kept in mind, however, that whereas Justin still assumed a creation by God from pre-existent matter,[56] and Tatian changed this in that he declared God first to have created matter and then the universe out of it,[57] Theophilus was the first who sought to prove the necessity of a creation from nothing, doing so by means of an argument which also occurs in the fourth chapter of the present treatise: 'Plato and his followers acknowledge that God is unborn and the Father and Creator of the universe; next they assume the existence of matter which, like God, is unborn, and they say that matter is equal in time[58] to God. But if God is unborn and matter is unborn, God is no longer the Creator of the universe, if we follow the Platonists, nor, as far as they are concerned, is the existence of a monarchy of God established. Further, as God, being unborn, is not subject to change, thus matter, if it was unborn, was also unchangeable and equal to God (*deo aequalis*, so Tertullian in more than one passage)' (*ad Autol.* 2.4).

b) As Professor Quispel (*op. cit.* 52) has pointed out, Theophilus' description of the Trinity as 'God, the Word (qualified as "the Servant"), and Wisdom' (*Ad Autol.* 2.10) is unique in his time. Now, as the same scholar observes, two statements in the *Adversus Hermogenem* tally with this description: in 22.3 Tertullian calls the Word *ministrum*, and in 18.3 (*sophia autem spiritus*) he, too, identifies the third *persona* of the Trinity with Wisdom. We may add that in the same context both authors not only assert that it is the Word (identified by both with Wisdom[59]) which, rather than matter, assisted God in the creation of the world,[60] but that both also quote Proverbs ch. 8 in this connection,[61] and interpret the 'beginning' of Gen. 1.1 as referring to the Word (-Wisdom).[62]

c) Finally, Professor Quispel has made it probable that Theophilus understood the expression 'the hands of God' as referring to both the Word and Wisdom (2.18);[63] now an interpretation entirely similar to this occurs in *Adv. Herm.* 45.1 (cf. also note 375 to the text) : *Denique 'sermone eius caeli confirmati sunt et spiritu ipsius universae virtutes eorum'* (Ps. 32.6). *Hic est dei dextera* (cf. Isa. 48.13) *et manus ambae.*

d) As Professor R. M. Grant has shown (*Vig. Christ.* 3 [1949] 229), four quotations from Genesis in the *Adversus Hermogenem* have characteristic features which are attested by no existing Greek manuscript but which also occur in the *Ad Autolycum.*

e) One may wonder whether not the sentence (*Adv. Herm.* 32.1), *Providit* (i.e. Scripture) *tamen et hebetes et insidiosos qui*, etc., is in imitation of a sentence in Theophilus' refutation of Hermogenes, *Ad Autol.* 2.10: 'For the Wisdom of God knew beforehand that some people were to say senseless things,' etc.

From the points discussed it may, in my opinion, be inferred that Tertullian used Theophilus' refutation of Hermogenes as an authority for his own work on the same subject. Our material is of course much too scanty to discern between arguments which he borrowed from Theophilus and such as he invented himself; yet it seems probable that the claim of contradictions in the doctrine of Hermogenes, which occurs especially often in the chapters concerning the condition and the motion of matter (35–40 and 41–43), should be ascribed to Tertullian.

Though the chronology of Tertullian's treatises has been

discussed by an ever-growing number of scholars,[64] only few definite results have been attained. With regard to the present treatise only the following points can, in my opinion, be made:

a) The *Adversus Hermogenem* does not show any traces of Montanism.[65] The first traces of this heresy are found in the 29th chapter of *Adv. Marcionem* I,[66] which chapter can hardly have been written after 207 A.D., since the 15th chapter of the same book was certainly composed in that year.[67] So we may conclude that the present treatise was composed before 207 A.D.

b) From the first sentence—*Solemus haereticis compendii gratia de posteritate praescribere*—it is clear that the *Adversus Hermogenem* is later than the treatise *De praescriptione haereticorum* which, in its turn, must be later than the *Apologeticum*, 198 A.D.[68] So we may conclude that the present treatise was composed between 198 and 207 A.D. Among the other arguments brought forward in favour of a more accurate datation not one, so it appears to me, is convincing.

At all events, it is clear that the *Adversus Hermogenem* was composed before the treatise *De censu animae adversus Hermogenem* [69] for the latter monograph must have been written almost immediately before[70] the *De anima* which in turn is undoubtedly posterior to *Adv. Marc.* 2 and probably composed between 210 and 213 A.D.[71]

2. ANALYSIS

A. Preface (1): The personality of Hermogenes and the origin of his doctrine.

B. The basic arguments of Hermogenes (2 f.):
   a) God made the universe either out of Himself or out of nothing or out of something. He cannot have made it out of Himself nor out of nothing—in the latter case He would be the creator of evil; therefore He must have made it out of something, that is, out of matter (2).
   b) God was always Lord, wherefore He must always have been Lord of something, that is, of matter (3.1). Refutation of this argument (3.2–7).

C. Refutation of Hermogenes' conception of matter (4–45.3).[72]
   I. Regarding the *existence* of matter (4–34).
      a) Refutation on logical grounds (4–16).
         1) Matter as equal to God (4–9).
            α) By proclaiming matter to be unborn, unmade, and eternal, Hermogenes makes it equal to God—which is impossible (4).

            β) Hermogenes says that 'the authority and substance of God remain intact,' because He 'retains undiminished His attributes of being the Only God and the First and the Creator of all things and the Lord of all, and of being incomparable to any being,' and that, therefore, matter, though sharing with God the attribute of eternity, is inferior to Him. But in reality Hermogenes makes matter equal to God (5–7).

            γ) By saying that God needed matter in order to create the universe, Hermogenes makes matter even superior to God (8).

δ) If matter was thus equal to God, God cannot have been its Lord (9).

2) Matter and evil (10–16).

α) If God permitted the existence of evil in matter, He is still the creator of evil (10).

β) If matter is eternal, it cannot be evil (11).

γ) If eternal matter should nevertheless be evil, it would be impossible to explain that good things were created out of it (12–14).

δ) From γ) it follows that good things must have been created out of nothing; but then the same must hold of evil things (15).

ε) Further proof for the assertion that God made evil things out of nothing (16).

Excursus: Positive proof from Scripture for a creation out of nothing (17 f.).

α) Rom. 11.34 ff. (17).

β) Prov. 8.22 ff.: God's 'associate' in the creation was not matter, but the Wisdom of God which is the Son (18).

b) Refutation of Hermogenes' interpretation of Scriptural passages (19–32).

1) Gen. 1.1 (19 f.).

α) Refutation of Hermogenes' interpretation (19).

β) The correct interpretation: *principium*= *dei sophia* (20).

Excursus: Refutation of the assertion that a creation out of nothing should have been explicitly mentioned in the Scripture (21 f.).

2) Gen. 1.2a (23–29).
3) Gen. 1.2b (30–32).

    Excursus: Positive proof for a creation out of nothing (33. f.).

    α) Even if all things were created out of matter, they would yet eventually draw their origin from nothing (33).

    β) Scripture states explicitly that the universe will eventually be reduced to nothing, wherefore it must also have been created from nothing (34).

II. Regarding the *condition* of matter (35–40).

  a) Corporeality (35 f.):

    1) Hermogenes' statement that matter is neither corporeal nor incorporeal (35).

    2) His statement to the contrary that it is partly corporeal and partly incorporeal (36).

  b) Good and evil (37): Hermogenes' assertion that matter is neither good nor evil.

  c) Locality (38): Hermogenes assigns a place to matter (by placing it below God); this contradicts his statement that it is infinite in space.

  d) Change (39 f.):

    1) Hermogenes says that the changes experienced by matter prove it to have been divisible—which contradicts the assertion of its eternity. Further difficulties concerning 'the parts of matter' (39).

    2) Contradiction between the statements that matter experienced a change for the better (i.e. by the creation) and that it was 'the model of the world.' Impossibility involved in the latter statement (40).

III. Regarding the *motion* of matter (41–43).

    a) This motion is described as both chaotic and equable. Further Hermogenes in this argument makes good and evil corporeal substances (41).

    b) Hermogenes says that this motion both aimed at formlessness and desired to be set in order by God. Next he observes that God was not equal to matter, but then subjoins that matter had something in common with God. Refutation of the latter point (42).

    c) Finally, this motion is described as both vehement and slow. The assertions that matter was not evil by nature and that after its regulation by God it lost its (evil) nature, lead to further contradictions (43).

IV. Regarding *the act of creation* (44–45.3).
Hermogenes' theory that God created the universe by merely appearing to and approaching matter (44). Scripture shows by which of His qualities God created the universe (45. 1–3).

D. Epilogue (45.4): Hermogenes' picture of matter is in reality a picture of Hermogenes himself.

3. Manuscripts, Editions, and Translations

Thanks to the intensive study of the manuscripts of Tertullian by various scholars, among whom Dr. Kroymann[73] and Dr. Borleffs[74] should receive first mention, the main lines of the history of the text are gradually becoming clear. It is to be assumed that because of Tertullian's Montanism his works, though still much read by authors of the third and fourth centuries (who, however, generally avoid mentioning his name), were not collected into one official *corpus*, but remained isolated [75] until three different collections were made. It seems probable that this took place in Gaul before the issuance of the directive *De recipiendis et non recipiendis libris* (preserved in the so-called *Decretum Gelasianum* of ca. 500 A.D.) which condemned all treatises of Tertullian as heretical works. [76]

The first of these collections, which is now represented only by the manuscript of Troyes 523 (*Trecensis*) of the twelfth century, [77] contained the following five treatises: *Adversus Iudaeos, De carne Christi, De resurrectione mortuorum* (=*De carnis resurrectione*), *De baptismo*, and *De paenitentia*. Kroymann [78] supposes it to be due to the Semipelagians, also called *Massilienses*; calling attention to the subscription found at the end of the *Adversus Iudaeos*—'*Nicasi vivas in XRo dno nro Amen*'—he ventures to assume that it was made at the instance of Vincent of Lerins (Nicasius=Vincentius), who is known to have been a fervent admirer of Tertullian. Several readings furnished by the *Trecensis* occur in the marginal notes of the edition by Martin Mesnart (1545).

The second collection is found in the *Agobardinus* (Paris, Bibl. Nat. lat. 1622), which manuscript was presented by Agobard, archbishop of Lyons (816–840 A.D.), to the church of St. Etienne in that city. According to the *indiculus*, the *Agobardinus* once contained twenty-one treatises; [79] its latter part, from the end of the *De carne Christi* onward, is lost—a particularly regrettable fact, since five of these works are found in no existing manuscript, [80] and so are lost forever. It seems probable that an *Ambrosianus* (G 58 sup., tenth or eleventh century) which contains chapter 9 ff. of the *De oratione*, derives from the same collection. [81]

The third collection consisting of *De carnis resurrectione*, Novatian's *De Trinitate*, the *De spectaculis, De praescriptione haereticorum, De pudicitia,* and *De ieiunio,* is probably due to a Montanist, a Tertullianist, or a student of Novatian.[82] It is represented by three manuscripts all of which are now lost: a codex of the Cathedral Library of Cologne (No. 833 in the oldest catalogue), a *Corbeiensis,* and the *Codex Ioannis Clementis Angli,* used by Jacques de Pamèle (Pamelius) for his edition (1579).[83] Dr. G. I. Lieftinck, Keeper of Manuscripts of the Library of Leyden University, has identified a fragment of the *De spectaculis* which exhibits a text very similar to that of the edition by Sigismond Ghelen (Gelenius, 1550).[84] He has made it very plausible—and further investigation by Dom Eligius Dekkers has advanced this probability to certainty[85]—that this fragment once formed part of the Cologne manuscript. As to the *vetustissimus codex* which Mesnart pretended to have used for the *editio princeps* of a part of the *De patientia,* nine other treatises of Tertullian,[86] and Novatian's *De Trinitate* and *De Cibis Iudaicis,* Dom Dekkers has made it highly probable that in reality Mesnart did not follow one old codex, but used—rather arbitrarily—a fairly great number of manuscripts.[87] Finally, as to the *Masburensis* '*ex ultima Brittannia,*'[88] which Gelenius affirmed to have used for the text of the treatises first edited by Mesnart and, further, of the *De carnis resurrectione,* the *De praescriptione haereticorum,* and the *De monogamia,* this remains a highly questionable matter: according to Dom Dekkers, Gelenius may have used only the *Coloniensis* besides Mesnart's edition.[89]

These three collections, mutually independent, have in common that they do not contain any of Tertullian's anti-heretical works. Much is to be said for Kroymann's supposition[90] that the latter treatises were always accepted by the Church because of their evident utility for the refutation of a great number of heretics—in this context it is justly pointed out that, in his praise of Tertullian, Vincent of Lerins mentions these treatises only—so that they did not require any special protection as furnished by the three collections mentioned.

Perhaps traces of a fourth collection may be found in the fragments of the *De pudicitia*, *De paenitentia*, *De patientia*, and *De spectaculis* which occur in the *Codex Ottobonianus latinus* 25 of the fourteenth century.[91] About the origin of this collection nothing can as yet be said, but the text frequently comes very near to that of the editions by Mesnart and Ghelen.

Thus the *Adversus Hermogenem* is found only in the last collection, the history of which has been studied with particular success by Dr. Kroymann. It must have been made—perhaps in Spain[92]—after the others, since, owing to the addition of the anti-heretical works, it contains a considerably greater number of treatises, namely, twenty-seven,[93] and since here for the first time an order taking into account the subject-matter of the treatises is observed.[94] It is to be supposed that the text was emended, supplemented, and also interpolated by a redactor. Apart from a number of Italian manuscripts of the fifteenth century which have all been copied from still existing manuscripts and which, therefore, are of no importance for the establishment of the text,[95] this collection is represented by seven manuscripts:

1) *Paterniacensis* 439, now *Selestatiensis* 88 (P), of the eleventh century; from the monastery of Payerne (Peterlingen) on the Lake of Neuchâtel, now in the municipal library of Sélestat (Schlettstadt) in Alsatia.[96]

2) *Montepessulanus* H 54 (M), of the eleventh century; from a monastery in Troyes.[97]

3) *Florentinus Magliabechianus Conv. soppr.* VI, 9 (N), of the fifteenth century.[98]

4) *Florentinus Magliabechianus Conv. soppr.* VI, 10 (F); written at Pforzheim in 1426 by two Franciscan monks, Thomas von Lymphen and Johannes von Lautenbach.[99]

5) *Luxemburgensis* 75 (X), of the end of the fifteenth century; from the abbey of Münster (Luxemburg).[100]

6) *Leidensis Bibl. Publ. Lat.* 2 (L), of the fifteenth century; written in Italy.[101]

7) *Vindobonensis* 4194 (V), now at Naples, whereas the second part of the same manuscript has always remained in that city (*Neapolitanus* VI, C, 36); fifteenth century, written in Italy.[102]

To these manuscripts must be added the first and third editions by Beatus Rhenanus which appeared respectively in 1521 and 1539. For his first edition Rhenanus used P and a manuscript from Hirsau (Württemberg), the now lost *Hirsaugiensis*. If a treatise was found in P, he took this as the base of his text, adding in the margin variants from H. For the thirteen treatises not found in P he based the text on H; and here his marginal notes are no more than conjectures.[103] In his third edition he made use of a collation of a manuscript from Gorze (near Metz), the *Gorziensis*. Unfortunately this collation seems to have been far from accurate and, moreover, not to have been used by Rhenanus systematically.[104]

As to the filiation of these manuscripts, I cannot enter here into details, and must limit myself to reproducing Kroyman's *stemma*: [105]

COMMON SOURCE OF THE FOURTH COLLECTION (lost)[106]

```
Cluny MS (lost)¹⁰⁷                    lost copy
        |                                 |
   ┌────┴────┐                         H (lost)
   P         M                            |
             |                  ┌─────────┼──────────┐
        ┌────┴────┐             X       Rhen.¹    Pforzheim
        G         N                               MS (lost)
        |                                             |
      Rhen.³                                    ┌──────┴──────┐
                                           lost copy          F
                                                |
                                           ┌────┴────┐
                                           V         L
```

Of the existing manuscripts all except the Montpellier codex, which probably is the first part of a manuscript in two volumes—as were the Cluny MS and H also [108]—contain the *Adversus Hermogenem*; it had the last place among the anti-heretical treatises and therewith in the entire collection. [109] In general it may be said that the 'left branch' of the family is superior to the right. [110] It is particularly to be regretted that the part of M containing the present treatise is lost, since P is full of mistakes. [111]

From the *stemma* it is clear that theoretically no existing manuscript can be neglected for the establishment of the text: G and N are necessary to reconstruct M, P and the reconstruction of M must lead to the readings of the Cluny MS. In the right branch, first the common source of V and L must be reconstructed, this reconstruction together with

F must lead to the lost Pforzheim MS, and from this, in combination with X and the readings of Rhenanus' first edition (in this case marginal notes, since the *Adversus Hermogenem* did occur in P) we must come to H. However, since V and L give a greatly corrupted text, the reconstruction of their common source is of no great importance;[112] it was neglected by Kroymann in his edition in which he based his reconstruction of H on the *consensus* of F and the first edition of Rhenanus; he then did not yet know of the existence of the Luxemburg MS. In 1935 attention was drawn to this codex by Dr. Borleffs who at the same time pointed out that among the sources for the reconstruction of H this manuscript must take first place.[113]

ɣ   ɣ   ɣ

With regard to the establishment of the text, only two editions deserve to be mentioned, those of Oehler (1854) and Kroymann (1906). Oehler unfortunately based his text on L, that is, the worst manuscript in existence, and the first edition of Rhenanus; further, he added all the divergent readings found in the editions of Mesnartius, Gelenius, Pamelius, and Rigaltius, thus only adding a great number of mostly erroneous conjectures.[114] Hence the basis of his edition could scarcely have been worse chosen; nevertheless, his knowledge of, rather, his feeling for, the style of Tertullian was such that his edition can still be used without too great risk or harm.

Kroymann's edition was based on P, N, F and the first and third editions of Rhenanus; he did not consult V and L, though in a former publication he had granted them a certain importance;[115] and, as we have seen above, he could not yet consult X.[116] Thus the base of Kroymann's edition is constituted on considerably more solid ground than Oehler's, but unfortunately his establishment of the text contains so great a number of erroneous or at least unnecessary conjectures that a discussion of all the divergences of my translation as compared with his edition would have unduly increased the bulk of the notes. It is for this reason that I have thought it preferable to note only the differences from Oehler's text.

Among existing translations the best is undoubtedly that by Heinrich Kellner which is based on Oehler's text.[117] It is still very readable and generally reliable, though a not inconsiderable number of misunderstandings is found in it; the most important of these passages are treated in the notes.

Oehler's text was also used for the translation by P. Holmes.[118] Compared with Kellner's version, this translation is now much more old-fashioned and the number of misunderstandings is also greater. In general it may be said that the English translation of other treatises of Tertullian by Thelwall in the same series is superior to the work of Holmes. Nevertheless, I gladly acknowledge my indebtedness to this version from which I have now and then borrowed the translation—rarely of complete sentences, yet of parts of them. I did not now consult the French translation by A. de Genoude,[119] since I found it practically worthless when I prepared my edition of the *De anima*.

The only commentary which somehow deserves the term is found in Oehler's notes; the older commented editions (Pamelius, Iunius, Rigaltius, even La Cerda) are particularly disappointing in the case of the *Adversus Hermogenem*.

As the present volume was about to go to press, it seemed well to add a few remarks by way of supplement.

I have just published an edition of the text based on new collations of all the important manuscripts and editions, this appearing as *Stromata* 5 (Utrecht-Antwerp 1956); I regret that I could not offer it with the present translation, but I hope that the full notes given for all difficult passages of the text will make up for its absence. The translation itself is as literal as possible. I realize that this striving to give above all an accurate rendering of the original has not infrequently compelled me to write down laborious and, in some cases, also immoderately long sentences; but I trust I may point out in my defence that in this very treatise, and especially in its first part, Tertullian's style is—even for his standard—particularly intricate and must have given great difficulties to his Roman readers, so that an 'easy' translation (especially by dividing up the long sentences) would in fact have been a falsification.

The notes are primarily devoted to the explication of the text as it stands; indeed in a treatise based on so few data (collected in the Introduction) and containing so many subtle and over-subtle arguments, the interpretation of these arguments (often combined with the establishment of the text) is for the present the commentator's principal task. I am, however, quite aware of the fact that my work, which is the work of a classical philologist, will in the future need to be supplemented by a more theological interpretation.

THE TREATISE AGAINST HERMOGENES

FOREWORD. WHO IS HERMOGENES?

Ch. 1] When[1] dealing with heretics, to shorten the discussion, we follow the practice of laying down against them a peremptory rule based on the lateness ⟨of their appearance⟩.[2] For in as far as the rule of truth is earlier, reporting as it did ⟨, among other things,⟩ the occurrence in the future of heresies,[3] just so far can all later doctrines *a priori* be regarded as heresies, as it is their future existence which was announced by the older rule of truth. 2. Now the doctrine of Hermogenes is such a new doctrine. He is,[4] briefly, a man who up to the present is living in the world, and, moreover, a born heretic; he is, further, a turbulent man, who takes loquacity for eloquence, regards impudence as staunchness of character, and considers the slandering of individuals the normal task of a good conscience. Apart from this, he exercises the art of painting, a thing forbidden ⟨by the Law⟩,[5] and marries continuously:[6] he defends the Law of God[7] in the interest of his lust, and despises it[8] in the interest of his art. He is a falsifier in two respects, with his cautery[9] and with his pen, and an adulterator in every respect, with regard both to his preaching and to the flesh. ⟨Nor is this surprising⟩: to begin with, the contagion coming from marrying people[10] produces a bad smell, and, secondly, the Apostle's Hermogenes did not stick to the rule of faith either.

3. But let us forget the man—it is his doctrine which I have to look into. He does not seem to acknowledge another Lord, but he makes a different being of Him whom

he acknowledges in a different way; nay, since He will not have it that it was out of nothing that He made all things, he takes from Him everything which constitutes His divinity.[11] 4. Thus he turned away from the Christians to the philosophers,[12] from the Church to the Academy and the Porch, and from there he took the idea of putting matter on the same level with the Lord—for in his opinion matter, too, has always existed, being neither born nor created, without any beginning or end, and it is from matter that the Lord afterwards made all things.

THE BASIC ARGUMENTS OF HERMOGENES

Ch. 2] To [13] this first and utterly lightless shade this very bad painter has given colour by means of the following arguments.[14] His fundamental thesis is that the Lord made all things either out of Himself, or out of nothing, or out of something, in order that, upon demonstrating that He could neither have made them out of Himself nor out of nothing, he may consequently affirm the remaining possibility—that He made them out of something; and, next, that that something was matter.

2.[15] He says that He could not have made ⟨all things⟩ out of Himself, because whatever things the Lord had made out of Himself would have been parts of Him; but that He cannot be divided into parts, since, being the Lord, He is indivisible and unchangeable and always the same. Further, if He had made something out of Himself, that something would have been part of Himself; but everything, both that which was made and which He was to make, must be considered imperfect, because it would be made of a part and because He would make it of a part. 3. Or if, being whole, He had made the whole, He must have been whole and not whole at the same time, since it would have befitted Him to be both whole, in order to make Himself, and not whole, in order that He might be made out of Himself. Now this is extremely difficult, for if He existed, He could not be made, but would exist ⟨already⟩, whereas if He did not exist, He could not ⟨in that case⟩ make anything because He would be nothing. But He who always exists, ⟨so he asserts,⟩[16] does not come into existence but exists for ever and ever. So ⟨he concludes that⟩ He did not make all things out of Himself, since He was [17] not of such a condition that He could have made them out of Himself.

4. Further, that He could not have made them out of nothing is asserted by him on the following argument: He defines the Lord as a good, even a very good, being, whose desire to make good and very good things is as strong as He is ⟨good and very good⟩;[18] nay, He desires and makes nothing that is not good and very good. Therefore, good and very good things only should have been made by Him, in accordance with His condition. It is found, however, that evil things as well have been made by Him—certainly not by His decision and His will, for then He would not have made anything unfitting or unworthy of Himself. Now that which He thus did not make by His own decision must be understood to have been made from the faultiness of something, which without a doubt means that it originated from matter.

Ch. 3] He [19] adds also another argument, that God, who was always God, was always Lord as well,[20] and that there never was a time when He was not Lord;[21] that further He could not possibly have been considered to be Lord always, as also He always was God, if in the past there had not always existed something of which He could be considered to have been always Lord, and that therefore matter was always together with God, who was Lord at the same time. 2. This concoction of his I shall hasten to refute here and now; I thought fit to add it at such length for the sake of such as are not informed on the matter, that they may know that his other arguments, too, can be understood and refuted with equal ease.

3. The name of *God*, so we say, has always been with Himself and in Himself, but not always that of *Lord*, for the state of being inherent in the one is different from that of the other: *God* is the name of the substance itself, that is, of the Divinity, but *Lord* is the name, not of a substance, but of a power. The substance has always existed together with its name, which is *God*, but ⟨the name⟩ *Lord* was a later addition, since it is the name of something coming in addition. 4. For ever since things began to exist upon which the power of a lord could operate, from that moment, by the accession of this power, He both became Lord and received that name. ⟨Nor is this surprising,⟩ for God is also a Father, and God is also a Judge, but He has not always been Father and Judge for the simple reason that He has always been God; for He could not be Father before the Son was, [22] nor Judge before there was sin. Now there was a time when for Him there existed neither sin nor the Son, the former to make God[23] a Judge, and the latter, a Father. In the same way He did not become Lord before the things existed of which He was to become the Lord. He was to become Lord but once in the course of time: as He became Father by the Son and as He became Judge by sin, so He also became Lord by the things which He had made to serve Him.

5. Do I seem to argue too subtly,[24] Hermogenes? Vigorous support is given to us by Scripture which has

conferred the two names on Him with proper distinction and which has made known each of them at its proper time. Thus it mentions ⟨the name of⟩ God, which He was always, at the very outset: *In the beginning God made heaven and earth*, [25] and in the sequel, as long as He was making the things of which He was to be Lord, it only writes 'God'— 'And *God* said,' 'and *God* made,' 'and *God* saw,' and nowhere yet do we find 'Lord.' But when He had completed the creation of all things, and above all man himself, who, being a lord himself [26] in the literal sense of the word, was to have a full understanding of His being the Lord, and who was also soon to give Him that surname [27]—at that moment Scripture, too, added the name 'Lord': *And God the Lord took man whom He had formed*; [28] *And God the Lord commanded Adam.* [29] From that moment He is Lord who before had been God only, since He had something of which He could be ⟨Lord⟩. For to Himself He was God, but to the things ⟨created⟩ He became God and Lord at one and the same time. 6. Hence, in just so far as Hermogenes will suppose matter to have always existed on the ground that the Lord existed always, in so far will it be certain that ⟨originally⟩ there existed nothing, because it is certain that the Lord ⟨as such⟩ did not always exist.

7. I shall also add an argument of my own for the sake of those who lack understanding, among whom Hermogenes represents the extreme; [30] I shall do so by turning back against him arguments taken from his own stock. [31] When, for instance, he denies that matter was either born or made, I find that, even on this premise, the name of Lord was not appropriate to God with regard to matter, for [32] matter must needs have been free: not having an origin, it did not have a creator; it owed its existence to nobody, and hence it was subservient to nobody. Therefore, the fact that matter

experienced God as its Lord ⟨only⟩ from the moment
when God began to exercise His power over it by creating
out of matter, demonstrates that He was not the Lord of
matter during all the time when He was so by all means![33]

REFUTATION OF HERMOGENES' CONCEPTION OF MATTER

HIS NOTION OF THE *Existence* OF MATTER IS UNTENABLE ON LOGICAL GROUNDS

a) *Matter as Equal to God*

Ch. 4]   At[34] this point I shall finally begin to discuss matter, that, according to Hermogenes, God makes disposition of it, when at the same time it is presented as equally
unborn, equally unmade, equally eternal, with neither beginning nor end. For what other essential property of God
is there than eternity?[35] What other essence[36] has eternity
than ever to have existed and to go on existing forever
because of its privilege of being without a beginning and
without an end? 2. If this is the special property of God, it
must belong to God alone, since it is His special property—
for clearly[37] if it should be assigned to some other being as
well, it will no longer be the special property of God, but a
property shared with that being to which it is also assigned.
3. For[38] *though there be that are called gods* in name, *whether
in heaven or in earth,* yet *for us there is but one God, the Father,
of whom are all things;*[39] and therefore it is still more necessary that in our conviction that should belong to God alone
which is the special property of God, and which, as I have
said, ⟨if shared with another being,⟩ would be no longer
His special property, since it would ⟨then⟩ belong to another being ⟨as well⟩. Now, if God is this (i.e. One), it

must necessarily be a unique property that it may belong to One. 4. Or what will be unique and singular, if not that to which nothing equal can be produced? What will be principal, if not that which is above all things and before all things and from which all things have originated?[40]

5. It is by having these qualities alone that He is God, and by having them alone, that He is One. If another being should possess them as well, then there will be as many gods as there are beings which possess the qualities proper to God. Thus it is that Hermogenes brings in two gods—he introduces matter as equal to God. 6. But God must be One, because that is God which is supreme; but nothing can be supreme save that which is unique; but nothing can be unique if something can be put on a level with it; but matter will be put on a level with God, when it is authoritatively declared[41] to be eternal.

Ch. 5] 'But[42] God is God, and matter is matter.' As if a difference in names could prevent equality, when an identity of condition[43] is asserted! Let their nature be different, let also their form be not the same, as long as the essence of their condition itself is one and the same. God is unborn—is not matter unborn as well?[44] God is eternal—is not matter eternal too? Both are without beginning, both without end; both, too, are the authors of the universe, both He who made it and ⟨matter⟩ out of which He made it—for it is impossible that matter should not also be considered to be an author of all things, seeing that the universe consists of it.

2. How will he answer? Will he say that matter is not *ipso facto* on the same plane with God if it possesses something of God, because, not possessing everything ⟨belonging to God⟩, it does not lead to a complete equalization?

What more then did he leave for God that he should seem not to have assigned to matter the full amount of ⟨qualities of⟩ God? ⟨'No, matter is not equal to God,'⟩ says he, 'were it only because, even if such be the condition of matter, the authority and substance of God remain intact by which He is the only and first Creator and is declared to be the Lord of all things.' 3. But Truth exacts the unity of God thus—by insisting that whatever belongs to God Himself, belongs to Him alone; for ⟨only⟩ then will it belong to Himself, if it belongs to Him alone, and so it will be impossible to admit the existence of another god, since no one is permitted to possess anything of God. 4. 'In that case,' you say, 'we do not possess anything of God either.' On the contrary, we do possess something of Him, and we shall do so, but by receiving it from Himself, not from ourselves. For we shall even be gods, if we deserve to be those of whom He pronounced: *I have said Ye are gods*,[45] and, *God stood in the congregation of gods*,[46] but by His grace, not by a property of our own, since it is He alone who can make gods. 5. But for matter he (Hermogenes) makes that which it shares with god its own property. Otherwise, if it received from God something that belongs to God—I mean the course of eternity—it can also be believed that it both shares something with God and yet is not God. But what are we to say when he declares that it shares something with God, and ⟨then⟩ proposes that what he does not deny matter to have, should belong to God alone?

Ch. 6] He [47] says that God retains undiminished His attributes of being the only God and the First and the Creator of all and the Lord of all, and of being incomparable to any being—qualities which he thereupon ascribes to matter as well. Now He is God. God will testify to this;

and sometimes He has sworn by Himself[48] that there is no other being like Him.[49] But Hermogenes will make Him a liar, for matter, too, will be like God—unmade, unborn, without beginning and without end. God will say: *I am the first*.[50] And how can He be the first, if matter is co-eternal with Him? But[51] between beings which are co-eternal and contemporary there is no sequence. Or is matter the first as well? *I*, says He, *stretched out the heaven alone*.[52] No, not alone, for[53] that took part in the expanding from which He made what He expanded.

2. When he asserts that matter existed without detriment to the condition of God, we may well ridicule him ⟨by asserting⟩ that it is no less true that God existed without detriment to the condition of matter, since nonetheless[54] the condition of both is common to them. Thus for matter, too, the fact will remain unabated that it did also exist by itself, but together with God, because God, too, existed alone, but together with it. And it was itself first with God, because God, too, was first with it, and further it was also[55] incomparable, like God, because God, too, is incomparable like it, and it was the creator of all things as well as their god and their lord together with God.

Thus ⟨he comes to conclude⟩ that God has something, but not the whole, of matter. 3. Accordingly Hermogenes has left Him nothing which he had not conferred on matter as well, so that it is not a case of matching matter with God, but rather of God with matter. Indeed, when those qualities which we maintain are God's very own—to have always existed, to be without beginning and without end, to have been the First, and Alone, and the Creator of all things—belong to matter as well, I ask what property is there different from, and alien to, God and therefore peculiar to it, that matter can have possessed because of which it could not be counted fully equal to God? If[56] in matter we find all the attributes which are special to God, these attributes are sufficient to decide *a priori* concerning their equality in other respects as well.

Ch. 7]   When[57] he contends that matter is less than God and inferior to Him, and therefore different from Him, and therefore, too, not capable of being counted fully equal to Him, He being a greater and a superior being, I lay down against him the rule that what is eternal and unborn does not admit of any diminution and humiliation, because it is this quality which also makes God to be as great as He is, inferior and subject to none, nay, greater and more august than all beings. For, just as all other things which are born or die and for that reason are not eternal, being once and for all exposed to an end, since they have also been exposed to a beginning[58]—just as these admit of things of which God does not admit (I mean diminution and inferiority), since they are born and made, so God, too, does not admit of these things because He is both absolutely unborn and unmade; but the condition of matter is of the same kind. 2. And so, of the two beings which are eternal because they are unborn and unmade, God and matter, we assert because of the identity of their common condition, possessing as they do in the same degree that which does not admit of diminution or subjugation, that is to say, eternity, that neither of them is less or greater than the other, neither inferior nor superior to the other; but that they both stand as equally great, equally sublime, equally possessing that complete and perfect felicity of which eternity is declared to consist.[59]

3. For we shall not affect the opinions of the heathens who when on occasion they are compelled to acknowledge

the existence of God, will yet have it that there are also other gods below Him. No, divinity has no degrees because it is unique; and if divinity is also present in matter, because matter is equally unborn and unmade and eternal, it must be present in both,[60] because it can in nothing be inferior to itself. 4. How, then, will Hermogenes dare to make a distinction and thereby subject matter to God, an eternal power to the Eternal, an unborn power to the Unborn, a creator to the Creator, a substance that has the courage to say: 'I, too, am the First—I, too, was before all things—I, too, am that from which are all things; equal we have been —together we have been—both without beginning and without end—both without a creator and without a god. Who subjects me to God,[61] my equal in time, my equal in age? If this is done because He is called God, then I, too, have my own name; or rather, I am God and He is mat-ter,[62] because we both are also that which the other is.' Do you think now that he[63] has not put matter on the same level with God because indeed he makes it subject to Him?

Ch. 8] Nay,[64] he even makes matter superior to God, and rather subjects God to it, while alleging that He made all things out of matter. For if He drew upon it for the work of ⟨the creation of⟩ the world, then, first, matter is clearly superior, since it provided Him with the material for His work; and, secondly, God is evidently inferior to matter, since He needed its substance. For there is no one but needs him whose property he makes use of; there is no one but is subject to him whose property[65] he needs in order that he may make use of it. Thus, on the one hand, there is no one who because of the fact that he makes use of another's property, is not inferior to him whose property he uses;

and, on the other hand, there is no one enabling another to make use of his property who is not in this respect superior to him whom he enables to make use of it. Thus matter itself was not in need of God, but rather lent itself to God who needed it, rich and opulent and liberal as it was—to one who, I suppose, was powerless and all too little adapted to make out of nothing what He wanted.

2. Great indeed is the service which matter rendered God, that to-day He should have something whereby [66] He can be known as God and be called the Almighty, save that He is no longer almighty, if His might did not extend to this also—to produce all things out of nothing! 3. To be sure, matter also conferred something on itself, namely, that it itself, too, can be acknowledged together with God as God's coequal and even as His helper; only it is a pity that Hermogenes alone has come by this knowledge along with the patriarchs of the heretics, the philosophers. For up to now it has escaped the prophets and the apostles and, I think, Christ besides.

Ch. 9]   He [67] cannot say that it was as its Lord that God made use of matter for the work of ⟨creating⟩ the world, for He could not be Lord of a substance which was coequal with Himself. 2. But it may be that He used it on sufferance and that He did so on sufferance, not on the ground of ownership, for such a reason [68] that, though matter was evil, He yet could endure to draw upon an evil substance— doing so, of course, under constraint of His weakness which made Him lack the power to draw His resources from nothing, [69] and not in consequence of His power; for if, as God, [70] He had possessed such at all over matter which He knew to be evil, He would, being the Lord and a good

God, first have converted it into a good thing[71] in order that thus He might draw upon a good thing, not an evil one. But because He was good, to be sure, but not Lord, He used matter such as He could dispose of, thereby demonstrating His unfree position which had to yield to the condition of matter,[72] which, had He been Lord, He would have amended.

3. This indeed is the answer to be given to Hermogenes when[73] he asserts that it was by virtue of His ownership that God made use of matter and thus drew upon a substance that was not His, since it had not been made by Him. ⟨If Hermogenes is right,⟩ then it follows that evil originated from Him who, if not the author of evil (for He did not create it), was at least its permitter because He was its owner. 4. But if matter, being evil, does not belong to God Himself, then He has drawn upon alien property, doing so either on sufferance, because He needed it, or even by violent possession, because He surpassed it in strength. For these are the three ways in which alien property is obtained: by right, by permission, or by violence, that is to say, by ownership, on sufferance, or by force. Now, with no title of ownership present, Hermogenes may choose what is suited to God, that He has created all things out of matter on sufferance or by violence. 5. Would not God then have thought better that nothing should be created at all than that the creation should take place on sufferance or by violence, and out of an evil thing into the bargain?[74] Even if matter had been as good as good can be, would He not have considered it equally unsuitable to Himself to draw His resources from alien property, granting even that it was good? It was, therefore, rather stupid[75] of Him that for the sake of His glory He made the world in such a way as to show His indebtedness to a substance not belonging

to Him and, what is more, a substance that was not good either!

b) Matter and Evil

Ch. 10] 'Was [76] He then,' says Hermogenes, 'to create from nothing that thus evil things too might be imputed to His will?' Great, to be sure, must be the blindness of the heretics in the presence of such an argument, when either they would have it believed that there is another supremely good God for the reason that, in their opinion, the Creator is the author of evil, or else represent matter together with the Creator so that they may derive evil from matter, not from the Creator: for there is no god at all who is spared this predicament, of how he—whoever he be—who, though he did not create evil himself, yet permitted its creation by some author or other and from some source or other, can then avoid the appearance of being the author of evil.

2. Thus Hermogenes, too, must hear for the present— for an accurate treatment of the essence of evil is given by us in another place [77]—that he, too, [78] has achieved nothing by this idea of his. For note that God is found to be, if not the author, yet the sycophant of evil, since by reason of His great goodness He tolerated before the creation of the world the presence of evil in matter which, being good and the enemy of evil, He should have corrected. 3. For either He was able to amend it but unwilling to do so, or else He was willing but unable because He was a weak God. [79] If He was able and would not, He was Himself evil because He favoured evil—and therewith that is to be regarded as belonging to Him on which, [80] though He did not create it, He yet, since nevertheless it would not have existed if He had not wished for its existence, conferred existence because He did not wish for its non-existence.

Now what is more shameful than this?[81] If He wished for the existence of that which He was unwilling to create Himself, He acted against Himself, since He both wished for the existence of that which He was unwilling to create and was unwilling to create that which He wished to exist. He regarded it as good when He wished for its existence and regarded it as evil when He was unwilling to create it:[82] what He judged to be evil by not creating it, He declared to be good by enduring its existence! By enduring the existence of evil, as if it were good, instead of rather exterminating it, He showed Himself to be its patron, wickedly, if by His own will, ignominiously, if through necessity. Thus God will be either the servant of evil or its friend, since He associated with the evil in matter and even created His works out of evil.

Ch. 11] But [83] still [84]—on what grounds does Hermogenes make it plausible to us that matter is evil? For it will be impossible for him not to call that evil to which he ascribes evil. Now we determine [85] that what is eternal cannot admit of diminution and subjection so as to be considered inferior to another coeternal being. Therefore we now say too that evil cannot be an attribute of it because it cannot even be subject ⟨to evil⟩ for this reason that it cannot be subject ⟨to anything⟩ in any way, because it is eternal. But since, on other grounds, it is certain that the highest good is what is eternal as God—for on this account He alone is God, because He is eternal, and therefore good, because He is God—how can there exist evil in matter which, since it is eternal, must be believed to be the highest good? 2. Otherwise, if that which is eternal can also be capable of evil, it will also be possible to believe this concerning God, and it will be without reason that he (Hermogenes) has been so eager to remove evil from God, that is to say, if, being an attribute of matter, it is also the attribute of an eternal Being. 3. But now, if what is eternal can be believed to be evil, then evil, being eternal,[86] will be invincible and insuperable—and in that case we vainly do our best *to put away evil from among ourselves*;[87] in that case it is also in vain that God gives this order and this precept—nay, it is also in vain that God has instituted His Judgment, for His punishment will then certainly be unjust.[88] But if, on the contrary, there will be an end of evil when its chief, the devil, shall *go away into the fire which God hath prepared for him and his angels*,[89] having been first *cast into the bottomless pit*;[90] when *the revelation of the sons of God*[91] shall have *delivered* from evil *the creature*[92] which in every respect had been *made subject to vanity*;[93] when, after the restoration of the innocence and purity of everything created, 'the cattle shall be at peace with the beasts of the field'[94] and 'little children shall play with serpents';[95] when the Father shall have 'put beneath the feet of His Son His enemies,[96] for being the workers of evil—in a word, if evil can have an end, then it must needs also have had a beginning, and[97] matter will have a beginning, since it also has an end of its evil. For[98] whatever things are ascribed to evil, are ⟨also⟩ to be attributed ⟨to matter⟩ in accordance with the fact that its condition is evil.

Ch. 12] Well[99] then, let us now believe that matter is evil, indeed very evil—by nature of course—just as we believe that God is good, even very good, likewise by nature. Now it will be necessary to regard nature as certain and fixed, no less persisting in evil when it occurs in matter, than in good when it occurs in God; it must of course be inconvertible and immutable,[100] because if in matter nature can be changed from evil to good, it can also be changed in God from good to evil. 2. Here one will say: 'Then will "children not be raised up to Abraham from the stones," and will "broods of vipers not bring forth fruit of penance,"[101] and will "children of wrath" not become "children of peace,"[102] if nature is not changeable?' You will achieve nothing, my friend, by directing your attention to such examples, for not applicable to the case of matter, which is unborn, are things which are born—stones and vipers and human beings; their nature, having a beginning, can also have an end. 3. But as for matter, keep in mind that it has been determined[103] once for all to be eternal, because it is unmade and unborn, and that therefore it must also be deemed to possess an immutable and incorruptible nature—this is also in accord with the opinion of Hermogenes himself which he opposes ⟨to our view⟩, when he denies that God could create ⟨anything⟩ out of Himself, because what is eternal does not change; obviously it would lose what it had been, by becoming by the change what it was not,[104] if it were not eternal. But keep in mind that the eternal Lord cannot be anything else than what He always is.

4. Now I too shall adopt this argument and use it to refute him as he deserves. I blame matter in the same way, when out of it, evil as it is, and even very evil, good and even very good things are made by God: *And God saw that they were good,*[105] *and God blessed them,*[106] because, of course, they were *very good*, certainly not because they were evil and very evil. But then change has been admitted by matter, and if this is so, it has lost its condition of eternity—it has, in short, died its natural death.[107] But eternity cannot be lost because, unless it cannot be lost, it is not eternity. For the same reason it could not have admitted of change

either, because if it is eternity, it cannot be changed in any way.

Ch. 13]   Now [108] it [109] will be asked how good things were made out of it, since these were by no means made by virtue of a change. Whence could the seed of what is good, even very good, occur in an evil, even a very evil, substance? At all events, *neither does a good tree produce fruit* because there also is no God who is not good, *nor an evil tree good fruit* [110] because there also is no matter except very evil matter. 2. Otherwise, if we grant to it a germ of good too, [111] it will no longer possess a uniform, that is, an utterly evil, nature, but in such case it will be twofold, that is, in possession of a nature both evil and good; and then the question will be again whether in one and the same subject there can have been a connection between good and evil, light and darkness, sweet and bitter. 3. Or, if it is possible that these two diverse qualities, good and evil, have come together, and the nature of matter can have been a double nature capable of bringing forth both kinds of fruit, then it will no longer be possible even to ascribe ⟨the origin of⟩ good things to God, just as evil things too are not imputed to Him; [112] but in that case both kinds of things will be taken from the proper nature [113] of matter, and ⟨so⟩ belong to matter. In this way we shall owe to God neither gratitude for good things nor resentment for evil things, because He will then have produced nothing from His own nature; and from this it will clearly be proved that He has been the servant of matter.

Ch. 14]   ⟨This [114] conclusion is irrefutable,⟩ for [115] even if it is said that, though with matter as His wherewithal, it was still of His own will that he brought forth the good things, by getting hold, as it were, of the good element of matter—although this, too, is ignominious—yet, since from the same matter He also produces evil things, He is the servant of matter, if only because surely He does not produce these things of His own will: ⟨for⟩ He can do nothing else than bring forth ⟨His creation⟩ from an evil source, doing so against His will, of course, because He is good, of necessity, because against His will, and as a servant, because of necessity. 2. What, then, is more dignified, that He created evil things of necessity or of His own will? For it was of necessity that He created them, if He made them out of matter, and of His own will, if He created them from nothing. Now indeed you labour in vain to keep God from being made the author of evil things, because if He made them from matter, they will still be imputable to Him who made them, precisely to the extent that He made them.[116] Plainly, the question whence He made them[117] amounts to the same as whether He had made them out of nothing;[118] nor does it make any difference whence He made them, provided that He made them from that from which it was more appropriate to Him to make them. Now it was more appropriate to Him to make them of His own will than of necessity—in other words, out of nothing rather than out of matter. It is more becoming to believe that God, even as the author of evil, is free than that He is subservient: power, of whatever kind it be, is more appropriate to Him than infirmity. 3.[119] Therefore, even if we grant that matter, to be sure, contained nothing good, but that the Lord, if He produced something good, produced it by virtue of His own power, there will with equal right arise other questions. In the first place, if there was no good at all in matter, good was not made out of matter for the simple reason that matter did not contain

it. Next, if it was not made out of matter, it was for that
reason made out of God. If it was not made out of God
either,[120] it was made out of nothing—for, according to
Hermogenes' classification,[121] this is the remaining possibility.

Ch. 15] Further,[122] if good was made neither out of
matter, because it was not in it, matter being evil, nor out
of God, because, following the statement made by Hermogenes, nothing could be made out of God, it is evident that
good was made out of nothing, since it was made out of
none—neither out of matter nor out of God. And if good
was made out of nothing, why not evil as well? Or rather,
if one thing was made out of nothing, why not all things?
Unless it be that the power of God was unequal to the production of all things after producing one thing out of nothing.[123] 2. Otherwise, if good proceeded from evil matter
because it sprang neither from nothing nor from God, it
will follow that it proceeded from a conversion of matter,
contrary to the statement that nothing eternal can admit
of a conversion. Thus Hermogenes will ⟨have to⟩ deny
that good could have proceeded from that from which,
⟨in his conviction,⟩ it drew its origin;[124] but good must
needs have proceeded from one of the sources from which
he has denied that it could have proceeded.

3. If, however, evil should not have sprung from nothing, lest it should come to belong to God, by whose will
it would ⟨still⟩ seem to have been made, but from matter,
in order that it may belong to the very thing from whose
substance it will then be made, in that case, too, as I have
already stated, God will be considered to be the author of
evil. For, whereas by His power, which is identical with
His will,[125] He should have produced all good things from

matter or at least good things only, yet He did not produce
from it good things only but also evil things—obviously
either willing that there should be evil things, if He could
prevent their coming into existence, or incapable of making only good things, if He was willing to make them and
could not—⟨a distinction which is immaterial,[126]⟩ for it
does not make any difference whether it was by weakness
or by His own will that the Lord became the author of
evil. Else what was the reason that after creating good
things, as being good Himself, He should also have
brought forth evil things as though He were not good,
seeing that He did not bring forth such things only which
were consistent with Himself? What need was there after
the production of His own work also to look after the
interests of matter by also producing evil in the same manner, in order that He alone might be known as good from
His good, but that matter might not be known as evil
from its evil? The good would have thrived better if evil
had not blown upon it.

4. ⟨Here it is not necessary to add more,⟩ for Hermogenes, too, refutes the arguments of certain people [127]
who say that evil things were necessary to shed light upon
the essence of good things, these to be understood from
their contrasts. 5. Wherefore this did not furnish a motive
either for the production of evil; or else, if some other
reason required its creation, why, then, could it not also be
created from nothing? For exactly the same reason would
shield the Lord from being regarded as the author of evil
which now excuses ⟨the production of⟩ evil things, when
He produces ⟨them⟩ from matter. If this reason does furnish an excuse,[128] then the question is driven on and on and
from every side into a corner [129] where those people do not
want ⟨it to be driven⟩ who, by failing to examine the

essence itself of evil and to distinguish how they should either attribute it to God or remove it from God, expose God to still more and still unworthier destructive arguments. [130]

Ch. 16] Accordingly,[131] in the preliminary discussion of this point [132] which perhaps will have to be treated elsewhere again,[133] I for my part state that either to God must be ascribed both good and evil, which He made out of matter, or to matter itself out of which He made them, or both to both of them together, because these two are bound to each other—He who created and that out of which He created, or one to one and the other to the other, for a third power besides God and matter does not exist.

2. Now if both belong to God, God will evidently be the author of evil too[134]; but God, being good, cannot be the author of evil. If both belong to matter, matter will clearly be the source of good as well; but since matter is evil throughout, it cannot be the source of good.[135] If both belong to both together, then matter will in this respect too be put on the same level with God and both will be equal, since ⟨in that case⟩ they will be equally allied to evil and to good; but matter must not be put on a par with God, lest it produce two Gods.[136] If one belongs to one and the other to the other—good, of course, to God and evil to matter—then evil cannot be ascribed to God nor good to matter; but God, making both good and evil things from matter, makes them in conjunction with matter.[137] If this is so, I do not see how Hermogenes can escape from my verdict, when he thinks that God, in whatever way He created evil out of matter, either of His own will or of necessity or for a ⟨certain⟩ reason, cannot be the author of evil. 3. Further, if He is the author of evil who actually

made it, matter being merely associated with Him by providing Him with its substance, you deprive the cause for ⟨the introduction of⟩ matter of its sense.[138] For it is clear that also assuming the mediacy of matter, God is nevertheless the author of evil, if matter is assumed in order to prevent God's appearing to be the author of evil.

Thus with matter excluded because the cause for it⟨s introduction⟩ has been excluded, it remains that God undoubtedly made all things out of nothing. 4. We shall see whether He also made evil things, when it will be clear what things are evil and whether those things are evil which for the present you regard as such. For it is more worthy of God that He produced these things of His own will by producing them too out of nothing than that He did so on the initiative of another, supposing that He produced them out of matter.[139] Liberty, not necessity, is appropriate to God. I would rather have it that He wanted to create evil things out of Himself than that He was unable to prevent their creation.

POSITIVE PROOF FROM SCRIPTURE FOR A CREATION OUT OF NOTHING

Ch. 17] The [140] fact of God being the One and only God [141] asserts this rule, for He is the One-only God for the only reason that He is the sole God, and the sole God for the only reason that nothing existed with Him. Thus He must also be the First, since all things are posterior to Him; all things are posterior to Him for the reason that all things are by Him; all things are by Him for the reason that they are from nothing, so that this passage of Scripture, too, is verified: [142] *Who hath known the mind of the Lord? Or who hath been His counsellor? Or with whom took He counsel? Or who hath shown Him the way of wisdom and knowledge? Who hath first given to Him and recompense shall be made?* [143] Surely no one, for there was no power, no material, no nature of another substance which assisted Him.

2. Further, if He created out of some substance, [144] He must needs have received from that very substance both the design and the method for its arrangement [145] as *the way of wisdom and knowledge.* For he had to operate in accordance with the quality of the thing, conformably to the nature of matter and not to His own will, so that indeed He must have made evil as well in accordance with the nature, not of Himself, but of that substance.

Ch. 18] If [146] any material is necessary to God for the creation of the world, as Hermogenes supposed, [147] God had a far worthier and more suitable material, one which was not to be determined from the writings of the philosophers, but could be known from the books of the prophets, [148] namely, His Wisdom; for this alone knew the mind of the Lord. For *who knoweth the things of God and the things in God but the Spirit which is in Him?* [149] Now that Spirit is His wisdom: this was His counsellor, this is the very way of knowledge and science; it is out of this that He created, creating by means of it and with it. *When He prepared the heavens,* Scripture says, *I was there with Him, and when He strengthened over the winds the clouds above, and when He secured the strong fountains of that which is under the heaven, I was moulding them with Him. I was he in whom He took delight; and daily I rejoiced in His person, when He rejoiced as He had completed the world and rejoiced among the sons of men.* [150]

Who would not rather approve of this power as the

source and origin of all things, the matter indeed[151] of matter, not subject to an end of its existence,[152] not changeable in its nature,[153] not restless in motion, not formless in appearance, but firmly rooted,[154] in possession of a nature of its own,[155] calm and beautiful, a substance such as God could have needed, needing what was His rather than alien property?[156] At all events, as soon as He felt its necessity for the creation of the world, He instantly created and generated it in Himself. *The Lord,* Scripture says, *created me as the beginning of His ways for the creation of His works: before the ages He founded me, before He made the earth, before the mountains were settled in their places; and before all hills He brought me forth and before the depths was I begotten.*[157]

2. Let Hermogenes then acknowledge that when the wisdom of God is proclaimed to be born and created, this is also for the reason that we should not believe that there exists anything unborn and uncreated except God alone. For if, within the Lord, that which was out of Him and in Him was not without a beginning, that is, His Wisdom, which was born and created at the moment when in the mind of God it began to be actuated for the arrangement of the works of the world, it is to a much higher degree impossible that anything should have been without a beginning which existed outside of God. 3. Now, if this Wisdom is at the same time the Word of God,[158] *without which nothing has been made,*[159] as also nothing has been arranged without His Wisdom, how could it be possible that, with the exception of the Father, anything should have been older—and thus, by all means, nobler—than the Son of God, the only-begotten and first-begotten Word? Not to mention that what is unborn is stronger than what is born, and what is not made, more powerful than what is made;

for that which for its coming into existence did not need an author, must be much more august than that which had an author for its existence. Therefore, if evil is unborn while the Word of God is born—for Scripture says, *He hath uttered the most excellent Word*[160]—I do not know but that evil can be employed[161] by a good power (i.e. Christ), ⟨for this would mean that⟩ a stronger power ⟨was used⟩ by a weak one, that is, an unborn power by a born one. 4. Thus on this score too Hermogenes ranks matter higher than God, because he ranks it higher than the Son. For the Son is the Word and *the Word is God*[162] and *I and the Father are one*[163]—only the Son will suffer with equanimity that that is put before Him which is put on the same level with the Father.

Hermogenes' Misinterpretation of Scripture in Support of his Notion of Matter

a) *Genesis* 1.1

Ch. 19] But[164] I shall also appeal to Moses' record of the origin of the world,[165] by which source the opposition too seeks in vain to support its suppositions,[166] in order, of course, to avoid the appearance of not seeking its instruction where it should. Thus it has seized upon the opportunities offered by certain words, as heretics generally have a habit of twisting everything simple. They will have it, for instance, that the very 'beginning' in which God made both heaven and earth, was something so to say substantial and corporeal, which can be interpreted as being matter.[167] 2. We, on the other hand, assert for every word its proper meaning, that *principium* means 'beginning' and that it was appropriate to be thus applied to things which began to exist; that as a matter of fact nothing which must come into being is without a beginning, nay, that the very moment of its beginning to exist is its beginning, and that, therefore, *principium* or *initium* is a word indicating the act of beginning, not the name of some substance. 3. Now if the heaven and the earth are the principal works of God, which God made before all things, that they should be the beginning—in the literal sense of the word—of His works,[168] since they were made before the rest, Scripture rightly says in its preface: *In the beginning God made heaven and earth*, just as it would have said: 'At the end God made heaven and earth,' if He had made them after all things.

Contrariwise, if the beginning is some substance, the end must somehow be material as well. 4. Now a substantial thing may indeed also be the beginning for some other thing which is to originate from it, as clay is the beginning of the vessel, as seed is the beginning of the plant. But when we use the word 'beginning' in this way as a designation of origin, not of order, we also make special mention of, and add, the name of the very thing which we regard as the beginning of the other thing. But[169] when we employ the word 'beginning' in this sense—for instance, 'In the beginning the potter made a basin or a jar'—'beginning' will not designate the material (for I have not mentioned the clay as the beginning), but the order of the work, because the potter made the basin and the jar first, before the rest, meaning to make the rest afterwards; it is to the order of the works that the word 'beginning' will refer ⟨in this case⟩, not to the origin of their substances.[170]

5. I can also give a different interpretation of the word 'beginning' which, however, is not inappropriate;[171] for in

Greek the term for 'beginning,' which is *arche*, designates the first place not only in order but also in power; hence, too, sovereigns and magistrates are called *archontes*. Thus, according to this second sense,[172] 'beginning'[173] can be used for 'sovereignty' and 'power'; for it was in His sovereignty and power that God made heaven and earth.

Ch. 20] But[174] in order ⟨to demonstrate⟩ that the Greek word means nothing else than 'beginning' and that 'beginning' admits of no other sense than 'commencement,'[175] we have to acknowledge that that power, too, is a beginning[176] which says, *The Lord created me for His works.*[177] For if it is through the agency of the Wisdom of God that all things were made, then it follows that when God made both the heaven and the earth *in the beginning* —that is, at the commencement—He made them in His Wisdom.[178] 2. And, finally, if 'beginning' designated matter, Scripture would not have employed the formula:[179] *In the beginning God made*, but '*From* the beginning'; for ⟨in that case⟩ He would not have made all things in matter but from matter. But with regard to Wisdom it was possible to say, *In the beginning.* For it is in His Wisdom that He made all things first, since, by inventing and arranging them, He had already made them in it.[180] ⟨This conclusion cannot be subverted⟩ because, even if He had intended to make ⟨all things⟩ out of matter, He certainly, by thinking them out and arranging them, would have made them already before in His Wisdom. For this was *the beginning of His ways*, because thinking and arranging are[181] the first operation of Wisdom, opening as it does the way from thought to action.

3. I claim for myself the support of this Scriptural passage [182] on this ground too that, while it mentions both God who made all things and the things which He made, [183] it does not equally attest whence He made them. For since in every operation there are three principal things, he [184] who makes and that which is made and that from which it is made, there are three names to be mentioned in a formal description of a work, that is to say, the person of the maker, the sort of thing made, and the kind of material. If the material is not mentioned, whereas both the work and the maker of the work are mentioned, it is evident that he made the work from nothing, for the source would have been mentioned as well, if he had made his work from something.

4. Finally, I shall adduce the Gospel as a supplement to the Old Testament. In the Gospel there was still more reason to show that God had made all things from some material, for the mere fact that there the Intermediary is also revealed through whose agency He made all things. [185] *In the beginning was the Word*[186]—in the beginning, of course, in which God made the heaven and the earth—*and the Word was with God and the Word was God . . . . All things were made by Him and without Him nothing was made.*[187] Therefore, when here there are clearly indicated both the maker, that is, God, and that which was made, namely, all things, and the intermediary, that is, the Word, would not the order of the record have required that also that from which all things were made by God through the intermediary of the Word, should be mentioned, if they had been made out of something? What, therefore, did not exist, Scripture could not mention, and, by not mentioning it, it has sufficiently proved that it did not exist, for it would have mentioned it, had it existed.

EXCURSUS: THE ASSUMPTION THAT SCRIPTURE SHOULD HAVE
    MADE EXPLICIT MENTION OF A CREATION OUT OF
    NOTHING IS GRATUITOUS

Ch. 21] 'But [188] then,' you say, 'if you decide beforehand that all things were made out of nothing on the ground that it is not clearly recorded that something [189] was made out of pre-existent matter, you must take care that the opposite party [190] does not contend that all things were made out of matter on the ground that it is not clearly indicated either that something was made out of nothing.' 2. Quite so, some arguments can easily be retorted, but they cannot by the same be promptly accepted as equally correct in their retorted form [191] when a basic difference is involved. For I say that, though Scripture did not clearly proclaim that all things were made out of nothing—just as it does not say either that they were made out of matter —there was not so great a need expressly to declare that all things had been made out of nothing as there would have been, if they had been made out of matter. 3. For in the case of that which is made out of nothing, it is clear that it was made out of nothing from the very fact that it is not shown to have been made out of something; nor is there any danger of its being thought to have been made out of something, when it is not indicated whence it was made. But in the case of that which is made out of something, unless the very fact that the thing in question was made out of something is clearly expressed by indication of whence it was made, [192] there will be danger—first, that it appears to have been made out of nothing because its source is not mentioned; secondly, though it be of such a condition that it could not appear not to have been made out of something [193], there will be like danger of its appearing to have

been made from a material far different from that out of
which it was actually made, since its source is not indicated.
4. Therefore, if God could make all things out of nothing,
Scripture could quite well omit to add [194] that He had
made them out of nothing, but it should have said by all
means that He had made them out of matter, if He had
done so [195]; for the first possibility would be completely
understandable, even if it was not expressly stated, but the
second would be doubtful, unless it were stated.

Ch. 22]   The [196] Holy Spirit has even established this rule
for His Scripture, that whenever something is made out of
something, He mentions both the thing which is made and
the thing from which it is made. *Let the earth*, says He, *bring
forth grass yielding seed after its kind and after its likeness, and the
fruit tree yielding fruit, whose seed is in itself, after its likeness.
And it was so. And the earth brought forth grass yielding seed
after its kind, and the fruit tree yielding fruit, whose seed was in
itself, after its likeness.*[197] And again: *And God said, Let the
waters bring forth the moving creatures that have life and fowl
that may fly above the earth through the firmament of heaven.
And it was so. And God created great whales and every living
creature that moveth, which the waters brought forth after their
kind.*[198] Again farther on: *And God said, Let the earth bring
forth the living creature after its kind—cattle and creeping things
and beasts of the earth after their kind.*[199] 2. Therefore, if God,
when producing things other than those already made,
makes them known through the prophet and says
what in each case He has produced from which source—
though we could regard these things as produced from
every source whatever except from nothing; for already
certain things had been made from which they could
seem to have been produced—if the Holy Spirit

bestowed so much care on our instruction [200] that we should know what proceeded from such and such source, would He not in the same way have informed us about both the heaven and the earth? ⟨He would have done so⟩ by indicating from which source He made them, if they had been drawn from some material, lest [201] He should seem to have made them out of nothing, the more so as nothing had yet been made from which He could seem to have made them. Therefore, just as in the case of such things as have been produced from something He has indicated their source, so in all things whose source He did not indicate He confirms their production out of nothing.

3. And so *in the beginning God made the heaven and the earth*. I worship the fullness of the Scripture by means of which He reveals to me both the Maker and the things made; but in the Gospel I find in addition Him who is both the Minister and the Intermediary of the Maker—the Word. But whether it was from some underlying matter that all things were made, I have as yet read nowhere. That Scripture has it, is for Hermogenes' workshop to show us. If it is not in Scripture, let him fear the *Woe* that was meant for all those *who add or take away*.

b) Genesis 1.2a

Ch. 23] But [202] he builds up an argument from the following words occurring in Scripture: *And the earth was invisible and unfinished*. To begin with, he refers the word 'earth' to matter, 'because,' so he says, 'it is the earth which was made out of it,' and he interprets 'was' as indicating [203] that it has always existed in the past, being unborn and unmade; finally, ⟨it is, in his opinion, called⟩ *invisible and unfinished* because—so he will have it—matter was shapeless, confused, and unordered.

2. Though I shall refute these suppositions of his singly, for the present I want to answer him as follows. Let us suppose [204] that by these terms matter is indicated: yet, Scripture does not signify, does it, that because it existed before all things, some such thing [205] was made out of it? On the contrary, it signifies nothing of the kind. Matter may have existed as much as it likes—or rather, as much as Hermogenes likes. It is possible too that it actually existed and that nevertheless God made nothing out of it, were it only because it was not proper that God should have been in need of something, or at least because it is not even indicated that He made anything out of matter. 'Then its existence would be without a cause,' you say. No, not quite without a cause, that is not quite true; for even if the world has not been made out of it, yet a heresy has sprung from it—one too which is the more impudent in that the heresy has not sprung from matter, but rather the heresy has made matter itself.

Ch. 24] I [206] return now to the several terms by which he thought that matter was signified, and first I shall take up with him the names. Of these, to be sure, we do find the one, that is to say, 'earth'; the other, that is, 'matter,' we do not find. I ask, therefore, since a designation of matter does not occur in Scripture, how the term 'earth' [207] can also be applied to it, a term already known in regard to another kind of substance. On this account [208] there is the more reason why there should have existed a ⟨special⟩ term for matter as well, if this had also acquired the designation 'earth,' [209] that I might know that 'earth' is a name shared ⟨by the earth⟩ with matter; that I might not claim

it for that substance alone of which it is the proper de-
nomination, in connection with which it is better known;
or that I might not be able, if I so wished, to confer it on
any and every other species ⟨of matter⟩ and not, indeed,
on matter in its entirety. [210] For when no proper name
exists for that thing to which a common name is ascribed,
the less apparent [211] the thing is to which it is ascribed, ⟨the
more⟩ can it be ascribed to any other thing whatever.
Therefore, even if Hermogenes could show that matter
has a ⟨special⟩ name, he would also have to prove that it
is surnamed 'earth' besides, in order that thus he might
claim both names for it.

Ch. 25] Therefore[212] he wants two earths to be represented in that passage of Scripture—one, which God
made in the beginning; a second, the matter from which
He made the earth, and about which it is said: *And the earth
was invisible and unfinished.* Of course, if I ask which of the
two must confer the name 'earth' upon the other, it will
be said that *this* earth which was made, derived its name
from the earth from which it was made, because it is more
probable that the offspring should be named after the
original than the original after the offspring. If this be so,
another question forces itself on us, namely, whether it is
becoming that this earth which God made should have
derived its name from that out of which He made it. 2. For
I learn from the works of Hermogenes and the other
materialist heretics that that other earth, to be sure, was
shapeless and *invisible and unfinished*, but that this our earth
obtained from God to an equal degree form as well as
appearance and equipment, and so was made a thing
different from that out of which it was made. Now,
having been made a different thing, it could not be

connected in its name with that earth from whose condition it had become divergent. If the proper name of that matter was 'earth,' then this our earth, which is not matter, since it has become a different thing, does not also admit of the name 'earth' which belongs to another and is alien to its nature.

3. 'But matter ⟨, so you tell me,⟩ subjected to the act of making, that is, our earth, had with its original a community of name as well as of kind.' Not at all! For though a pitcher is made out of clay, I shall no longer call it clay, but a pitcher, and though electrum is compounded of gold and silver, I shall yet call it neither gold nor silver, but electrum. When a thing becomes different from the nature of another thing, it also loses the name of that thing, thus acquiring a designation all its own, as it has also acquired a nature all its own.[213] Now, how much this earth has changed from the nature of that other earth, that is, matter, is evident from the mere fact that in Genesis this our earth has received a testimony to its being good—*And God saw that it was good*[214]—whereas the other is considered in the doctrine of Hermogenes to be the origin and cause of evil things.

4. Finally, if this earth is earth for the reason that the other is earth, why, then, is not this earth matter too, because the other is? Nay, on this assumption the heaven, too, and all things, if they consist of matter, should have been called 'earths' and 'matters.'

5. This is sufficient regarding the term 'earth' by which he wanted matter to be understood. This, everybody knows, is the name of one of the elements. So we are taught, first by nature, then by Scripture—unless we should give credence to that Silenus who spoke with an air of authority about another world to king Midas, according

to the narrative by Theopompus; [215] but the same author also records that there are many gods.

Ch. 26] For [216] us, however, there exists but one God and one earth only, which God made in the beginning. When Scripture begins to give an ordered account of it, it first establishes the fact that it was made, and next discusses its quality. So, too, with regard to the heaven, it first declares that it was made: *In the beginning God made heaven*; and next it subjoins an account of its arrangement: *And he divided the water which was under the firmament from that which was above the firmament, and God called the firmament heaven* [217]—the very heaven which He had made in the beginning. In like manner concerning man too: *And God made man, to the image of God He made him.* [218] Next it records how He made him: *And God formed man of the slime of the earth, and breathed into his face the breath of life, and man became a living soul.* [219]

And certainly it is proper to set up a narrative in this way—first to give a preface, then to proceed to the actual treatment; first to mention the name, then to give the description. To proceed otherwise is absurd, to suppose that ⟨Scripture⟩ [220] suddenly revealed the form and condition of the thing of which it had made no mention before, that is, matter, not even ⟨mentioning⟩ its name; if it describes its quality before showing whether it existed ⟨at all⟩, if it draws its figure, but conceals its name. 2. But how much more credible is our view that Scripture subjoined a description of the arrangement of that thing only after having prefixed an account of its creation together with its receiving a name! Finally, how complete is the meaning of the words, *In the beginning God made the heaven and the earth. And the earth was invisible and unfinished*—that is, the earth which God made and about which Scripture had just made a statement! For the very word 'And' has been appended to the narrative as a clasp, that is to say, as a conjunctive particle serving to effect the connection [221]—'*And the earth . . . .*' It is by this word that Scripture returns to the earth about which it had spoken before, thus connecting the meaning ⟨of the second sentence with that of the first⟩. Indeed, take away the word 'And' from this text, and the connection is removed, so that then it may seem that another earth is spoken of in the words, *the earth was invisible and unfinished.*

Ch. 27]   But [222] you raise your eyebrows with a corresponding gesture of your finger, toss back your head, and say: [223] 'We read "was" because' [224]—so you say—'it always existed, being of course unborn and unmade, and for that reason worthy of being believed to be matter.' 2. Now I shall answer simply, without resorting to any affectation of speech, that 'was' can be predicated of everything—also of a thing which is made, which is born, which once did not exist, and which is not matter. For of everything which has existence, no matter whence it received it, whether by a beginning or without a beginning, we can, for the very reason that it *is*, also say that it *was*. If the first tense of a verb is applicable to a thing for its definition, the conjugated forms of that same verb will also bear upon a relation of that thing: [225] 'is' constitutes the chief part of a definition, 'was' of ⟨the expression of⟩ a relation.

3. Such are the quibbles and subtleties of the heretics who twist the simple meaning of ordinary words into something problematic. It is, of course, a momentous problem whether the earth that *is* made, also *was*! [226] However, the real matter for discussion is whether to

have been *invisible and unfinished* is to be predicated of the
earth which was made or rather of that of which it was
made, in which case the word 'was' actually belongs to the
very thing of which it was taken and with which it was
identical. [227]

Ch. 28] But [228] we shall prove not only that this condition was suited to this our earth, but also that it was not
suited to that other one. For if matter was thus in its pure
state at the disposition of God, that is to say, without the
obstructing presence of any element—for as yet nothing
existed except matter itself and God—it could by no means
be invisible. [229] For though Hermogenes will have it that
darkness was present in the substance of matter—a statement which we shall have to refute in its proper place—
yet darkness is visible even for a human being (for the very
presence of darkness can be seen), [230] much more so for
God; and in any case, if it were invisible, its quality certainly could not have become known. How, then, did
Hermogenes come to know that that substance was without a form and confused and restless which, being invisible,
was hidden entirely? Or if this has been revealed by God,
he must prove it.

2. Likewise I want to be informed whether it could be
termed unfinished. For certainly that is unfinished which
is imperfect, and certainly nothing can be imperfect but
what is made, for that is imperfect which is not fully
made. 'Certainly,' you say. Matter, therefore, which was
not made at all, could not be imperfect, and when it was
not imperfect, it was not unfinished either. Having no beginning, since it had not been made, it did not have an unfinished state either, [231] for an unfinished state is accidental
to a beginning. The earth, on the other hand, which was

made, deserved to be called 'unfinished,' for as soon as it was made, it had prior to its perfection the state of being imperfect.

Ch. 29] For [232] God perfected all His works in a definite order: first He so to say staked out the universe, the elements still being in a rough state. Then He inaugurated it, as it were, by bringing the elements to perfection: [233] He did not at once inundate light with the splendour of the sun, nor at once mitigate darkness by the assuaging luster of the moon; and He did not at once signalize the heaven with constellations and stars nor at once populate the seas with its monsters, and the earth itself He did not at once endow with its ability to produce various things: no, first He conferred on it being, then He added this that its existence would not be in vain. [234] Indeed thus also Isaias says: *He did not create it in vain, He formed it to be inhabited.* [235]

2. Therefore, after it was made, waiting to be made perfect also, it was in the meantime *invisible and unfinished*: unfinished, to be sure, also for the very reason that it was invisible—for it was not perfect to the sight and at the same time not yet provided with its further qualities; and invisible, since it was still enveloped by masses of water as by a rampart of procreative moisture, in the same way that our flesh too which is akin to it, is produced. [236] Indeed David also speaks in the same vein in his songs: [237] *The earth is the Lord's and the fulness thereof; the world, and all they that dwell therein. He hath founded it upon the seas and hath prepared it upon the rivers.* [238] For it was after the segregation of the waters into their hollow recesses [239] that the dry earth emerged, which hitherto was covered by the waters. It is therefore from that moment that it is also made visible, when God says: *Let the waters be gathered together in*

one gathering and let the dry land appear. [240] 'Appear,' He says, not, 'be made'; for it had already been made, but, being invisible up to that moment, it was waiting to appear. Further, ⟨He says⟩ 'dry land,' because it was to become so by its separation from the water, but yet ⟨He says⟩ 'earth': *And God called the dry land Earth* [241]—not matter. [242]
3. And thus, when afterwards it has attained perfection, it ceases to be called 'unfinished' when God proclaims: *Let the earth bring forth the herb of grass, bearing seed after its kind and after its likeness, and the fruit tree yielding fruit, whose seed is in itself, after its likeness.* [243] Again: *Let the earth bring forth the living creature after its kind, cattle and creeping things and beasts of the earth after their kind.* [244] 4. Thus Divine Scripture has fully accomplished its order. For on that which it had earlier termed *invisible and unfinished*, it conferred both visibility and completion. Now no other matter was *invisible and unfinished*; [245] therefore matter must from then on be visible and complete. And so I wish to see matter, for it has become visible. I also wish to recognize it in its complete state, so that I may also gather from it the herb bearing seed and the tree yielding fruit, and that living creatures created out of it may serve my need. But in fact matter is nowhere, whereas the earth is this our earth— here before my eyes. This earth I see, this earth I enjoy, ever since it ceased to be *invisible and unfinished*.

5. It is obviously about this earth that Isaias says: *Thus saith the Lord that created the heaven, He is the God that made visible the earth and made it.* [246] Certainly He made visible the same earth which He also made. How did He make it visible? Undoubtedly by saying: *Let the dry land appear.* Why does He command it to appear, if not because previously it was not visible, ⟨and⟩ that by making it visible and thereby usable [247] He might not have made it in vain?

6. Thus it is proved to us by every possible means that this earth which we inhabit is the same which was both created and made visible by God, and that none other was *unfinished and invisible* than that which was both created and made visible. And so the words, *And the earth was invisible and unfinished*, refer to that earth which God made separately [248] along with the heaven.

c) *Genesis* 1.2b

Ch. 30]   So, [249] too, the following words apparently will lend support to the supposition of Hermogenes: *And darkness was upon the deep, and the Spirit of God moved over the waters* [250]—as though these blended substances lent arguments for the existence of that massive body of matter. Since, however, Scripture designates precisely and severally 'darkness,' 'the deep,' 'the Spirit of God,' and 'the waters,' so detailed an account of certain and distinct elements precludes a supposition of ⟨the existence of⟩ anything which was confused and, because of such confusion, uncertain. Still more, when it ascribes to them separate places, speaking of 'darkness *upon the deep*,' 'the spirit *over the waters*,' it denies a confusion of the substances, because by demonstrating their different places [251] it also demonstrates their distinction. 2. Finally, it is completely absurd that matter, which is represented as formless, should be asserted to be formless on the basis of so many terms designating forms, without any indication of what that confused body is, which obviously must be regarded as constituting a unity, if it is formless. [252] For that which formless has one form, and that is formless which is blended together from various elements: that must of necessity have one appearance, which does not have an appearance, since it has one appearance ⟨resulting⟩ from ⟨a combination of⟩ many. For the rest, matter either had within itself those formed parts from whose names it had to be understood—I mean 'darkness,' and 'the deep,' and 'the spirit,' and 'the waters'—or it did not have them. Now,[253] if it had them, how can it be presented as not having any form? If it did not have them, from what[254] can it be known?[255]

Ch. 31]   But[256] this point, too, will certainly be made much of, that the Scripture intimated of the heaven only and this earth of ours that God made them[257] in the beginning, but that it said nothing of the sort about the abovementioned parts, and that therefore these, which are not signified as having been made, belong to unmade matter. To this objection, too, we shall make reply. 2. Divine Scripture would be explicit enough if it had established concerning only the principal parts of creation, heaven and earth, that they were made by God, equipped of course with what was specifically their own, which latter could be understood as included in the principal parts themselves. 3. Now the equipment of heaven and earth in that period were[258] the darkness and the deep, the spirit and the waters. For the earth had under it the deep and darkness: if the deep was under the earth, but darkness over the deep, both darkness and the deep were undoubtedly under the earth. Further, the heaven had under it the spirit and the waters: for if the waters were over the earth, since they had covered it, and the spirit was over the waters, both the spirit and the waters were over the earth; but that which is over the earth, is undoubtedly under the heaven. And as the earth lay over the deep and the darkness, so the heaven lay over the spirit and the waters and enclosed them.

4. Nor is it so novel that that alone is mentioned which contains, constituting as it does a principal part, while in the same there is understood to be present that which is contained, this being a subordinate part. For instance, if I were to say: The city built a theatre and a circus, but the stage was of such and such a kind, and there were statues on the canal, and an obelisk rose above all—would it follow that, because I did not say expressly that these specific objects, too, were made by the city, they were not made by it together with the circus and the theatre? Or did I fail to add that these parts, too, were made for the simple reason that they were contained in the things which I had already said were made, and ⟨so⟩ could be understood to be present in the things in which they were contained? But this example may be just idle talk, since it is taken from the human sphere. I shall take another from the authority of Scripture itself. *God*, it says, *made man of the earth, and breathed into his face the breath of life, and man became a living soul.*[259] It does mention his face here, but it has not mentioned that this was made by God; and later it speaks of his skin and bones and flesh and eyes and sweat and blood, of which it then did not intimate either that they had been made by God. What will Hermogenes answer? Surely the limbs of man will not also belong to matter, because they are not expressly mentioned as having been made? Or are they, too, rather included in the creation of man? 5. In the same way the deep and darkness, the spirit and the waters were members of the heaven and the earth, for in the bodies the limbs were made, in the names of the bodies the names of the limbs, too, were included. There is no element but that is a member of that element in which it is contained; and all elements are contained in the heaven and the earth.

Ch. 32] This [260] is what I would answer in defence of the present passage from Scripture as here appearing, to establish the creation of the bodies of the heaven and the earth alone. It [261] knew [262] that there were those who would spontaneously understand in the bodies their members as well, and so it used concise language. Nevertheless, it also foresaw that there would be stupid and at the same time astute men who, though understanding, yet affecting not to understand what is not expressly stated, [263] would also require for the individual members an indication of their creation. It is therefore because of such people that in other passages it also furnishes information concerning the creation of individual parts. 2. You have Wisdom saying, *And before the depths was I begotten,* [264] that you may believe that the depth, too, was begotten, that is, made (for we also 'make' sons, though we 'beget' them). It makes no difference whether the depth was made or born, [265] provided it is accorded a beginning, which could not be the case if the depth were incorporated in matter. [266] Further, of darkness the Lord Himself says by the mouth of Isaias: *I, who formed the light and created darkness.* [267] Of the spirit, too, Amos says: *He that strengtheneth the thunder, and createth the spirit, and declareth His Christ unto men,* [268] showing that that spirit was created which was reckoned to belong to the ⟨equally⟩ created earth, [269] the spirit which swept over the waters—the power which balances, refreshes, and animates the universe—and that not, as some think, God Himself was signified by the 'spirit' [270] because *God is a spirit;* [271] no, the waters would not be strong enough to bear the Lord. He means that spirit from which the winds have also sprung, as He says by Isaias: *Because my spirit went forth from me and I have made every breath.* [272] Further, the same Wisdom says of the waters: *And when* [273] *He secured the fountains, things which are under the sky, I was moulding them with Him.*[274]

3. Now, when we thus [275] prove that those subordinate parts were also made by God, though in Genesis there is a mere recording of their names without mention of their creation, it will perhaps be replied by the opposition that they were made, to be sure, but out of matter, so that the passage [276] in Moses, *And darkness was over the deep, and the spirit of God moved over the waters,* refers to matter,[277] whereas the further relevant passages of Scripture designate separately the specific parts made out of matter.

4. ⟨But⟩ then ⟨it follows that⟩ as earth originated from earth, so depth must also have originated from depth, and darkness from darkness, and spirit and waters from spirit and waters.[278] And, as we stated above, matter could not have been without a form, if it contained specific parts,[279] so that other parts [280] were also made out of it.[281] Only the latter were not other parts, but the same ⟨specific parts⟩ proceeding from themselves—for it is impossible that they should have been different, when they are brought forth with the same names—and on this account[282] God's activity might also seem to be superfluous, if it made things which existed already, whereas ⟨, moreover,⟩ these things would have been more august if they had not been made than if they had been made.[283] 5. Therefore, to conclude, either Moses signified matter when he wrote, *And darkness was over the deep, and the spirit of God moved over the waters—* but [284] ⟨then⟩, when afterwards in other places it is shown that these parts were made by God, it ought also to be shown that they were made out of that matter which Moses had mentioned before—or, if Moses signified those parts and not matter, I ask where the existence of matter has been demonstrated.

FURTHER POSITIVE PROOF FOR A CREATION
OUT OF NOTHING

Ch. 33] But [285] until Hermogenes has found it among his colours [286]—for in the books of God's Scriptures he cannot find it—it is enough that, first, it is certain that all things were made by God, and that, secondly, it is not certain that they were made out of matter. But even if matter had existed, we would believe that it had also been made by God, for by laying down the rule that nothing is unborn except God, we would win our case [287] (up to this point ⟨only⟩ is there room for doubt—until the endeavour to prove the existence of matter is brought to the test of the Scriptures and has to be given up [288]). The main point is clear now: I find that nothing was made except from nothing, because I know that what I find was made, once did not exist. Also if something is made out of something, it draws its origin from something made: thus from the earth originated the grass and the fruits and the cattle and the form of man himself, so from the waters the swimming and flying animals. Such origins of things produced out of such things [289] I may call 'materials' ('matters'), but on the understanding that these, too, were made by God.

Ch. 34] The [290] fact that everything sprang from nothing will ultimately [291] be made plausible by the dispensation of God which is to return all things to nothing. 2. For *the heaven shall be rolled together as a scroll,* [292] nay, it will disappear along with the earth itself, with which it was made in the beginning. *Heaven and earth shall pass,* [293] says Scripture, *the first heaven and the first earth passed away,* [294] *and there was no place found for them* [295]—because, of course, that which ceases to exist also loses its place in space.[296] Thus, too, David : *The heavens are the works of Thy hands* and *they shall perish*; for if *as a vesture He shall change them, and they shall be changed,*[297] yet to be changed is to fall from that former state which, by being changed, they lose. [298] *And the stars shall fall from heaven, as the fig tree loseth its untimely figs, when it is shaken by a mighty wind,*[299] and *the mountains shall melt like wax at the presence of the Lord,*[300] that is, *when He ariseth to shatter the earth.*[301] But He also says, *I will dry up the pools,*[302] and *they shall seek for water, and they shall not find it;*[303] also *the sea shall be no more.*[304]

3. Now, even if he should think that all these passages ought to be interpreted in a different way,[305] he will yet not be able to explain away the reality of things which are to happen exactly as they were written. For if ⟨in these passages⟩ there are some allegories,[306] they must necessarily arise from existing, not from non-existing things, because nothing can furnish anything of its own for a similitude, unless it itself be such that it lends itself to such a similitude.[307]

4. I return, then, to my propostion which defines[308] that all things produced from nothing will in the end come to nothing. For from an eternal being, that is, from matter, God would not have made anything perishable; nor out of greater things would He have created smaller ones, since it is more appropriate to Him to produce greater things out of smaller ones—that is to say, out of something perishable that which is eternal. 5. This it is which He also promises our flesh, and of this His goodness and power He has moreover willed to deposit this pledge in us, that we might believe that He also raised up the universe from nothing into existence, when, since it did not exist, it was, as it were, dead.

THE TREATISE AGAINST HERMOGENES

HERMOGENES' NOTION OF THE *CONDITION* OF MATTER IS CONTRADICTORY AND ABSURD

Ch. 35] But[309] as to the further condition of matter, though there is no need to treat this subject—for first the fact of its existence should be established—yet we must, as though this had been established, adhere to the sequence in order that its non-existence may be the more certain as its further condition cannot be established either,[310] and also that Hermogenes may acknowledge his own contradictions.

2. 'At first sight,' he says, 'matter seems to us to be incorporeal; but when it is examined by the right method, it is found to be neither corporeal nor incorporeal.' But what is that 'right method' which proclaims nothing right, that is, nothing certain? For, if I am not mistaken, everything must necessarily be either corporeal or incorporeal—even granting for the moment that there is something incorporeal,[311] at least in substances, though the substance in itself is the body of every single thing; at all events, besides the corporeal and the incorporeal there is no third ⟨class of things⟩. 3. But to grant a third, detected by that 'right method' of Hermogenes which makes matter neither corporeal nor incorporeal—where is it? What sort of thing is it? What is it called? How is it described? What is understood by it? All that the 'method' has stated is that matter is neither corporeal nor incorporeal.

Ch. 36] But[312] see, he promptly adds a contrary proposition (or perhaps another 'method' has suggested itself to him!), declaring that matter is partly corporeal and partly incorporeal. Then must matter now be thought to be both, lest it should be neither?[313] For if it is both corporeal and incorporeal, this will be contrary to the declaration of that 'right method'[314] which, to be sure, does not account for its statement, as it does not account for other things either.[315] 2. Anyway, he wants the corporeal part of matter to be that from which bodies are created, whereas the incorporeal part is its irregular motion. 'For if,' he says, 'it were only a body, nothing incorporeal would appear in it, that is, no motion; if, on the other hand, it had been entirely incorporeal, no body would have been made out of it.' 3. How much 'righter' is this 'method'! Only, if you draw your lines as right, Hermogenes, as you make your method, there is no painter more stupid than you. Indeed, who assents to your regarding motion as the second part of a substance, while it is not a substantial thing because it is not corporeal either, but an accident—if it be even that— of a substance and a body, just as are action and impulsion, as is a slip and a fall,[316] and so also motion? 4. For if a thing is set in motion, be it even by itself,[317] its motion is an action and certainly not a part of a substance in the sense you make motion a substance by making it an incorporeal part of matter. After all, all things are set in motion, either by themselves as animals, or by others as inanimate things; but we shall not call a man and a stone both corporeal and incorporeal, because they have both a body and motion: we shall rather say that all things have one form of simple corporeality, which is a substantial thing;[318] if some incorporeal things are incidental to them, such as actions or passions or functions or desires, we do not regard these as parts of them. 5. What, then, is the sense of assigning the status of a part of matter to motion, which does not belong to the category of substance but rather to a condition of substance? Indeed, if it had pleased you to represent matter

as immovable, certainly its immobility would not be regarded by you as the other half of its form.[319] Therefore,
neither can motion be such. But concerning motion I shall
have occasion to speak in another context.

Ch. 37] Well[320] now, I see you are returning to that
'method' which has a habit of telling you nothing certain.
As a matter of fact, just as you represent matter as neither
corporeal nor incorporeal, you allege that it is neither good
nor evil, and, arguing on in the same strain, you say: 'For
if it were good, it would, having been so always, not require to be set in order by God. If it were evil by nature, it
would not have admitted of improvement; nor, if it were
such by nature, would God have applied to it any regulation by Himself, for He would have laboured in vain.'
    2. These are your words which you should have remem-
bered as also occurring in other passages, to avoid making
contradictions of them. But since in what has gone before
we have already discussed to some extent the ambiguity
of good and evil as touching matter,[321] I shall now reply
only to your present proposition and argument. I shall not
say here again that you ought to have declared yourself
unequivocally—that matter was either good or evil or ruled
by some third quality; but ⟨I must point out⟩ that even
here you failed to keep to the statement it pleased you to
make. 3. Thus you revoke your statement that it is neither
good nor evil, when, saying, 'If it were good, it would not
require to be set in order by God,' you imply that it is evil,
and, adding, 'If it were evil by nature, it would not admit
of a change for the better,' you suggest that it is good. And
thus you have established an affinity of matter to both good
and evil, even though you have declared it to be neither
good nor evil.

4. Further, in order to refute also[322] the argument whereby you thought to confirm your proposition, I also have this objection to make: If matter had always been good, why should it not have wanted to be changed for the better? Does that which is good not want or desire or admit of progress, so as to change from good to better?[323] In like manner, if it had been evil by nature, why could it not have been changed by God as the more powerful Being, as the Power which can even convert the nature of stones into children of Abraham? 5. Certainly you thus not only put God on the same level with matter, but you even make Him inferior to it, since according to you the nature of matter could not have been subdued by Him and trained to something better. But again when here you will not have it that it is evil by nature, in other passages you will deny having made such an admission.[324]

Ch. 38]   Regarding [325] the site of matter I bring forward observations similar to those I have also made on its mode of being, in order to expose your erroneous views. [326] You put matter below God and thus, of course, you assign[327] a place to it, because it is below God. Matter, therefore, is in a place; if it is in a place, then it is bounded by the place within which it is; if it is bounded, it has an outline which, being a painter by profession, you acknowledge to be the boundary of everything of which it is the outline. Therefore matter will not be infinite because, being in a place, it is bounded by that place and since, being bounded by it, it experiences this circumscription on its outline.[328] 2. But you make it infinite when you say: 'Further, it is infinite for the reason that it always exists.' 3. And if one of your pupils proposes to argue that you will have it understood that matter is infinite in time, not in the quantity of its body, then the words which follow show that it is, on the contrary, infinite in regard to its body, since it is regarding its body that it is unmeasurable and unbounded. 'Wherefore, too,' you say, 'it is worked up, not as a whole, but in its parts.' Hence it is infinite in body, not in time, and you will stand refuted [329] when you make it infinite in body, whereas ⟨, on the other hand,⟩ by assigning a place in space to it, you include it within that place and its outline. 4. But yet I do not understand why God did not form it entirely, unless it be that He was either powerless to do so or envious. And thus I want to become acquainted with the ⟨other⟩ half of matter, which was not wholly formed, that I may understand how it was in its entirety. Indeed, God should have made it known as an example [330] of antiquity for the glory of His work.

Ch. 39]   Let [331] matter now be distinct, as is your more correct view, on account of its changes and transpositions; let it also be comprehensible, since, as you say, 'it is worked up by God,' because it is also convertible and changeable and divisible ('For its changes,' you say, 'show it to be divisible') : Here you have once again deflected from your own lines, [331a] which you have drawn with regard to the person of God by setting up the rule that God did not make matter out of Himself, since He could not be divided into parts for the reason that He is eternal and existing forever and therefore unchangeable and indivisible. If matter is considered to possess the same eternity because it has neither a beginning nor an end, it will be incapable of division and change in the same way that God, too, is: having been placed in the joint possession of eternity ⟨with God⟩, it must needs share with Him the powers and the laws and the conditions of eternity.

2. Likewise, when you say: 'Further, its parts contain simultaneously all things taken from all ⟨its constituents⟩, so that the whole can be known from its parts,' you want, of course, those parts to be understood which were produced out of it and which we see to-day. How, then, do those parts contain all things taken from all ⟨its constitutents⟩—meaning, of course, the original ⟨constituents⟩ —when the parts of matter seen to-day are different from the original constituents? [332]

Ch. 40] You [333] say that matter was re-formed for the better—meaning, of course, from a worse condition—and you will have it that better things bear the image of worse things? [334] It was a confused thing, but now it has been reduced to order—and you will have it that order reflects disorder? [335]

2. No one thing is the image of another thing, that is to say, of a thing that is not its coequal. [336] Nobody ever saw himself in the barbershop as a mule instead of a man—unless one should think that formless and unordered matter is reflected in the matter which is now arranged and made into beautiful things [337] in this bountifully furnished world. What is there to-day that is without form in the world, what was there before that was formed in matter, so that the world could be the image of matter? [338] When among the Greeks the world is known by a name meaning 'ornament,' how can it present an image of unadorned [339] matter, so that you might say that the whole can be known from its parts? 3. At all events, to that whole will also belong that part which has not become formed (and you stated earlier [340] that matter was not worked up in its entirety). Therefore this rude and confused and unarranged part cannot be recognized [341] in the polished and

distinct and well-arranged things, which it is not even
suitable to call parts of matter, since, by being separated
from it in consequence of their transformation, they have
abandoned its condition.[342]

HERMOGENES FURTHER CONTRADICTS HIMSELF REGARDING *MOTION* IN MATTER

Ch. 41] I[343] return to the subject of motion in order to
show that you are slippery everywhere. The motion of
matter was disorderly and confused[344] and turbulent. This is
why you apply to it the picture of a pot boiling over. Now,
how is it that in another passage this motion is asserted by
you to be different? For when you want to represent matter
as neither good nor evil, you say: 'So matter, which lies at
the root ⟨of creation⟩, possessing as it does motion of uniform momentum, does not strongly incline[345] towards
either good or evil.' If this motion had a uniform momentum, then it was not turbulent nor like the water in the
pot,[346] but well-ordered and steady because, moving as it
did between good and evil of its own accord, yet without
inclining and tending to either side, keeping the tongue
of the balance, as they say, in the center,[347] it manifested
itself in a well-balanced course. This is not unrest,[348] this is
not turbulence and confusion: it is the regularity and con-
trol and normalcy of a motion inclining to neither side. If
it moved this way and that way, or if it inclined more to
one side, then it would obviously deserve to be labelled for
unevenness and inequality and turbulence.

2. Furthermore, if motion in matter did not tend more
to good nor to evil, yet it certainly was there, impelled between good and evil, so that from this circumstance, too,
it is evident that matter was contained within fixed limits:

for its motion, not tending to either good or evil, because
it did not incline [349] to [350] either side, went on between the
two at a distance from either and for that reason was de-
limited by the two.

3. But, what is more, you make both good and evil local,
when you say that the motion of matter inclined to neither
of them: for when matter, which was local, inclined
neither to the one nor to the other, it refrained from inclining to the *places* in which good and evil were. Now, when
you assign a place in space to good and evil, you make them
corporeal by making them local, since things which have a
place in space must first be corporeal. After all, incorporeal
things could not have a place of their own except in a
body, when they have access [351] to a body. But with matter
not inclining [352] to good and evil, it was as corporeal or
local things that it did not incline to them. [353] You are
wrong, therefore, when you will have it that good and
evil are substances; [354] for you make substances of things to
which you assign locality; and you assign locality to them
when you keep motion in matter suspended within two
directions.

Ch. 42]   You [355] have given out your tenets in wide dis-
persion lest by their being correlated it become clear, how
they contradict each other; but I shall gather the several
notions together and compare them.

You assert that the motion of matter is irregular,
and you subjoin that matter aims at formlessness; then, in
another passage, that it wants to be set in order by God.
Does it want to receive a form, if it aims at formlessness?
Or does it aim at formlessness, if it wants to receive a
form?

2. You will not have it that God seems to be made equal

to matter,[356] and you subjoin that it has a common condition with God. 'For it is impossible,' you say, 'when it does not have something in common with God, that it be adorned by Him ⟨with a form⟩.' But if it had something in common with God, it did not want to be adorned by Him, for in that case it was a part of God by reason of this participation in Him. Or else God could also be adorned by matter since He, too, has something in common with it. Further,[357] you herein make God subject to necessity, if there was something in matter because of which He should form it.

3. Moreover, you make them share this in common, that they are both set in motion by themselves and that they are always in motion.[358] What less do you ascribe to matter than to God? This freedom and eternity of motion makes for a complete joint possession of divinity. 'But God's motion is regular, that of matter, irregular.' Nevertheless, matter is something equally divine,[359] since its motion is equally free and eternal. Nay, you grant even more to matter: it had freedom of moving itself in a way not permitted to God.

Ch. 43]   Concerning[360] motion I would make this further observation. Immediately after using the simile of the boiling pot you say: 'Such was the motion of matter before it was regulated—confused, restless, and incomprehensible by reason of its excessive commotion.' Then you add: 'But it waited to be set in order by God, and it kept its irregular motion comprehensible[361] due to[362] the slowness of this irregular motion.' In the former instance you impute commotion—here, slowness, to motion.

2. Now,[363] regarding the nature of matter, note how many slips you make. In an earlier passage you say: 'But if

6—A.C.W. 24

matter were evil by nature, it would not have admitted of improvement, nor . . . would God have applied to it any regulation . . ., for He would have laboured in vain.' Thus you have formed two definitive statements—that matter is not evil by nature, and that its nature could not have been transformed by God. Then you forget them and draw the inference: 'But when it was adjusted by God and was adorned ⟨with a form⟩, it lost its nature.' If it was re-formed to something good, it was at all events reformed from something evil, and if in consequence of adjustment by God it lost its nature of evil, it consequently lost its nature as such. And so [364] we may say that it was evil by nature before its adjustment, and that it could also lose its nature after that reformation.

HERMOGENES' THEORY ON *THE ACT OF CREATION* REFUTED

Ch. 44] But [365] next I must show also how you say that God has worked. You are obviously keeping aloof from the philosophers; but yet you are doing the same with regard to the prophets. Thus the Stoics hold that God pervaded matter as honey the honeycombs. [366] You, however, say: 'It is not by pervading matter that He makes the world, but merely by appearing to it and approaching it, just as beauty [367] affects something by merely appearing to it, and a magnet by merely approaching it.' 2. But what similarity is there between God fashioning the world and beauty wounding the soul, or a magnet attracting iron? For even if God did appear to matter, He yet did not wound it, as beauty does the soul; and if He did approach it, He did not adhere to it, as the magnet does to iron.

3. But suppose now that your examples are apposite: then, at all events, if it was by appearing to and approaching matter that God made the world out of it, He certainly made it since the moment when He appeared to it and when He approached it. Therefore, since He had not made it before that moment, He had neither appeared to it nor approached it. And who can believe that God did not appear to matter ⟨at any time⟩, were it only because matter shares the same substance with Him because of its eternity? Or that He had been far removed from it whom we believe to be present everywhere and to appear everywhere, and whose praises are sung even by inanimate and incorporeal things in Daniel?[368] How immense the place must have been where God kept himself so far aloof from matter that He neither appeared to it nor approached it before the creation of the world! I suppose He had to make a long journey to reach it when He wanted to make his first appearance and approach to it!

Ch. 45] But[369] it is not thus that the prophets and apostles tell us that the world was made by God, by merely appearing to and approaching matter. Indeed, they did not even mention any matter but stated that first Wisdom was created, *the beginning*[370] *of His ways for His works*[371] and that next the Word was also brought forth, *by whom all things were made and without whom nothing was made.*[372] Indeed, *by His Word the heavens were established, and all the hosts of them by His breath,*[373] He is God's *right hand,*[374] indeed both His hands,[375] by which He worked and built the universe—for *the heavens*, says Scripture, *are the works of Thy hands*[376]—by *which* He *also hath measured the heaven, and the earth with a span.*[377]

2. You must not try to flatter God[378] to the extent of

asserting that He produced substances so numerous and so great by a mere look and a mere approach instead of creating them by His own powers. Thus it is also represented by Jeremias: *God hath made the earth by His power, He hath prepared the world by His wisdom, and hath stretched out the heavens by His understanding.*[379] These[380] are His powers by which He worked and created this universe. The greater is His glory if He really laboured. After all, on the seventh day He rested from His works: both things are in accordance with His way of acting. Or, supposing that He made this world by merely appearing to it and approaching it—did He, when He stopped creating, cease to appear and to approach it again?[381] On the contrary, from the time the world was made, He began to appear still more and to be addressed everywhere as God. 3. Thus you see how the universe exists by the operation of God who *made the earth by His power, prepared the world by His wisdom, and stretched out the heaven by His understanding*;[382] who did not merely appear or approach, but applied in wondrous labour His mind, His wisdom, His power, His understanding, His Word, His Spirit, His might.[383] These faculties would not have been necessary to Him if He had set out on a journey in order to merely appear ⟨to matter⟩ and to approach it.[384] But these are *the invisible things of Him*, which—so the Apostle—*from the creation of the world are clearly seen . . . by*[385] *the things that are made*:[386] they are not matter in some form or other, but operative functions of His mind.[387] *For who hath known the mind of the Lord*[388] of which ⟨the Apostle⟩ proclaims: *O the depth of His riches and wisdom! How incomprehensible are His judgments and how undiscoverable His ways?*[389] What else do these words convey than: 'How true—all things were made out of nothing!' For[390] they could not be comprehended nor discovered save by God alone; otherwise,[391] if they derive from matter, they would admit of discovery and comprehension.

EPILOGUE

4. And thus, in as far as it has been established that matter did not exist (also for the reason that it cannot have been such as it is represented), in so far is it proved that all things were made by God out of nothing. I would add only that[392] by delineating a condition of matter quite like his own—irregular, confused, turbulent, with a disordered, rash, and violent motion—Hermogenes[393] has put on exhibition a sample of his art: he has painted his own portrait.

NOTES

In the notes below α stands for the consensus of the manuscripts P and N, β for the consensus of X, F, V, and L. The smaller groups FVL and VL are indicated respectively by γ and δ. For further details, see the third chapter of the Introduction.

INTRODUCTION

[1] *Hist. eccl.* 4.24.1. In this connection it may be observed that the *Adversus Hermogenem* contains six quotations from the Apocalypse of St. John and that these are found in no other work of Tertullian. Thus the possibility suggests itself that Tertullian borrowed them from, or owed them to, Theophilus, as is certainly the case in regard to a number of ideas occurring in this author; see the end of the present chapter.

[2] J. L. Mosheim, *Commentarii de rebus christianis ante Constantinum Magnum* (Helmstedt 1753) 453, and C. W. F. Walch, *Ketzergeschichte* 1 (Leipzig 1762), 552 ff., questioned the identity of the Hermogenes refuted by Theophilus with Tertullian's opponent. This supposition was refuted by G. Uhlhorn in his article, 'Hermogenes,' in Herzog-Hauck, *Realencyklopädie* 7 (3 ed. 1899) 756–58; moreover, we shall see at the end of this chapter that several of Tertullian's arguments also occur in Theophilus' *Ad Autolycum*, so that we may infer that Tertullian borrowed these from his predecessor (cf. also the end of n. 1 above).

[3] Tertullian, *Adv. Herm.* 1.2 (cf. n. 5 to text). Allusions to Hermogenes' profession occur in 3.7 (cf. n. 30 to text), 36.3, 38.1, and 45.4; see also *De monog.* 16: *Hermogenem aliquem, plures solitum mulieres ducere quam pingere.*

[4] *Adv. Herm.* 1.2: *ad hodiernum homo in saeculo.*

[5] Cf. my discussion of the contents of this treatise in my edition of the *De anima*, pp. 7*–14*.

[6] This inference may, in my opinion, be drawn from the first sentence of the *De anima*: *De solo censu animae congressus Hermogeni . . . iam ad reliquas conversus quaestiones*, for these words seem to imply that the *De censu animae* was composed shortly, if not immediately, before the *De anima*, which treatise was written between 210 and 213 A.D. (cf. my edition, p. 5* f.), whereas the *Adversus Hermogenem* seems to have been composed before 207 A.D. (cf. the end of the present chapter). It is, further, more plausible that Tertullian, when his attention had been drawn to the doctrine of Hermogenes, first attacked the fundamental

thesis, that is, the creation of the universe by God out of matter, and that in the course of this refutation he decided to reserve the treatment of Hermogenes' doctrine of the soul for a special treatise; in fact, nothing is said about this subject in the *Adversus Hermogenem*.

[7] Cf. n. 5 above.

[8] For a particularly striking example, cf. my note on *De an.* 6.1— p. 132 f.

[9] For the use of *occupatio* in Tertullian's works, cf. my note on *De an.* 35.5—p. 416.

[10] *Adv. Herm.* 2.1: *praestruens dominum de semetipso fecisse cuncta aut de nihilo aut de aliquo.*—From now on quotations from the present treatise are given with the numbers of the respective chapter and paragraph only.

[11] 2.2 f. Cf. the analysis of this lengthy argument in n. 15 to text. Other testimonies for the first syllogism (I.A in n. 15) are found in 12.3 and 39.1; cf. also 15.1: *quia nihil potuit ex deo fieri, sicut definit Hermogenes.*

[12] The 'official' record of the argument is given in 2.4. Further, cf. 10.1: '*Ergo*,' inquit, '*ex nihilo faceret, ut mala quoque arbitrio eius imputarentur?*'; 16.2: *Hermogenes qui deum, quoquo modo de materia malum condidit, sive voluntate sive necessitate sive ratione, non putet mali auctorem.*

[13] These statements occur throughout the present treatise: cf. especially ch. 10 and 14.2.

[14] 2.4: *Quod ergo non arbitrio suo fecerit, id intellegi oportere ex vitio alicuius rei factum, ex materia sine dubio.* It is greatly to be regretted that this record (which at the end undoubtedly abbreviates the argument of Hermogenes) does not bring out how, after concluding that the universe must have been created out of something, Hermogenes demonstrated that this 'something' must be matter. Hence we do not know whether his statement that matter is the origin of evil (11.1: *malum adscribit*—that is, to matter; 11.3: *secundum mali statum*—on this difficult passage, cf. n. 98 to text; 25.3: *illa autem apud Hermogenem in originem et causam malorum deputatur*) was a premise of his argument ('now, since matter is the origin of evil, this "something" must be matter') or an inference drawn from the conclusion ('now this "something" can only have been matter, and since evil must have been created out of this "something," matter must be the origin of evil'); the latter possibility is by far the more probable one; cf. below, n. 27.

[15] 21.1: '*Ergo*,' inquis, '*si tu ideo praeiudicas ex nihilo facta omnia quia non sit manifeste relatum de materia praecedenti factum quid, vide ne diversa pars ideo contendat ex materia omnia facta, quia proinde non aperte significatum sit ex nihilo quid factum.*'

[16] 3.1: *Adicit et aliud: deum semper deum ⟨semper⟩ etiam dominum fuisse, numquam non dominum. Nullo porro modo potuisse illum semper dominum haberi, sicut et semper deum, si non fuisset aliquid retro semper, cuius semper dominus haberetur. Fuisse itaque materiam semper deo domino.* Further, 9.1: *Non potest dicere deum ut dominum materia usum ad opera mundi*; 9.3: *cum ex dominio defendit deum materia usum*; Hippolytus, *Elench.* 8.17.1: 'and that God is always Lord . . . and matter always His slave.'

[17] 4.1: *eam* (i.e. matter) . . . *non natam,* . . . *non factam,* . . . *aeternam, sine initio sine fine propositam*; 39.1: *Si et materia eadem aeternitate censetur neque initium habens neque finem; De praescr. haer.* 33.9: *Idem apostolus, cum improbat elementis servientes* (Gal. 4.3; Col. 2.8), *aliquid Hermogenis ostendit, qui materiam non natam introducens deo non nato eam comparat, et ita matrem elementorum deam faciens potest ei servire, quam deo comparat.* I regard it as certain that Hermogenes qualified the soul as 'unborn,' but I have serious doubts whether, as Tertullian says, he also called it 'unmade': for one thing, Tertullian has an outright habit of adding *non factus* (or *infectus*) after *non natus* (or *innatus*)—thus in *De an.* 4 he says that Plato called the soul *innatam et infectam*, whereas Plato only called it an 'unborn substance' (cf. my note *ad loc.*, p. 121). Again, Hippolytus states merely that Hermogenes qualified matter as unborn —*Elench.* 8.17.1: 'A certain Hermogenes . . . declared that God had made everything out of matter which was equal to Him in time and unborn; that it was impossible that God should not make the things which come into being from existing things' (cf. also Theodoret, *Haer. fab. comp.* 1.19); almost the same text occurs in *Elench.* 10.28, where, however, Hippolytus speaks of 'underlying,' not of 'unborn,' matter. From the passage quoted it is, in my opinion, evident that Tertullian has omitted a second argument of Hermogenes in favour of his statement that God cannot have created the universe out of nothing, that is, the general impossibility 'not to make the things which come into being from existing things.' This purely logical argument tallies with the equally purely logical refutation of the conception that God created all things out of Himself (cf. above, n. 11).

[18] 5.1: '*Sed deus deus est et materia materia est*'; 5.2: '*Vel qua,*' inquit, '*et sic habente* (the Grecism should be noted) *materia* (that is to say, even if it should be eternal), *salva sit deo et auctoritas et substantia, qua solus et primus auctor est et dominus omnium censeatur*'; 6.1: *Dicit salvum deo esse, ut et solus sit et primus et omnium auctor et omnium dominus et nemini comparandus*; 6.3: *semper fuisse sine initio sine fine, et primum fuisse et solum et omnium auctorem*; 7.1: *Si minorem et inferiorem materiam deo et idcirco diversam ab eo et idcirco incomparabilem illi contendit ut maiori, ut superiori.*

[19] 15.4: *Nam et Hermogenes expugnat quorundam argumentationes dicentium mala necessaria fuisse ad inluminationem bonorum ex contrariis intellegendorum.*

[20] 19.1: *Nam et ipsum 'principium' in quo deus fecit et caelum et terram aliquid volunt fuisse quasi substantivum et corpulentum, quod in materiam interpretari possit.*

[21] 23.1: *Sed ex sequentibus argumentatur, quia scriptum sit: 'Terra autem erat invisibilis et incomposita.' Nam et 'terrae' nomen redigit in materiam, quia terra sit quae facta est ex illa, et 'erat' in hoc dirigit, quasi quae semper retro fuerit innata et infecta, 'invisibilis' autem 'et rudis,' quia informem et confusam et inconditam vult fuisse materiam.* Thus Hermogenes came to distinguish the earth of Gen. 1.1 (= this earth) from the earth mentioned in Gen. 1.2 which he identified with matter—25.1: *Vult igitur duas proponi terras in ista scriptura, unam quam in principio deus fecit, aliam materiam ex qua fecit, de qua dictum sit: 'Terra autem erat invisibilis et rudis'*; 25.3: *'Sed materia facta, id est terra, habuit cum sua origine consortium nominis, sicut et generis'* (from the context it seems probable that this is not a literal quotation but rather a statement which Tertullian puts into Hermogenes' mouth). Cf. also 27.1: *'Erat' inquis, quasi semper fuerit, scilicet innata et infecta et idcirco materia credenda.*

[22] 30.1: *Sic et sequentia coniecturam Hermogenis instruere videbuntur: 'Et tenebrae super abyssum et spiritus dei super aquas ferebatur,' quasi et hae confusae substantiae massalis illius molis argumenta portendant.* From the future tense of the main verb (*videbuntur*) one might infer that Tertullian has thought out this argument himself in order promptly to refute it, but on second thought it seems to be out of the question that Hermogenes should not have brought into the discussion the second half of a verse the first half of which he had so thoroughly interpreted. Moreover, the idea to regard the four 'elements' mentioned in Gen. 1.2 as constituent parts of matter is so obvious (especially because nothing is said there about their creation), that we cannot but assume that this idea was indeed advanced by Hermogenes.

[23] 31.1: *Sed et illud utique captabitur, de caelo solo et de terra ista scripturam significasse, quod ea in principio deus fecerit, de speciebus autem supra dictis* (i.e. the four 'elements' of Gen. 1.2) *nihil tale, et ideo eas quae factae non significentur ad infectam materiam pertinere.* This idea, too, is so closely connected with Hermogenes' further interpretations, that the future tense of *captabitur* will have to be understood as a symptom of Tertullian's temperament (indeed, he frequently uses this tense both in reports and in conclusions, as he also makes extensive use of the 'gnomic future'), not as an *occupatio*. On the other hand, a case of *occupatio* must, in my opinion, be seen in 32.3: *Cum ergo et eas species*

(namely, the darkness, the abyss, the spirit, and the waters) *probamus a deo factas, . . . respondebitur fortasse ex diverso plane factas eas, sed ex materia, ut stilus quidem Moysei* (Gen. 1.2) *. . . materiam sonet, ceterae vero scripturae quae ex materia factae sunt species in disperso demonstrent.*

²⁴ 35.2: '*Prima*,' inquit, '*facie videtur nobis incorporalis esse materia, exquisita autem ratione recta invenitur neque corporalis neque incorporalis.*'

²⁵ 36.1: *Sed ecce contrarium subicit (aut alia fortasse ratio [cf. n. 24] ei occurrit) ex parte corporalem renuntians materiam et ex parte incorporalem.*

²⁶ 36.2: *Corporale enim materiae vult esse de quo corpora edantur, incorporale vero inconditum motum eius.* '*Si enim,*' ait, '*corpus tantummodo esset, nihil ei incorporale appareret, id est motus; si vero in totum incorporalis fuisset, nullum corpus ex ea fieret.*'

²⁷ 37.1 f.: *. . . nec bonam nec malam adlegas, et proinde superargumentans,* '*Si enim,*' inquis, '*esset bona, quae semper hoc fuerat, non desideraret compositionem dei; si esset natura mala, non accepisset translationem in melius, nec quicquam compositionis suae adplicuisset illi deus tali natura; in vacuum enim laborasset.*' *Verba haec tua sunt.* With slight variations, 37.3: '*Si esset bona, non desideraret componi a deo . . . . Si esset mala natura, non admitteret in melius translationem*'; 43.2: '*Si autem esset materia natura mala, non accepisset translationem in melius nec deus aliquid compositionis accommodasset illi; in vacuum enim laborasset.*' In the same vein is the statement in 41.1: '*Igitur,*' inquis, '*subiacens materia aequalis momenti habens motum neque ad bonum neque ad malum plurimum vergit.*' Tertullian infers from this sentence that Hermogenes regarded the motion of matter as generally equable which, as he is not slow to point out, contradicts his former statement about a chaotic motion. But Hermogenes undoubtedly meant to say that this motion is *aequalis momenti* only in so far as it does not incline to either good or evil.

²⁸ 14.1: *Nam et si dicatur, licet ex occasione materiae, suo tamen arbitrio bona protulisse, quasi nactus bonum materiae.*

²⁹ 38.2 f.: *At tu infinitam facis dicens:* '*Infinita est autem eo quod semper est.*' *Et si qui discipulorum tuorum voluerit argumentari, quasi infinitam aevo, non modo corporis intellegi velis, atquin corporaliter infinitam, ut corporaliter immensam et incircumscriptam, sequentia ostendunt:* '*Unde,*' inquis, '*nec tota fabricatur, sed partes eius.*' *Adeo corpore infinita, non tempore est.*

³⁰ Hippolytus, *Elench.* 8.17.2: 'when He saw it (i.e. matter) boiling like hot water'; Tertullian 41.1: *Inconditus et confusus et turbulentus fuit materiae motus. Sic enim et ollae undique ebullientis similitudinem opponis* (*ibid.* this motion is qualified as *caccabacius*, for which adjective cf. n. 346 to text); 42.1: *Inconditum adseveras motum materiae eamque adicis sectari informitatem.*

³¹ Hippolytus, *Elench.* 8.17.2: 'for it (i.e. matter) was continuously in

a wild and unordered motion, but He regulated it in the following way: when He saw it boiling like hot water, He divided it into (two) parts, and, taking one part out of the whole, He regulated it, but the other part He let persist in its unordered motion. And the regulated part, he (Hermogenes) says, is the cosmos, but the other part retains its wildness and is called unordered matter; that, he says, is the essence (οὐσία) of the universe.' It is this regulation by God which is meant in Hermogenes' statement that matter was improved (40.1: *Dicis in melius reformatam materiam*; cf. also 43.2: '*At ubi accepit compositionem a deo, cessavit a natura*'). These passages are important for Uhlhorn's reconstruction of Hermogenes' doctrine on the origin of evil (cf. n. 39).

³² 44.1: *At tu, 'Non,' inquis, 'pertransiens illam facit mundum, sed solummodo apparens et adpropinquans ei, sicut facit quid decor solummodo apparens et magnes lapis solummodo adpropinquans.*'

³³ 42.3: '*Impossibile enim,' inquis, 'non habentem illam commune aliquid cum deo ornari eam ab ipso*'; 42.4: *Commune autem inter illos facis, quod a semetipsis moveantur et semper moveantur; ibid.: 'Sed deus composite, materia incondite movetur.*'

³⁴ 38.3: '*Unde,' inquis, 'nec tota fabricatur, sed partes eius*' (*Unde* refers to 38.2: *At tu infinitam facis dicens: 'Infinita est autem eo quod semper est.*'—Tertullian also asserts that, in Hermogenes' description, matter was *subiacens deo*, from which he concludes that Hermogenes assigned a place to it—38.1: *Subiacentem facis deo materiam, et utique locum adsignas illi, qui sit infra deum* (for *subiacens*, cf. also 41.1: '*Igitur,' inquis, 'subiacens materia . . . neque ad bonum neque ad malum plurimum vergit*'). In my opinion, this is no more than a sophistic interpretation by Tertullian of the predicate 'underlying' attributed to matter by Hermogenes (cf. above, n. 17); the real meaning of this adjective in the present context is evident from the sentence immediately following in Hippolytus (*Elench.* 10.28.1=*ibid.* 8.17.1): 'and that God is always Lord . . . and matter always His slave.'

³⁵ 39.2: *Aeque cum dicis: 'Partes autem eius omnia simul ex omnibus habent, ut ex partibus totum dinoscatur*' (for the different interpretations of this passage, cf. n. 332 to text). The correct explanation has been given by J. A. W. Neander, *Antignostikus, Geist des Tertullianus und Einleitung in dessen Schriften* (2 ed. Berlin 1849) 347: 'Hermogenes behauptete: Die Bildung der Materie durch Gott ist eine unendliche Aufgabe, und immer bleibt ein der Bildung widerstrebender Rest zurück. So, sagt er, lässt sich, wie das Ganze in den Theilen, die Materie als das zum Grunde Liegende in der Welt erkennen, theils was sie durch die göttliche bildende Kraft werden konnte, theils was in ihr das aller Bildung Widerstrebende ist. Das alte Chaos lässt sich bei aller Schönheit und Ordnung

in der Welt doch immer noch als das zum Grunde Liegende erkennen; es scheint durch mitten durch die hergestellte Ordnung.'

[36] From 40.2: *Nulla res speculum est rei alterius, id est non coaequalis,* and *ibid.*: *ut speculum sit mundus materiae,* we may infer that Tertullian is refuting a statement by Hermogenes which contained this metaphor (cf. also Neander, *op. cit.* 347 n. 1).

[37] 39.1: *Sit nunc definitiva, sicut rectius tibi videtur* (allusion to Hermogenes' appeal to the *recta ratio*—cf. n. 24), *per demutationes suas et translationes, sit et comprehensibilis, ut quae 'fabricetur,' inquis, 'a deo,' quia et convertibilis et demutabilis et dispartibilis.* '*Demutationes enim eius,*' inquis, '*dispartibilem eam ostendunt*' (*fabricatur* must belong to the quotation since it is followed by *inquit* and since, if it formed part of Tertullian's sentence, it should have had a subjunctive after *ut quae*; the clause *quia ... dispartibilis* does not belong to the quotation, because in that case the *inquit* in the next sentence would have been superfluous; one may doubt whether the *enim* after *Demutationes* belongs to the quotation or not).

[38] 43.1: *Nam secundum* ('immediately after') *ollae similitudinem* (cf. n. 30), '*Sic erat,*' inquis, '*materiae motus antequam disponeretur, concretus, inquietus, inadprehensibilis prae nimietate certaminis.*' *Dehinc subicis:* '*Stetit autem in dei compositionem, et adprehensibilem habuit inconditum motum tarditate inconditi motus.*'

[39] Uhlhorn, *op cit.* 757: 'Hier liegt wohl der Punkt, von wo aus Hermogenes das Vorhandensein des Bösen erklären zu können glaubte. Die Materie wird nämlich nicht ganz, sondern nur teilweise gebildet (c. 38: 'Nec tota materia fabricatur, sed partes ejus'). Gott durchdringt sie nicht, es kommt also nur zu einer Bildung auf der Oberfläche. In jedem Teile der Materie ist aber zugleich das Ganze enthalten (c. 39), es bleibt daher in allem etwas von der ungeordneten Bewegung, und da wird Hermogenes, obwohl das aus Tertullians Angaben nicht ganz klar wird, die Ursache des Bösen gesehen haben.' Cf. also the quotation from Neander's *Antignostikus* in n. 35, and the same, p. 348: 'Nach der Lehre des Hermogenes ist nun also das, was in der Materie der Bildungskraft widerstrebt, was erst allmälig überwunden werden kann, der Grund des Mangelhaften und des Bösen; darin, dass die Bildung der Materie eine unendliche Aufgabe ist, liegt die Nothwendigkeit des Bösen.'

[40] *Op. cit.* 757 f.

[41] Hippolytus, *Elench.* 10.28.3: 'He (Hermogenes) acknowledges that Christ is the son of God, the Creator of the universe; he also acknowledges, in accordance with the statement of the Gospels, that He was born of the Virgin and the Spirit.'

[42] Hippolytus, *ibid.* (immediately after the sentence quoted in n. 41): 'and that, after His Passion, He rose from the dead and, in the possession

of His body, appeared before His disciples; and that, at His ascension to the heavens, He left His body in the sun, but had gone to the Father Himself' (in support of this statement Hermogenes quoted Ps. 18.6). Cf. also Clement of Alexandria, *Ecl. proph.* 56.2; Theodoret, *Haer. fab. comp.* 1.19.

⁴³ *De haer.* 26(54) (p. 28.10–14 Marx): *Sabellius post istum* (i.e. Noetus), *de Libia, discipulus eius, similitudinem sui doctoris itidem secutus est et errorem, unde et Sabelliani postea sunt appellati, qui et Patripassiani, et Praxeani a Praxea et Hermogene, qui fuerunt in Africa, qui et ita sentientes abiecti sunt ab ecclesia catholica.*

⁴⁴ *De haer.* 41 (PL 42.33), quotation of Filastrius, *loc. cit.*, with several divergences; with regard to Hermogenes: *et Praxeani a Praxea et Hermogeniani ab Hermogene, qui . . . catholica.*

⁴⁵ I borrow this qualification from C. Bäumker, *Das Problem der Materie in der griechischen Philosophie* (Münster 1890); the 'primary' matter of the *Timaeus* is, of course, space. The passages quoted in the following have been borrowed from the chapter, 'Die sogenannte "secundäre" Materie des Timaeus' (142–51).

⁴⁶ 3.2 (300b.16–19): 'if we accept the account of the *Timaeus*, that before the creation of the cosmos the elements were in disorderly motion' (tr. by W. K. C. Guthrie).

⁴⁷ Cf. especially Chalcidius' commentary on the *Timaeus*, c. 300 Wrobel: . . . *quando ante inlustrationem quoque motu instabili atque inordinato dixerit* (i.e. Plato) *eam fluctuasse, cum motus intimus genuinusque sit viventium proprius* (cf. also Tertullian, 42.4: *Commune autem inter illos* [i.e. God and matter] *facis, quod a semetipsis moveantur et semper moveantur*).

⁴⁸ Cf. my edition of the *De anima*, pp. 41*–44*.

⁴⁹ Texte und Untersuchungen 1.2 (1882) 289.

⁵⁰ G. Quispel, *De bronnen van Tertullianus' Adversus Marcionem* (Leiden 1943) ch. 3 (pp. 34–51).

⁵¹ Cf. n. 1.

⁵² The passages are the following: Apoc. 6.13—*Adv. Herm.* 34.2; 20.3—11.3; 20.11—34.2; 21.1—34.2 (two separate quotations); allusion to 22.18 ff. in 22.3.

⁵³ This idea, too, was borrowed by Tertullian, *Adv. Prax.* 5: *ante omnia enim deus erat solus, ipse sibi et mundus et locus et omnia.* For further details, cf. E. Evans, *Tertullian's Treatise against Praxeas* (London 1948) 212.

⁵⁴ The idea that God wanted to be known to man was borrowed by Tertullian for one of his ironical arguments (8.2): *Grande revera beneficium deo contulit* (i.e. matter), *ut haberet hodie per quae deus cognosceretur.*

55 Perhaps a reminiscence of a comparison of God with a human craftsman in Theophilus' refutation of Hermogenes may be found in the example of the *figulus* in *Adv. Herm.* 19.4.

56 1 *Apol.* 10.2; 59.1; 67.7. Cf. J. M. Pfättisch, *Der Einfluss Platons auf die Theologie Justins des Märtyrers* (Paderborn 1910) 93 ff.

57 *Orat. ad Graec.* 12 (12.22–24 Schwartz).

58 Theophilus uses the verb συνακμάζειν, which also occurs in the passage quoted above from 2.10. We may assume that it was a term of the Platonists borrowed from them by Hermogenes.

59 Theophilus 2.10. In other passages Theophilus makes a clear distinction between the Word and Wisdom, e.g. 1.7, 15, 18, but in the present passage he means (like Tertullian) to apply the statements concerning Wisdom in Proverbs 8.22 ff. to the Word which performed the act of creation.

60 Theophilus 2.10—Tertullian 18.

61 Theophilus 2.10—Tertullian 18.1.

62 Theophilus 2.10—Tertullian 20.

63 *Op. cit.* 38 n. 3.

64 Cf. the literature collected by Harnack, *Die Chronologie der altchristlichen Literatur bis Eusebius* 2 (Leipzig 1904) 256 n. 1.

65 Harnack, *op. cit.* 282. Harnack's treatment of the subject is greatly superior to all other discussions of it, but he is wrong in finding a reference to the present treatise in *De an.* 16 and 21 (Tertullian there refers to the *De censu animae*).

66 Harnack, *op. cit.* 281.

67 *Adv. Marc.* 1.15: *ad XV iam annum Severi imperatoris.*

68 Harnack, *op. cit.* 274.

69 See above, n. 6.

70 I concede this to C. Becker, *Gnomon* 25 (1953) 53.

71 I again agree with Becker (cf. the note preceding) that the exhortation to martydom in *De an.* 55 need not refer to an actual situation but may be explained from Tertullian's Montanism; on the other hand, I still regard the similarities between the *De anima* and the *De pallio* as so characteristic that I maintain my hypothesis that the two treatises were composed at about the same time.

72 One may wonder whether ch. 2 f. should not be added to the main part of the treatise; but in 4.1 Tertullian says: *Hic denique incipiam de materia retractare.*

73 E. Kroymann, 'Die Tertullian-Überlieferung in Italien,' *Sitzungsber. d. kais. Akad. d. Wiss.*, Philos.-hist. Cl. 138 (Vienna 1898) III. Abh. (quoted as Kr. I); 'Kritische Vorarbeiten für den III. und IV. Band der neuen Tertullian-Ausgabe,' *ibid.* 143 (Vienna 1901) VI Abh. (=Kr. II);

Prefaces to volumes 47 and 70 of the *Corpus scriptorum ecclesiasticorum latinorum* (=respectively Kr. III and IV).

74 J. W. P. Borleffs—cf. the preface of his edition of the *Ad nationes* (Leiden 1929); also: 'Observationes criticae in Tertulliani de paenitentia libellum,' *Mnemosyne* N. S. 60 (1933) 41–106; 'Un nouveau manuscrit de Tertullien,' *Vigiliae Christianae* 5 (1951) 65–79; further, cf. nn. 77 and 100.

75 Cf. Kr. IV p. XXIX.

76 Cf. Kr. IV p. XXXII; J. de Ghellinck, *Patristique et Moyen Age* 2 (Brussels-Paris 1947) 257 f., with notes.

77 The best description of this manuscript was given by Borleffs, *Mnemosyne* N. S. 59 (1932) 1–9. Cf. also his paper, 'La valeur du Codex Trecensis de Tertullien pour la critique du texte dans le traité De baptismo,' *Vig. Chr.* 2 (1948) 185–200.

78 IV p. XXX.

79 For a description of this manuscript, cf. M. Klussmann, *Curarum Tertullianearum particula I* (Halle 1881), and Reifferscheid's preface to CSEL 20. The treatises mentioned by the *indiculus* are the following: *Ad nationes, De praescriptione haereticorum, Scorpiace, De testimonio animae, De corona, De spectaculis, De idololatria, De anima, De oratione, De cultu feminarum, Ad uxorem, De exhortatione castitatis, De carne Christi, De spe fidelium, De paradiso, De virginibus velandis, De carne et anima, De patientia, De paenitentia, De animae submissione,* and *De superstitione saeculi.*

80 The *De spe fidelium, De paradiso, De carne et anima, De animae submissione,* and *De superstitione saeculi.*

81 On this manuscript, cf. the edition of the *De oratione* by G. F. Diercks (diss. Amsterdam: Bussum 1947) X–XII.

82 Cf. E. Dekkers, 'Note sur les fragments récemment découverts de Tertullien,' *Sacris Erudiri* 4 (1952) 372–83, esp. 377.

83 Cf. Dekkers, *art. cit.* 374.

84 'Un fragment du De Spectaculis de Tertullien provenant d'un manuscrit du neuvième siècle,' *Vig. Chr.* 5 (1951) 193–203.

85 Cf. Dekkers, *art. cit.* 372–76.

86 That is, *De testimonio animae, De anima, De spectaculis, De baptismo, Scorpiace, De idololatria, De pudicitia, De ieiunio,* and *De oratione.*

87 *Art. cit.* 381: 'Quoi qu'il en soit, Mesnart a disposé, en dehors de l'*Agobardinus*, du *Trecensis*, du manuscrit de Sainte-Geneviève et d'un exemplaire de la collection de Corbie, encore d'un ou, plus probablement, de plusieurs autres manuscrits. Ce qu'il décrit d'un mot fort laconique *ex vetustissimo codice desumpta* a été en réalité une opération bien complexe.'

[88] J. M. Lupton (in his separate edition of the *De baptismo* [Cambridge 1908] XXXVI) for the first time pronounced the supposition that the *Masburensis* came from the abbey of Malmesbury (Wiltshire).

[89] *Art. cit.* 382; on the entire collection, cf. also Kr. IV pp. XVIII–XXVIII.

[90] IV pp. XXIX–XXXI.

[91] Borleffs, *Un nouveau manuscrit de Tertullien* (cf. n. 74).

[92] This suggestion was first made by Kroymann, IV p. XXXV; Dom Dekkers rightly points out (*art. cit.* 373 n. 2) that Isidore of Seville was acquainted with several works of Tertullian which do not form part of this collection.

[93] Cf. Kr. I.

[94] Cf. Kr. IV p. XXXIII f.

[95] All data concerning these manuscripts are to be found in Kr. I.

[96] For this manuscript, cf. Kr. II pp. XV–XVII; IV p. X. For the contents of P, M, N, and F, cf. III p. VII n. 3.

[97] Cf. Kr. III p. XIV f.

[98] Cf. Kr. I p. 12 f.; II *passim*; III p. XXI f.; IV p. XXXV.

[99] Kr. I p. 13 f.; II p. 3 f.; III p. XX f.; IV p. XXXV.

[100] Borleffs, 'Zur Luxemburger Tertullianhandschrift,' *Mnemosyne* ser. III. 2 (1935) 299–308. Cf. *ibid.* 300: 'Die Handschrift ist . . . in einem eckigen Duktus geschrieben, ob in Italien oder in Deutschland ist auf Grund der Schriftform allein schwer zu sagen; doch dürfte letzteres aus anderen Gründen wahrscheinlicher sein.'

[101] Cf. Kr. I pp. 26–30.

[102] Cf. Kr. I pp. 27–30.

[103] Cf. Kr. II p. 3.

[104] Cf. Kr. II pp. 7–11.

[105] Cf. Kr. IV p. XXXVI. A more complete *stemma*, also containing the later Italian manuscripts, is found in *Corpus Christianorum, series latina* 1.1 (1953) p. XXVII.

[106] Following the advice given by Paul Maas in his excellent short monograph, *Textkritik*, I avoid the term *archetypus* used by Kroymann, since this term should be reserved to the common source of *all* existing 'families' of manuscripts.

[107] The catalogue of the library of Cluny (written in 1158–1161) contains the following items: *Nr. 73. Volumen, in quo continentur libri Tertulliani decem ad diversos et apologeticum eius. Nr. 74. Volumen, in quo continentur eiusdem libri XVII.* Kroymann (II p. 14 f.) is certainly right in supposing that this collection was the source of P (the monastery of Payerne was founded by monks from Cluny) and of M. He first

assumed that H also derived from this manuscript (*loc. cit.*); afterwards he came to a different conclusion, as is evident from his *stemma*.

108 Cf. Kr. II p. 3.

109 Cf. Kr. II p. 17 f.

110 Cf. Kr. IV p. XXXV f.

111 Cf. Kr. IV p. X.

112 Still they cannot be neglected entirely—cf. n. 116.

113 Cf. n. 116 (X and the first edition of Rhenanus are the most important sources for the reconstruction of H, and X is of course superior to the edition which may contain conjectures by the editor).

114 As we have seen above, the *Adversus Hermogenem* was not included in the manuscripts used by Mesnartius, Gelenius, and Pamelius.

115 In I p. 30.

116 Cf. p. 23.—In the preface of CSEL 70 which appeared seven years after Borleffs' article on the Luxemburg manuscript, Kroymann writes (p. XXXV n. 67): 'Qui liber ms. (i.e. X) saeculo XV. exeunte exaratus etsi ex ipsis Hirsaugiensibus descriptus est, cum Florentinus F ex apographo eorum fluxerit olim in coenobio Pforzhinensi asservato, tamen, quia iam praesto erat Florentini collatio a memet ipso confecta consensusque primae editionis Rhenani (R¹) cum Florentino F meram imaginem Hirsaugiensium praebere visus est, his duobus testibus contenti esse voluimus.' But from the article by Borleffs it is evident that a consensus of R¹ and X (about which of course nothing is to be found in Kroymann's *apparatus criticus*) undoubtedly reproduces readings of H, so that the consensus of R¹ and F can by no means procure *meram imaginem Hirsaugiensium*. With regard to F, Borleffs observes (*op. cit.* 307): 'da F an allen entscheidenden Stellen, wo er von X abweicht, ausnahmslos eine schlechtere Lesart aufweist als jener—Beispiele dafür hat der Leser oben in Hülle und Fülle angetroffen—so kann man ihn ruhig beiseite lassen: sein Wert ist nur noch ein rein historischer'; cf. also *ibid.* 307 f.: 'Für die Konstitution des Textes also muss F seinen Platz im Apparat in Zukunft der Handschrift X einräumen, und das sogar noch eher als LV, obgleich diese durchweg fehlerhafter sind als F' (that is to say, because Oehler, whose text has served as the base of several special editions of treatises of Tertullian, had founded his edition of those treatises on LV and R¹).

117 K. A. H. Kellner, *Tertullians sämtliche Schriften* (Cologne 1882) 2.59–100.

118 P. Holmes, *The Writings of Quintus Sept. Flor. Tertullianus* 2 (Ante-Nicene Library 15, Edinburgh 1870) 55–118.

119 Paris 1852.

TEXT

[1] **Chapter 1**: 'The doctrine of Hermogenes, when tested by the pre-scriptive rule of antiquity, is found to be heretical (§1). Hermogenes is a painter and, moreover, a falsifier in two respects (§2). He denies a creation out of nothing (§3): following the example of the Stoics, he puts matter on the same level with God and says that out of it the Lord made all things (§4).'

[2] *Solemus haereticis compendii gratia de posteritate praescribere.* For the conception of *praescriptio* which plays so prominent a part in Tertullian's refutations of heretics, cf. T. H. Bindley's edition of the *De praescriptione haereticorum* (Oxford 1893) 3–5; P. de Labriolle, 'L'argument de prescription,' *Rev. d'hist. et de litt. relig.* 11 (1906) 408 ff. and 497 ff.; J. L. Allie, *L'argument de prescription dans le droit romain, en apologétique et en théologie dogmatique* (Ottawa 1940); E. Evans, *Tertullian's Treatise Against Praxeas* (London 1948) 194; and especially the detailed monograph by J. K. Stirnimann, *Die Praescriptio Tertullians im Lichte des römischen Rechts und der Theologie* (Paradosis 3; Fribourg 1949). The last-mentioned scholar has demonstrated that in the time of Tertullian three types of *praescriptio* were usual in legal practice. In his opinion, Tertullian's argument is based on the *praescriptio* of the law-suits *per cognitionem* ('der Kognitionsprozess'), the normal form of legal proceedings in the imperial age. Here the prescript was an appeal (in any form) by the accused to a prescription preventing the suit; if the correctness of this appeal was proved, the plaintiff was dismissed. It is not the place here to enter into this highly controversial subject; but I would like to draw attention to the fact that, as Bindley has observed, 'in the case of the Church v. Heresy' the Church has, according to Tertullian, the position of the plaintiff, not of the accused. Therefore, one may ask whether Tertullian did not at least *also* think of the so-called *praescriptio pro actore*, which, as Bindley describes it, 'denoted a clause prefixed to the "intentio" of a "formula" for the purpose of *limiting the scope of an enquiry*, which the "intentio" would otherwise have left open for discussion before the "judex"' (Stirnimann 173: 'ein ausserordentlicher Bestandteil der Formel im Formularprozess und dazu bestimmt, den in der intentio formulierten klägerischen Anspruch abzugrenzen'). Stirnimann is undoubtedly right in pointing out that, as is evident from *De praescr. haer.* 21, Tertullian acknowledged two *praescriptiones* which he regarded as an entirely conclusive refutation of the heretics:

1) *Si dominus Christus Iesus apostolos misit ad praedicandum, alios non esse recipiendos praedicatores quam Christus instituit, quia nec alius patrem novit nisi filius et cui filius revelavit, nec aliis videtur revelasse filius quam apostolis, quos misit ad praedicandum, utique quod illis revelavit.*

2) *Quid autem praedicaverint, id est quid illis Christus revelaverit, et hic praescribam, non aliter probari debere nisi per easdem ecclesias, quas ipsi apostoli condiderunt, ipsi eis praedicando tam viva, quod aiunt, voce quam per epistulas postea.*

In the present passage (as generally in Tertullian's refutations of individual heretics) we have only to do with a further conclusion of the doctrine of the *De praescr. haer.*, namely, that inasmuch as the Apostles alone possessed the true Rule of Faith and, moreover, were earlier than the heretics, one may state a *principalitas veritatis et posteritas mendacitatis* (*De praescr.* 31); cf. especially *Adv. Marc.* 1.1 (292. 4–10 Kr.): *In tantum enim haeresis deputabitur quod postea inducitur, in quantum veritas habebitur quod retro et a primordio traditum est. Sed alius libellus* (= *De praescr. haer.*) *hunc gradum sustinebit adversus haereticos, etiam sine retractatu doctrinarum revincendos, quod hoc sint de praescriptione novitatis* (however, he decides first to describe his opponent's doctrine, *ne compendium praescriptionis—* cf. the present passage—*ubique advocatum diffidentiae deputetur*); *Adv. Prax.* 2 (229. 17–20 Kr.): *Quo peraeque adversus universas haereses iam hinc praeiudicatum sit id esse verum, quodcumque primum, id esse adulterum, quodcumque posterius.*

[3] An allusion to 1 Cor. 11.19, a passage frequently quoted by Tertullian in his antiheretical treatises (cf. my comment on *De anima* 3.1— p. 114).

[4] Tertullian likes to open his antiheretical treatises with a vivid and caustic description of the heretic in question. We refer to the picture of Praxeas, *Adv. Prax.* 1, of the Valentinians, *Adv. Val.* 1, and especially to his masterpiece, the portrait of Marcion in *Adv. Marc.* 1.1.

[5] *pingit illicite.* I cannot agree with Rigaltius (*ad loc.*) and Neander (*Antignostikus*[2] 344 n. 1) that *illicite* refers, not to the art of painting in general, but to the subjects chosen by Hermogenes; cf. n. 8.

[6] Neander (*loc. cit.*) is certainly right in finding a reference here, not to polygamy, but to remarriage, of which Tertullian had such a profound aversion, as is evident from his three treatises *Ad uxorem, De exhortatione castitatis*, and *De monogamia* (cf. ACW 13). The correctness of this interpretation is proved by *De monog.* 16: *Hermogenem aliquem, plures solitum mulieres ducere quam pingere.*

[7] See Gen. 1. 28, a passage frequently quoted by Tertullian—*De an.* 27.9; *De exh. cast.* 6; *De monog.* 7; *Adv. Marc.* 1. 29 (331. 14 Kr.); *De pud.* 16 (255.9 f. Reiff.-Wiss.).

8 See Exod. 20.4, which is also frequently quoted by Tertullian. In *De spect.* 23 he observes with regard to theatrical masks: *Iam vero ipsum opus personarum quaero an deo placeat, qui omnem similitudinem vetat fieri, quanto magis imaginis suae?* Further, cf. *De idol.* 4 (33.10 R.-W.) and 5 (35.18); *Scorp.* 2 (147.15 R.-W.); *Adv. Marc.* 2.22 (364.23 f. Kr.).

9 The *cauterium* was used in painting for the purpose of burning in the wax colours.

10 *siquidem et nubentium contagio foetet.* Kroymann reads: *Si quid et nominum contagio* ('nominativum intellego') *foetet, nec . . . perseveravit*: 'If a contagion on account of names (i.e. of having the same name) can also produce a bad smell, we may point out that the Apostle's Hermogenes (2 Tim. 1.15; also mentioned by Tertullian in *De fuga* 2 and *De praescr. haer.* 3), too, did not remain faithful to the Creed.' However ingenious this conjecture may be, it is quite possible to interpret the text furnished by the manuscripts: 'Hermogenes is *adulter et praedicationis et carnis.* This is by no means surprising: to begin with (correspondence with *carnis*; the chiasm should be noted), the contagion coming from marrying (probably=remarrying—cf. n. 6) people produces a bad smell, and, secondly (~*praedicationis*), Hermogenes' namesake in the New Testament also abandoned the rule of faith' (cf. also H. Hoppe, *Beiträge zur Sprache und Kritik Tertullians* [Lund 1932] 152 f.). Holmes translates: 'since he is rank indeed with the contagion of your marriage-hacks'; but Tertullian always uses *contagio*, not *contagium.* Much better is Kellner's translation: 'wie denn die Verwandtschaft mit Heiratslustigen immer nicht sauber ist,' though his rendering of the words *nubentium contagio* is too free. The meaning is, 'the contagion coming from marrying people'—cf. the similar use of an adjective with *contagio* in *De an.* 38.2: *ad instar ficulneae contagionis*='in analogy of the contagion caused by the fig-leaves' (see my note *ad loc.*, p. 436).

11 I read *dominum non alium videtur agnoscere, alium tamen facit quem aliter agnoscit.* The manuscripts read *Christum dominum*; Kroymann deletes *Christum* and for *dominum* reads *deum.* I agree with the deletion of *Christum*, because in the last sentence of this chapter *dominus*, which there occurs twice, undoubtedly denotes God (Christ cannot possibly be qualified as *non natus*—cf. ch. 18 and especially 33.2: *nihil innatum praeter deum praescribentes*), and it would be very strange indeed if in the preceding sentence not God but Christ were mentioned as the creator of the world. (Kellner tries to avoid the difficulty by translating: 'Hermogenes scheint denselben Christus und diesen in keiner andern Weise anzuerkennen wie wir, und doch nimmt er einen andern an und stellt sich ihn anders vor, ja er beseitigt alles was Gott ist, da er nicht

will, dass derselbe das Weltall aus nichts geschaffen habe'; but in my opinion, if *Christum* were indeed the first word of the sentence, the natural interpretation would be that after *aufert* we should understand *a Christo* and that *illum* should refer to Christ; it is also in this way that the passage is translated by Holmes). We must also bear in mind that *deum agnoscere* and *agnitio dei* is frequently found in Tertullian's works, while *Christum agnoscere*, as far as I know, occurs nowhere. It seems probable therefore that *Christum* originally was a marginal or interlinear note explaining—wrongly—*dominum* which has crept into the text. It is true, of course, that according to Tertullian Christ also took part in the creation of the world (cf. the full treatment of this subject in *Adv. Prax.* 12 which culminates in the sentence *habes duos* [that is, *deos*], *alium dicentem ut faciat* [= God], *alium facientem* = Christ; cf. the commentary by Evans 258–62), but throughout the present treatise the relation between God and matter, as postulated by Hermogenes, and God's creation of the world are the main subjects, so that it would be quite surprising, if in this preface Christ were mentioned before God in reference to the creation. Finally, it seems not improbable that if *dominum* refers to God, the words *dominum non alium videtur agnoscere* contrast Hermogenes with Marcion—cf. e.g. *Adv. Marc.* 2.1 (333.9 f. Kr.): *quatenus ita Pontico placuit alterum (deum) inducere alterum excludere*). Up to this point I agree with Kroymann; I cannot, however, subscribe to his alteration, beginning with this passage until well into ch. 2, of all forms of *dominus* into the corresponding forms of *deus*. It is true that Tertullian, in accordance with the New Testament practice (cf. Evans 267 f.), usually writes *deus* for 'God' and *dominus* for 'Christ,' as he also says himself in *Adv. Prax.* 13(249.18–21 Kr.): *Itaque deos omnino non dicam nec dominos, sed apostolum sequar, ut, si pariter nominandi fuerint pater et filius, patrem deum appellem et Iesum Christum dominum nominem*; but this does not imply that he cannot also denote God by *dominus* (it should be noted that in the passage just quoted the distinction is said to be used in cases where both the Father and the Son are mentioned). Here the choice of *dominus* instead of *deus* may have been influenced by the fact that the creation is the primary subject of the treatise and that it is the creation which made God *dominus* (cf. ch. 3).—For *agnoscere* (β and Kroymann), Pamelius (followed by most of the editors, also Oehler) reads *aliter agnoscere*, α *aliter cognoscere*, Latinius *sed aliter cognoscere*. In my opinion, this *aliter* is no more than an erroneous anticipation of the *aliter* before *agnoscit*; it should also be noted that *videtur agnoscere* gives a better clausula (2) than *aliter agnoscere* (2¹). In the first sentence of § 4 I read with Kroymann *inde sumpsit materiam cum deo ponere*, deleting the words *a Stoicis* after *sumpsit*; cf. my discussion of the entire passage in 'Observations on Tertullian's Treatise against Hermogenes,' *Vig. Chr.* 9 (1955) 129 f.

[12] Cf. *De carn. res.* 11 (40.7–9 Kr.): *nam et quidam . . . de materia potius subiacenti volunt ab illo (i.e. deo) universitatem dedicatam secundum philosophos.*

[13] **Chapter 2**: 'Hermogenes' fundamental argument runs as follows: "the Lord made all things either out of Himself, or out of nothing, or out of something" (§1). Now He could not make all things out of Himself, neither if He created the universe in parts (§2), nor if He created the whole universe at one time (§3). Nor could He have created the universe out of nothing, for in that case He would never have created evil; but He did create evil. It follows that He must have made the universe out of matter (§4).'

[14] *Hanc primam umbram plane sine lumine pessimus pictor illis argumentationibus coloravit.* Holmes: 'Our very bad painter has coloured this his primary shade absolutely without any light, with such arguments as these.' But *sine lumine* certainly has the function of an adjective and should be connected with *primam*, for *sine* with a substantive frequently follows an adjective to which it is juxtaposed—e.g., Ovid, *Met.* 8.518: *ignavo . . . et sine sanguine leto*; for this reason I also disagree with Kellner who correctly interprets *sine lumine* as an adjective, but connects it with *pictor*: 'Diesen Urschatten hat der völlig lichtlose, ungeschickte Maler mit folgenden Beweisführungen gefärbt.' Kroymann changed the text into *pessimis pictor ille argumentationibus.*

[15] The argument is fairly confused, and it is quite possible that this confusion is not due to Hermogenes alone but, to say the least, also to Tertullian who often, either purposely or not, gives inexact reports of the arguments of his opponents. A very striking sample is his record of the Platonic argument for the incorporeality of the soul, the original text of which is still known to us, in *De an.* 6.1 (cf. my commentary 132 f.). Here two arguments are mentioned for the thesis that the Lord cannot have created the universe out of Himself; the first of these is again subdivided into two syllogisms, the second, into three:

I.A. a. Everything made by the Lord out of Himself would have been a part of the Lord.
    b. Parts of the Lord cannot exist, for the Lord is indivisible.
    ⟨c. Consequently, the Lord cannot have made anything out of Himself.⟩

I.B. a. (the same premise as in I.A. a, but now, in *pars ipsius*, the stress is not laid on *pars* but on *ipsius*). If the Lord had made something out of Himself, that something would have belonged to Him (would have been part of *Him*).

    b. It would, moreover, have been out of a part of Him, and
       hence it would be imperfect.
   ⟨c. Consequently, something imperfect would belong to the
       Lord, which is impossible. Hence the Lord cannot have
       created something out of Himself.⟩

(The quite unnecessary juxtaposition of the active and passive
form of *facere* in I.B. b [*et quod fieret et quod faceret; quia ex parte fieret
et ex parte faceret*] may be an addition by Tertullian and due to the
mere fact that, as frequently, he was already thinking of what was
coming next.)

II.A. a. If the Lord had not produced the universe in separate parts
       from parts of Himself, but as a whole at the same time out of
       the whole of Himself, He must have been whole and not whole
       at the same time: whole, in order to bring forth Himself
       (= the entirety of the universe which was produced out of
       Him), and not whole, in order that He (= the universe) might
       be brought forth out of Himself.
    ⟨b. But it is impossible that the Lord should have had two con-
       tradictory predicates at the same time.
    c. Consequently, in this case too it is impossible that the Lord
       should have produced the universe out of Himself.⟩

II.B. a. If God existed, He would not come into existence, and if He
       did not exist, He would be unable to create.
    ⟨b. But God should both have created and have come into exist-
       ence, *si totus totum fecisset de semetipso* (cf. II.A. a).
    c. Thus again it is impossible that God should have created *totus
       totum de semetipso.*⟩

II.C. ⟨a. If God had created *totus totum de semetipso*, he should have
       come into existence (cf. II.A. a).⟩
    b. But God has always existed, so He could not come into ex-
       istence.
    ⟨c. Consequently, God cannot have created *totus totum de
       semetipso.*⟩

The conclusion bears upon the entire argument, for the words *eius . . .
condicionis* refer both to God's indivisibility (I.A.) and perfection (I.B.)
and to the conclusions of II.

    ¹⁶ When recording arguments of others, Tertullian frequently
changes over from the *oratio recta* to the *oratio obliqua* without any

apparent reason (cf. *De an.* 5.5 f. and 6.1 with my notes—pp. 130 and 133 f.). I have endeavoured to render this as exactly as possible by inserting 'so he asserts (concludes)' before the *or. obl.*; only in §4, which is one long sentence depending on *concludit*, I have substituted the *oratio recta*.

[17] *fuerit* (Latinius Kroymann; *fieret* MSS and Oehler).

[18] *qui bona atque optima tam velit facere quam sit* (i.e. *bonus atque optimus*). Holmes' and Kellner's translations are quite erroneous here: 'who must will to make things as good and excellent as He is Himself'; 'und wolle die Dinge so gut und so trefflich schaffen als er selbst sei': *tam* refers to *velit* alone. For the last sentence of this chapter, read my discussion in *Vig. Chr.* 9 (1955) 141 f.

[19] **Chapter 3**: 'To this Hermogenes adds a further argument: God, who was always God, was always Lord as well; hence He must always have been Lord of something, and from this we may deduce that something has always existed. Now this something can only be matter (§1). This argument can be refuted promptly (§2): God has not always been Lord (§3), as He also was not always Father and Judge (§4). This is also evident from Scripture (§5). Therefore, if Hermogenes assumes matter to have always existed because God was always Lord, we may reply that since God was not always Lord, it is certain that in the beginning there existed besides God, not matter, but nothing (§6). Moreover, Hermogenes can be refuted by an argument of his own: when he says that matter was unborn and unmade, it must once have been entirely free—and therefore God cannot always have been its Lord (§7).'

[20] *semper etiam dominum* (Kroymann; *etiam dominum* MSS; *etiam semper dominum* Iunius). At the end of the sentence it is not necessary to read with Kroymann *Fuisse itaque materiam semper ⟨cum⟩ deo domino*, for the meaning is: 'that matter (always existed and, therefore) was always at God's disposal'; cf. my discussion of this passage in *Vig. Chr.* 9 (1955) 142.

[21] *numquam non dominum* (Iunius Kroymann; *numquam non deum* MSS).

[22] Cf. *Adv. Prax.* 7 (235. 19–21 Kr.; I quote the text as established by Evans): *exinde eum patrem sibi faciens* (i.e. *sermo*) *de quo procedendo filius factus est primogenitus* (cf. the comment by Evans 225); *ibid.* 10 (240.23 f. Kr.): *habeat necesse est pater filium, ut pater sit, et filius patrem, ut filius sit.*

[23] *deum* Latinius Kroymann; *dominum* MSS.

[24] *argumentari* (MSS), not *argutari* (Iunius Kroymann); cf. my note on *De an.* 2.5 (p. 109) and Evans 290.

[25] Gen. 1.1: *In principio fecit deus caelum et terram* (= the *Vetus Latina*) and Tertullian's quotations in ch. 19 and *De bapt.* 3.2; in ch. 22 and

twice in ch. 26 Tertullian writes *deus fecit*; cf. also *Adv. Prax.* 5 (233.3 f. Kr.): *aiunt quidam et Genesim in Hebraico ita incipere: In principio deus fecit sibi filium*).

²⁶ That is, of the creation (Gen. 1. 28).

²⁷ For this difficult passage I adopt the text of the manuscripts with two corrections by Engelbrecht: *qui, proprie dominus,* (punctuation by Engelbrecht) *et* (*dominus, et dominum* R³ Oehler, *deum et* Kroymann) *intellecturus erat dominum* (Kroymann; *dominus* MSS Oehler, *deum* Engelbrecht) *et iam* (N Engelbrecht, *etiam* Pβ) *cognominaturus* (*cognominatur* R² Oehler; the latter has the following punctuation: . . . *hominem, qui proprie dominum intellecturus erat, dominus etiam cognominatur*). Engelbrecht was the first to note the allusion to Gen. 1.28 (*dominamini*); on the other hand, his substitution of *deum* for *dominum* is wrong, for the *cognomen* of God is *dominus*, whereas *deus* is His *nomen proprium,* as is often said by Tertullian. Cf. *Apol.* 17.4: (*anima*) *deum nominat hoc solo quasi proprio nomine* (imitated by Min. Fel. 18.10, from whom it was borrowed again by the author of Ps.-Cyprian, *Quod idola* 9, and by Lactantius, *Div. inst.* 1. 6.5); *Adv. Marc.* 1.10 (303. 9 Kr.); *De test. anim.* 2 (136.3 R.-W.).

²⁸ Gen. 2.15: *Et accepit deus dominus hominem, quem finxit.* The *Vetus Latina* reads: *Et sumpsit* (*cepit, accepit, adprehendit*) *dominus deus hominem quem fecerat* (*fecit, finxit, plasmavit*).

²⁹ Gen. 2.16: *Et praecepit dominus deus Adae* (= the *Vetus Latina*).

³⁰ *quorum Hermogenes extrema linea est.* Beatus Rhenanus was certainly right in finding here an allusion to the art practised by Hermogenes; cf. 38.1: *si determinatur* (= matter), *habet lineam extremam, quam tu, quantum proprie pictor, agnoscis finem esse omni rei.*

³¹ I read *ex penita scientia* (the MSS give *ex penitentia*). Cf. my discussion of this passage in *Vig. Chr.* 9 (1955) 142 f. Oehler wrote *experimenta,* which deserves to be considered, since Tertullian has a habit of qualifying Hermogenes' assertions as mere suppositions—cf. e.g. 3.2: *Hanc coniecturam eius,* and nn. 147, 166, and 286.

³² *qua* (α X F Kroymann; *quam* δ; *quia* R Oehler). At the end of the sentence I follow van der Vliet in reading *quod erat nemini debens* (*debet* MSS).

³³ *Itaque ex quo deus potestatem suam exercuit in eam, faciendo ex materia, ex illo materia dominum deum passa demonstrat hoc illum tamdiu non fuisse quamdiu fuit hoc* (*hoc utique* γ, but *utique* is deleted in F by the copyist himself). Holmes: 'Therefore ever since God exercised His power over it, by creating (all things) out of matter, although it had all along experienced God as its Lord, yet Matter does, after all, demonstrate that God did not exist in the relation of Lord to it,⁸ although all the while

He was really so[9]' (on which he remarks in n. 8: 'Matter having, by the hypothesis, been *independent of God*, and so incapable of giving Him any title to Lordship'; and in n. 9: 'Fuit hoc utique. In Hermogenes' own opinion, which is thus shown to have been contradictory to itself, and so absurd'). This translation overlooks the correspondence of *ex quo . . . ex illo*: matter experienced the Lordship of God only from the moment when God began to exercise His power over it, and so, prior to that moment, it was independent of God. The word *tamdiu* clearly refers to the time *before* God exercised His power over matter, so that the contradiction pointed out by Tertullian must refer to that time only: God 'was not the Lord of matter during all the time (i.e. before the creation) when (according to Hermogenes, who said that God had always been Lord—cf. 3.1) He was so by all means.' Kellner, following Iunius, reads *quamdiu fuit haec utique* or *quamdiu fuit haec illud* (i.e. *libera*), and translates: 'dass er dieses (that is, Lord) so lang nicht war, als sie (that is, matter) jenes (that is, free) war.' But this requires a fairly important alteration of the text, and, moreover, even if Tertullian had written this, *illud* could not as easily refer to *libera*, which does not occur in the present sentence, as *hoc* refers to *dominum*.

³⁴ **Chapter 4**: 'If matter is unborn, unmade, and eternal, as is asserted by Hermogenes, it is in all respects equal to God, for eternity is the very essence of God's being (§1). But if eternity is a quality proper to God, it must, for that very reason, belong to God alone (§2); further —and this argument is particularly important for Christians—if God is One, eternity must be something quite unique in order that it may belong to the One and Only God (§3), for what belongs to One must be unique (§4). Finally, if another being also possesses eternity, there will be as many gods as there are beings possessing eternity, and it is thus that Hermogenes introduces a second God—matter (§5). But from the fact that God is One it can be concluded that matter cannot be eternal (§6).'

The complicated argument of this chapter may be summarized by the following schema:

Hermogenes declares matter to be eternal. Now eternity is *Dei census* (= *id quod Deus esse censetur*—§1) ⟨and hence matter cannot be eternal, for:⟩

A. eternity must belong to God alone (§§2–4), since—
    a) otherwise it would not be *Dei proprium* (§2).
    b) God is One, and that which belongs to One must be unique (§3 f.).

B. ⟨eternity is so divine a quality, that⟩ if matter were eternal, it would
   become equal to God (§5), but since God is One, matter cannot be
   eternal (§6).

It may not be superfluous to add a more detailed paraphrase:

According to Hermogenes, God used eternal matter as His resource
for the creation of the world. Now if matter were eternal, it would
share (cf. the threefold *proinde* in the first sentence) this quality with
God, for eternity is *Dei census* (cf. above) (§1). ⟨But this is impossible,
for⟩

A. eternity must belong to God alone (§§2–4), for—
   a) else it would not be *proprium Dei*, but *commune Deo cum alio* (the
      argument being taken from the very sense of *proprius*— §2).
   b) (*Nam etsi*, etc.; for *Nam* we would, as so frequently in Tertul-
      lian's arguments, expect *Porro*) God is One, and so—apart from
      a), which is repeated here in the clause *et ut dixi . . . alterius esset*
      —Christians (*nos*), who know this very well, have one reason
      more to believe that what belongs to God, belongs to Him
      alone (=unique), for what belongs to One is unique (§3).
         Demonstration of the last statement: that is unique with which
         nothing can be compared (, and *principale* is that, 'which is
         above all things and before all things and from which all
         things have originated'); now, since these two predicates are
         predicates of God, that which is unique must belong to
         God (§4).
B. It is by having alone the predicates just mentioned that God is God
   and is One (inversion of the conclusion of §3: 'what belongs to One
   must be unique'), for if He does not have them alone, there will be
   more than one God. It is thus that Hermogenes introduces two
   Gods, that is to say, by making matter equal to God (§5). But matter
   cannot be eternal and thereby equal to God, as is evident from the
   following argument:
I. 1. *Deus=summum*; 2. *summum=unicum*; 3. *Ergo Deus est unicum*
   (*unus*).
II. 1. *unicum=cui nihil adaequabitur*; 2. *Deus est unicum* (=I.3);
    3. *Ergo Deo nihil adaequabitur*.
III. 1. *Materia, si aeterna est, Deo adaequabitur*; 2. *Deo nihil adaequabitur*
     (=II.3); 3. *Ergo materia non aeterna est* (§6).

[35] *Hinc denique incipiam de materia retractare, quod eam deus sibi comparet proinde non natam, proinde non factam, proinde aeternam, sine initio,
sine fine propositam. Quis enim alius dei census quam aeternitas?* Holmes:

'At this point, then, I shall begin to treat of Matter, how that, according to Hermogenes, God compares it with Himself as equally unborn,' etc. Kellner: 'So will ich denn nun meine Untersuchungen über die Materie mit dem Punkte beginnen, dass Gott sich derselben bemächtigt haben soll, während sie doch gleich ihm nicht entstanden . . . gedacht wird.' In my opinion, Kellner's translation of the words *sibi comparet* is to be preferred. One might consider a translation 'that God puts it on a level with Himself,' 'makes it equal to Himself' (not 'compares it with Himself'), for this sense of *comparare* is not infrequent in Tertullian's works (cf. my note on *De an.* 2.2—p. 102) and is, moreover, often found in the present treatise (cf. e.g. ch. 7 end); but in the present passage this translation would not be appropriate: Tertullian quotes Hermogenes, as is shown by the subjunctive, and Hermogenes had said that matter was eternal, to be sure, but that at the same time it was inferior to God—it is this statement which Tertullian proposes to refute in the following chapters by demonstrating that in reality Hermogenes makes matter equal and even superior to God. It would, therefore, be surprising if Tertullian's eventual conclusion had been advanced with this first record of Hermogenes' view: it is indeed much more probable that Tertullian only prepares his refutation by the more modest insertion of a threefold *proinde* and that the *enim* in the second sentence (*Quis enim alius dei census*) only refers to this *proinde.*—Of the second sentence Kellner gives this translation: 'Denn es gibt keinen andern Ursprung für Gott als die Ewigkeit.' It is true that *census* frequently means 'origin' in Tertullian's works (cf. my note on *De an.* 1.1—p. 82), but here the meaning of *dei census* is undoubtedly '*id quod deus esse censetur*' (Holmes: 'estimate of God'). For *censeri = vocari*, cf. my note on *De an.* 21.3 (p. 293).

³⁶ *Quis alius aeternitatis status.* On *status* cf. the excellent note by Evans 50–52. Here the meaning is 'essence' rather than 'existence.'

³⁷ *scilicet quia* (Oehler; *sed quia* MSS, *quia* R³ Kroymann), *et si* (MSS, rightly defended by E. Löfstedt, *Zur Sprache Tertullians* [Lund 1920] 42, and G. Thörnell, *Studia Tertullianea* 1 [Uppsala 1918] 64 n. 1; *si et* all editors) *alii adscribatur.*

³⁸ Kroymann has no fewer than four objections against the text given by the manuscripts: 'gravius corrupta esse puto quae abhinc (i.e. from *Nam*, which is the first word of §3) sequuntur his de causis: 1) hiscit sententia ante verba: *nam etsi* . . . . 2) abundare videntur verba: *et, ut dixi,—alterius esset.* 3) non liquet, quo referendum sit illud *quod* (i.e. in the last sentence of §3). 4) non iuste procedit oratio inde a verbis: *aut quid* sqq. (' = the first two sentences of §4).' I cannot agree at all with Kroymann's 'restitution' of the text which, as he says himself, is

realized 'haud levibus sane medelis adhibitis,' and which need not to be discussed here, but it may prove useful to answer his four objections: 1) in the first sentence of §3 we would indeed prefer to read *porro* instead of *nam*, but, as has been observed earlier, Tertullian's syllogisms are full of such sins against logic (cf. the ample discussion of this subject by Thörnell, *Stud. Tert.* 1.20 ff.). We may also say that between the two syllogisms there is a certain connection which may be expressed by understanding before *nam*: 'and this is impossible (for . . .)'; 2) this clause contains a repetition of argument I.A. a inserted into I.A. b— such repetitions are quite usual in Tertullian's syllogisms (cf. the Index of my edition of *De anima* s.v. 'syllogisms, abundant,' p. 637). 3) *quod si deus est* simply means 'now, if God is this, that is, One': Tertullian very often writes *id*, *hoc*, or *quod* as a nominal predicate, the pronoun referring to an adjective or substantive mentioned in one of the preceding sentences. Thus in 3.7: *hoc* (i.e. *dominum*) *illum tamdiu non fuisse* (cf. n. 33); *Adv. Prax.* 26 (278. 25 Kr.): *hoc* (i.e. *filium dei*) *et satanas eum* (i.e. Christ) . . . *novit*. Cf. my note on *De an.* 24.1 (p. 308). 4) This objection is sufficiently answered by the paraphrase of this chapter (n. 34): Tertullian wishes to furnish a proof for the thesis, *unicum est quod unius est*, and does so in a somewhat unusual way by starting from *unicum*, not from *unus(-um)*.

³⁹ 1 Cor. 8.5 (also quoted in *Adv. Marc.* 3.15 (400. 25 f. Kr.) in a slightly different form: *nam et sunt qui dicuntur dii sive in caelo sive in terris*). In the present quotation as it is given by the manuscripts (*etsi sunt qui dicuntur dii sive in caelo sive in terra nomine*), the addition of the ablative *nomine*, which has no correspondence in the Greek text, is surprising.

⁴⁰ *super omnia*: allusion to Rom. 9.5; *ante omnia*: Col. 1.17 (there referring to Christ); *ex quo omnia*: 1 Cor. 8.6 (just quoted).

⁴¹ *censetur*: cf. the note on *censeri* by Evans 214–16.

⁴² **Chapter 5**: 'Hermogenes says: Nevertheless God is God and as such superior to matter; but by qualifying matter as unborn and eternal, and even as a creator of the universe, he makes it equal to God (§1). He may answer that matter is not *ipso facto* equal to God, if it possesses one of His qualities (i.e. eternity), and that it lacks several other qualities of God—but he has left God nothing which he has not also granted to matter! "The authority and substance of God," he says, "remain intact by which He is the only and first Creator and is declared to be the Lord of all things" (§2). But whatever belongs to God, must belong to Him alone: nobody and nothing is permitted to possess anything of God (§3). To this he may answer again that if this is true, man cannot possess anything of God either. But neither does this assertion

hold good, for man does indeed possess something of God—but by receiving it from God, not out of himself (§4). In the case of matter, however, Hermogenes makes that which it shares with God (i.e. eternity) a property of matter itself. He is thus clearly inconsistent: on the one hand he says that matter shares with God a property which it owes to itself, on the other hand he asserts this property to belong to God alone (§5).'

This and the two following chapters treat the same argument of Hermogenes which may be summarized as follows: 'Matter is eternal, but since it lacks the other qualities proper to God, it is inferior to Him.' In the present chapter the chief stress is laid on the first part of this statement ('matter is eternal'); in chapter 6, on the second ('matter lacks the other qualities proper to God'); in chapter 7 on the third ('matter is inferior to God'). In the present chapter, §1 repeats the statement of 4.5 that if matter is eternal, it is equal to God; according to his habit, Tertullian adds a conclusion of his own, namely, that if matter shares with God the quality of eternity, it also shares with Him the character of *auctor universitatis*. In §2 Hermogenes is made to reply that God possesses qualities, not eternity alone. It is averred that Hermogenes has in fact granted all qualities proper to God to matter, to which Hermogenes replies again—and here Tertullian seems actually to quote his words—that even if matter shares the predicate of eternity with God, God retains undiminished His predicates of Only and First Creator and of Lord of all things (it should be noted that this statement contradicts the assertion in §1 that Hermogenes regards matter, too, as *auctor universitatis*, so that we have a second proof for our supposition that this assertion is a mere conclusion by Tertullian himself). Thereupon (§3) Tertullian repeats the conclusion reached in 4.2, that whatever belongs to God must belong to Him alone, so that no one can possess anything of God. Hermogenes' reply (§4) that in that case man cannot possess anything of God either, is easily refuted; moreover, it gives an opportunity to make a distinction between divine things received by the grace of God and divine things which are in reality the property of some other being. This leads to the next argument (§5): Hermogenes declares eternity to be a property which matter did not receive from God but which it possessed of its own. Tertullian concludes that Hermogenes is grossly inconsistent: on the one hand, he says that matter shares something with God; on the other hand, he will have it that that belongs to God alone which he does not deny matter to possess. Here it should be noted that the inconsistency does not exist between statements of Hermogenes himself but between a statement of Hermogenes and an inference drawn by Tertullian. Hermogenes had actually said that matter shares with God the predicates of being unborn, unmade, and eternal, but not the predicates of being the First and Only Creator and the Lord of all things (since we find this quoted as an assertion of Hermogenes in §2 and, moreover, in almost the same words in 6.1, we may indeed suppose that these were Hermogenes' actual words). Now Tertullian had inferred that if matter is eternal, it is equal to God, and so possesses *all* the predicates of God. Hence the present antithesis which, also in its form, reveals its provenance from a contamination: 'On the one hand, Hermogenes says that matter shares an attribute with God (=eternity); on the other hand—so we would expect to hear—he says that eternity belongs to God alone.' But Hermogenes had explicitly said that matter is eternal too, so that Tertullian could not possibly add this. He therefore adds another statement which in itself contains a contrast: 'on the other hand, he will have it that that belongs to God alone (that is, the predicates of Only and First Creator and Lord of all things) which he does not deny matter to possess (that is, these very predicates—but this has only been inferred by Tertullian).' The sophism is concealed by the choice of pronouns instead of substantives: the reader does not immediately realize (or is supposed not immediately to realize) that the *aliquid* in the first part of the sentence and the *quod* in the second part refer to different things: *aliquid* to eternity, *quod* to the other predicates of God.

43 'identity of condition': *idem status*. On *status*, cf. above, n. 36.

44 *an non et innata et materia?* (Nβ and Thörnell, *Stud. Tert.* 2 [1920] 81; *an non et innata materia?* P and all older editions; *an non innata et materia?* Kroymann).

45 Ps. 81.6. The same passage is quoted in *Adv. Prax.* 13 (248.3 ff. Kr., with the addition *et filii altissimi*) in order to prove that the Son had *a fortiori* a right to the name 'God,' and in *Adv. Marc.* 1.7 (298.20 Kr.; in both passages together with Ps. 81.1).

46 Ps. 81.1, quoted in the same form in *Adv. Prax.* 13 and more fully in *Adv. Marc.* 1.7: *deus deorum stetit in ecclesia deorum, in medio autem deos diiudicabit* (*deus deorum*: LXX only Ὁ θεός; *diiudicabit*: present tense —διακρίνει—in the LXX).

47 **Chapter 6**: 'Hermogenes says that God retains undiminished His attributes of being the Only God and the First and the Creator and the Lord of all things, together with the quality of not being comparable to any being; but all these qualities are ascribed by him to matter as well (§1). Therefore, if he asserts that matter existed without any detriment to the condition of God, we may as well turn the tables on him and say that God existed without detriment to the condition of matter. Likewise, when he says that matter had some, not all, of God's

qualities, we may say that God had some, not all, of God's qualities (§2). In reality, Hermogenes has left God nothing which he has not also conferred on matter: according to his description, it possesses merely attributes which are the special property of God, nor can we discover in it any property which is foreign to God (§3).'

In this chapter Tertullian continues the discussion, begun in 5.2, of the predicates which God possesses in addition to eternity. §1 gives a further elaboration of the thought already expressed in 5.2, namely, that Hermogenes has left God no special prerogative, because he has ascribed all His qualities to matter as well; in §§2 and 3 this same idea is given more striking expression.

48 Allusion to Isa. 45.23 (never quoted by Tertullian).

49 Allusion to Exod. 20.3 (quoted in *Scorp.* 2 [147.3 f. R.-W.]: *non erunt tibi dii alii praeter me*).

50 Isa. 44.6 (48.12; cf. 41.4 and Apoc. 1.17). According to Oehler, this passage is also quoted in *Adv. Marc.* 1.11 and 4.39 and *Adv. Prax.* 17 and 18, but not one of these chapters contains a quotation of it.

51 *autem*. Kroymann reads *enim* which is certainly wrong, for we find here one of those 'inverted syllogisms' which are so frequent in Tertullian (cf. the list of confused syllogisms in the index of my edition of the *De anima*, p. 637). The argument, which is best given in Latin, runs as follows: a. *Materia dei coaetanea est*; b. *Inter coaetaneos autem et contemporales ordo non est*; c. *Ergo inter deum et materiam ordo non est, unde deus primus esse non potest.* The irregularity consists in the fact that the conclusion (*Et quomodo primus . . . ?*) has been put before the premises.—I read *cuius* (Nβ Kroymann, *cui* P Oehler) *materia coaetanea est.*

52 Isa. 44.24 (also quoted in *Adv. Prax.* 19 [261.2 Kr.] and alluded to *ibid.* 18 end; cf. Evans 291).

53 *enim* (*etiam* Oehler, which is quite unnecessary).

54 That is, in spite of Hermogenes' assertion that God is superior to matter.

55 *et ipsa* (Nβ Kroymann; *et illa* P and most editors, also Oehler).

56 *In qua omnia dei propria recensentur, satis praeiudicant de reliqua comparatione.* Kroymann reads *in qua si*, but the relative clause is equivalent to a *si*-clause which is not infrequent in Tertullian: cf. my note on *De an.* 30.5 (p. 377). After stating in the two preceding sentences that Hermogenes has left God nothing which he has not also granted to matter, in other words, that matter possesses all the *propria dei*, Tertullian comes to the question whether matter possesses any qualities besides those which it shares with God. The answer is in the negative (this is not explicitly said, but the question with which ch. 6 ends is to be regarded as a rhetorical one). If in matter we find all the special qualities

of God, they show (or rather: their presence shows) sufficiently that for the rest, too, matter is equal to God (Kellner: 'Da alle Eigenschaften Gottes bei ihr vorkommen, so gibt das für sonstige Gleichheit genügende Anhaltspunkte'); and with that it is demonstrated that matter is completely equal to God, since it not only possesses all the *propria dei*, but also nothing besides the *propria dei*. In reality, though, this sentence does not furnish a proof at all (the fact that matter has all the *propria dei* does not imply that it could not have other qualities besides; this is also tacitly indicated by the words *de reliqua comparatione* which now are meaningless, since there is no 'rest'). Tertullian not infrequently concludes a chapter with an impressive but utterly false thesis, so at the end of *De an.* 7: *In quantum enim omne corporale passibile est, in tantum quod passibile est corporale est*; or at the end of *ibid.* 10: *Ipsum est enim quid, per quod est quid.*

57 **Chapter 7:** 'Hermogenes says that matter is inferior to God; but whatever is eternal and unborn, as he asserts matter to be, does not admit of any diminution or humiliation (§1). So the only reasonable conclusion is that God and matter are completely equal to each other (§2). We cannot avoid this conclusion by saying that below God there exists a lesser God, as this would be a pagan statement: for Christians Divinity has no degrees (§3). Therefore Hermogenes will never succeed in making a distinction between God and matter, when he confers on matter all those divine qualities (§4).'

The only new element which this chapter adds to the discussion given in chs. 5 and 6 is the rejection of the possibility that matter be regarded as divine, but as a lesser divinity; the first and second paragraphs repeat the argument of chs. 4 and 5, the third that of ch. 6.

58 *semel opposita fini, quae et initio* (*quae* α and Thörnell, *Stud. Tert.* 2.70, *qui* β, *quia* Iunius, *qua* Oehler and Kroymann).

59 *ex pari solidae et perfectae felicitatis, quae censetur aeternitas.* On *censeri*, cf. above, n. 41.

60 Thörnell, *Stud. Tert.* 1.26, reads ⟨*eadem*⟩ *aderit utrobique*, Engelbrecht *aderit* ⟨*tota*⟩ *utrobique*. With P, I read *aderit utrobique*.

61 We must read *deo* with Iunius (*deus* MSS).

62 *Aut ego sum deus et ille materia* (*et* Iunius, *aut* MSS). Matter says: 'I am in no respect inferior to God. One might think that God is superior to me because His name is "God," but to this I reply that I, too, have a name which is all my own (on *deus* as a *nomen solius dei proprium*, cf. n. 27). Nay, I also have a right to bear the name "God" (and likewise God has the right to bear the name "matter"), for in consequence of our complete equality, we can each of us bear the other's name besides our own.' If we adopt the reading given by the manuscripts

(*aut ille materia*), the first *aut* cannot establish the necessary connection with the preceding sentence.

⁶³ That is, Hermogenes.

⁶⁴ **Chapter 8**: 'If God really needed matter for the creation of the universe, matter was even superior to God (§1). So matter has rendered God a great service: thanks to it, God nowadays has something by means of which He can be known as the Almighty God—though His power was indeed far from being omnipotence, if He was unable to create the world out of nothing (§2). But matter also rendered itself a service in that it could be acknowledged as God's coequal and His helper; though this has become known only to Hermogenes and the philosophers, whereas the prophets, the apostles, and Christ know nothing about it (§3).'

⁶⁵ *de cuius* (β Kroymann; *cuius* α and most editors) is clearly required by the parallelism with *de cuius utitur* in the preceding sentence.

⁶⁶ *Grande revera beneficium deo contulit, ut haberet hodie per quae* (which I read instead of the meaningless *quem* given by the MSS) *deus cognosceretur.* Kroymann follows E. Bruhn who indicated a lacuna before *ut*, and mentions as a possible supplement: *cum ad hominem procreandum se ei obtulit*, whereas Engelbrecht substitutes *hominem* for *hodie*. It is true that if we keep *quem*, man should be mentioned somewhere, but the end of the sentence (*si non et hoc potens: ex nihilo omnia proferre*) shows that Tertullian is not thinking of the creation of man, but of creation in general.

⁶⁷ **Chapter 9**: 'If matter was thus equal to God, God cannot have used it as its Lord and owner (§1). He may, however, have used it *precario*—on sufferance; this is even probable, for in drawing on an evil substance for the creation of the universe, God demonstrated His weakness which prevented Him from creating the world out of nothing. If He had possessed any power over matter, He would have amended it prior to the creation (§2). Therefore Hermogenes is certainly wrong in saying that God used matter by virtue of His ownership. If we agree with Hermogenes, we must indeed regard God as the creator or at least the "permitter" of evil (§3). But it is better to say that matter, for being evil, did not belong to God, so that God must have used it either on sufferance or by means of violence—let Hermogenes himself choose between these alternatives (§4). We may say that under such conditions God might have preferred not to create anything at all (§5).'

In this chapter three ideas have been combined:

a) If matter was equal to God, God cannot have been its owner and so, if He made use of it, He must have done so *precario* (in §4 this is extended to: 'either *precario* or *vi*').

b) If God used matter, which is an evil substance, as its Lord for the creation of the world, He is, if not the creator, at least the 'permitter' of evil.

c) If God had to draw upon matter for the creation of the world and could not create the world out of nothing, He was weak. The combination is made in the following way: God's weakness, as proved by (c), obliged Him to use an evil substance (b) for the creation of the world, and so to use it *precario* (a)—for if He had possessed any power over it, He would have amended it. This tallies with the conclusion that matter is equal to God (a).

68 *ideo*. E. Bruhn, followed by Kroymann, reads *adeo*; Holmes' translation is in the same line: 'and to such a degree that . . . .' Kellner retains the *ideo*, but wrongly connects it with *cum*, not with *ut* (*et ideo precario, non dominio, ut, cum ea mala esset, de mala tamen sustinuerit uti*: 'und zwar darum leihweise, nicht als Eigentum, weil sie böse war, damit er sich dazu verstehen könne, auch vom Bösen Gebrauch zu machen'). After *ideo* we would indeed expect to find the reason mentioned why God made use of matter *precario, non dominio*, but instead we find a consequence, namely, that God was now obliged to draw His resources from an evil substance. Nevertheless the *ideo* is, in my opinion, sound: the cause of the fact that God used matter *precario*, that is to say, the *mediocritas dei*, is also the ultimate cause of what is said in the *ut*-clause (cf. n. 66), and so the cause of *precario* is qualified by the description of another of its consequences which, because it is more concrete, is more evident. Therefore *ideo* should not be translated 'for this reason,' but 'for such a reason': *ideo . . . ut=ob talem causam, ut* (cf. *is sum qui dicam*). In the sequence (*scilicet ex necessitate mediocritatis suae*, etc.) the *mediocritas dei* is immediately connected with this *secondary* consequence.

69 *ex nihilo uti*. Kroymann puts a *crux* before *uti* and writes: '*facere vel operari* rescribendum puto'; but cf. 8.1: *Nemo . . . non eget eo de cuius utitur*; cf. Thörnell, *Stud. Tert.* 2.58 n. 2, and my note on *De an.* 35.1 (p. 411).

70 *ut deus*. We would expect *ut dominus*; this is also put into the text by Kroymann, but since Tertullian's use of *deus* and *dominus* is not always accurate, it seems preferable to change nothing.

71 *in bono convertisset: bonum* R² Oehler Kroymann, but there is no reason to reject the reading of the manuscripts, for *in* with an ablative, where we would expect an accusative, is quite frequent in Tertullian (cf. my note on *De an.* 8.2—p. 157).

72 *necessitatem suam ostendit cedentem condicioni materiae*. Holmes: 'He . . . showed the necessity He was under of yielding to the condition of

Matter.' Apart from being much too free, this translation overlooks the fact that Tertullian had already spoken in this chapter about the *necessitas mediocritatis* of God. For the same reason we should not adopt Engelbrecht's *cedens*; moreover, such personifications ('*necessitas cedit*') are frequent in Tertullian, cf. nn. 181 and 308.

73 *cum ex dominio defendit deum materia usum, et de re non sua, scilicet non facta ab ipso.* Holmes: 'when he maintains that it was by virtue of His Lordship that God used Matter—even of His non-possession of any right to it, on the ground, of course, of His not having Himself made it.' Holmes regards the words *de re non sua* as determining *materia usum* and so as being in parallel with *ex dominio*; but *de re non sua* is only to be connected with *usum* (cf. n. 69) and refers to matter, as is also evident from the following *scilicet non facta ab ipso*: 'from a thing which was not His (because He had not made it),' not: 'from the fact that the thing was not His.'

74 I agree with Kroymann that this and the following sentence, which in the editions constitute the beginning of ch. 10, should be added to the present chapter.

75 I read *bono? Fatue satis itaque* (*bono factae satis. itaque* PNR¹; *bona fact(a)e satis* [*satis.* F] *itaque* XF; *bona factis satis itaque bono? fatue satis, ita* R³).

76 **Chapter 10**: 'Hermogenes says that if God had created the universe out of nothing, He would clearly have willed that evil should exist: the heretics indeed want to remove from the good God the creation of evil, and therefore they either postulate a supremely good God besides the Creator who is the author of evil, or they put matter on a level with the Creator that thus they may derive evil from matter (§1). With regard to the alternative, we may reply that if God permitted the existence of evil in matter, He still is, if not the author, at least the sycophant of evil (§2). For either He could amend evil matter but would not, or He would but could not—which means that He either was the friend of evil or its servant (§3).'

Tertullian begins by quoting an argument of Hermogenes: If God had created the world out of nothing, He would also be the creator of evil; therefore God cannot have created the world out of nothing. Tertullian observes that this argument is one commonly found among heretics who in consequence seek two different solutions for the question of the origin of evil: they say either that God is different from the Creator (as was done by Marcion), or that God created the world out of matter (as was said by Hermogenes). After briefly observing that neither of these solutions removes the difficulty, Tertullian concentrates again on the doctrine of Hermogenes and observes that if God

suffered evil to exist in matter and did not amend it, He must either
have been powerless (as had already been stated in 9.2) or unwilling to
amend it—both possibilities being, of course, unacceptable.

[77] *distinguimus.* Kroymann reads *distinguemus,* but in references to his
own writings—whether already published or being prepared—Tertullian frequently uses the present tense: he sees his works as a continuous
whole which is always present to his mind and should be so to the
minds of his readers. Cf. my discussion in *Mnemosyne* Ser. III.3 (1936)
168, of *De carn. res.* 17 (47.22 f. Kr.): *Nos autem animam corporalem et hic
profitemur et in suo volumine* (i.e. the earlier treatise *De anima) probamus
(probavimus* M. Schanz Kroymann). Moreover, as was pointed out by
E. Löfstedt (*Zur Sprache Tert.* 80 f.), the *lectio tradita* is defended by the
clausula.

[78] *se quoque (quoque se* Kroymann): (like Marcion) Hermogenes, too,
has been unsuccessful.

[79] The possibility that God wished to amend matter but could not,
is treated very briefly: its impossibility is sufficiently evident from the
consequence that in that case God would be weak; moreover, this subject was already amply discussed in 9.2.

[80] *habetur eius* MSS Kellner p. 70 n. 1; *habetur reus* Oehler; *habetur
⟨auctor⟩ eius* Ursinus Kroymann.

[81] *Quo quid est turpius?* α and most editors. Kroymann follows F—and
XL—(*quo quidem turpius*) with a slight variation: *quod quidem turpius,* but
the *quidem* of F is certainly owing to a misreading of *quid ē* (= *est*).

[82] *Quasi bonum voluit esse et quasi malum noluit fecisse.* The translation
by Holmes is very strange: 'As if what He willed was good, and at the
same time what He refused to be the Maker of was evil.'

[83] **Chapter 11**: 'Whatever is eternal does not admit of diminution
and subjection, and therefore evil cannot be an attribute of it, for it
cannot be subject to evil; further, what is eternal is the highest good,
and the highest good cannot possibly be evil (§1). If that which is
eternal is capable of evil, then God is also capable of evil and Hermogenes' endeavour to remove evil from God has been in vain (§2).
Finally, if what is eternal can be evil, then evil will be eternal; but
Scripture clearly shows that evil will once have an end, which implies
that it has also had a beginning; and then evil matter, too, must have
had a beginning (§3).'

[84] The first paragraph consists of two arguments, the second of which
is subdivided into two syllogisms:

I. a. *Quod aeternum est, nulli rei subici potest (nam diminutionem et
    humiliationem non capit).*

⟨b. *Cui porro malum competit, id subicitur malo.*⟩
  c. *Ergo ei quod aeternum est, malum competere non potest.*

II.A. a. *Deus est solus Deus, quod aeternus est.*
     b. *Deus est bonus, quod Deus est.*
     c. *Ergo Deus, quod aeternus est, est solus bonus deus= summum bonum; et inde* (!) *quod aeternum est, summum bonum est.*

II.B. a. (=II.A. c.): *Quod aeternum est, summum bonum est.*
    ⟨b. *Malum non competit bono, nedum summo bono.*⟩
     c. *Ergo ei quod aeternum est, malum non competit.*

From I. c and II.B c it follows that eternal matter cannot be evil.

85 *definimus; definivimus* Engelbrecht Kroymann, but cf. n. 77.

86 One may find here one of those inadmissible inversions which are not infrequent in Tertullian (cf. the quotation from *De an.* 7 at the end of n. 56): '*quod aeterum est malum potest credi* (*esse*), *ergo quod malum est aeternum est*'; but in my opinion the meaning is slightly different—'if an eternal substance can be evil, then the evil *present in that substance* will be eternal': this interpretation tallies with the end of the chapter—cf. n. 98.

87 Cf. 1 Cor. 5.13 (also alluded to in *De pud.* 13: *incesto . . . quem scilicet auferri iussisset de medio eorum*).

88 *iniustitia utique puniturus.* Holmes: 'when He means, indeed, to inflict punishment with injustice'; but the future participle does not denote an intention here but an objective consequence.

89 Cf. Matt. 25.41 (alluded to in *De carn. Chr.* 14, and *De carn. res.* 58); cf. G. J. D. Aalders, *Tertullianus' Citaten uit de Evangeliën en de Oud-Latijnsche Bijbelvertalingen* (Amsterdam 1932) 78 f.

90 Cf. Apoc. 20.3 (cf. *De carn. res.* 25).

91 Cf. Rom. 8.19.

92 Allusion to Rom. 8.21.

93 Allusion to *ibid.* 8.20 (also alluded to in *De cor.* 6 and 8).

94 Allusion to Isa. 11.6.

95 Allusion to *ibid.* 11. 8 (also alluded to in *Adv. Marc.* 4.24–502.15 Kr.).

96 Allusion, not to Ps. 109 (110).1, as is indicated by the editors, but to the quotation of this passage in 1 Cor. 15.25. In *Adv. Prax.* 4 (232.10 ff. Kr.) Tertullian makes a clear distinction between the two passages: *. . . siquidem apostolus scribit de ultimo fine: Cum tradiderit regnum deo et patri. Oportet enim eum regnare usque dum ponat inimicos eius deus sub pedes ipsius,—scilicet secundum psalmum: Sede ad dexteram meam, donec ponam inimicos tuos scabellum pedum tuorum.* Further

quotations are found in *Adv. Prax.* 30 (288.5 f. Kr.) and *Adv. Marc.* 5.9 (602.21 f. Kr.).

97 With Oehler I read *et erit materia habens initium* (*et* om. MSS, *eritque* Latinius; Kroymann marks a lacuna before *materia*: '*igitur et* desideratur.'

98 *Quae enim malo deputantur, secundum mali statum ⟨materiae⟩ computantur* (*computantur* α; *deputatur* β; *competunt* Oehler; *competunt ei* (or *illi*) Kellner; *computantur* ⟨*materiae*⟩ Kroymann); with regard to the clausula, I prefer to put *materiae* before *computantur*, for this gives a ditrochaic, which is the legitimate form of the third clausula of the classical period in Tertullian. Holmes, adopting Oehler's text, translates: 'For whatever things are set to the account of evil, have a compatibility with the condition of evil.' Kellner writes: 'Denn die Eigenschaften, die dem Bösen beigelegt werden, die kommen dem Zustande des Bösen entsprechend ihr zu.' This interpretation hits the mark, for the trend of thought is as follows: 'If evil has an end—and from Scripture it is evident that it has—it must needs have a beginning as well; but then matter also has a beginning, for the evil in it has one.' Now the correctness of the last statement has to be proved: 'For the things which are ascribed to evil (in this case, a beginning and an end) are also to be ascribed to matter on account of its *mali status*, that is, on account of the fact that its condition is evil' ('its condition which consists in evil': *mali* is an explicative genitive—cf. 43.3 *natura mali* and n. 141). For the variation of *deputantur* and *computantur*, cf. 13.3: *deputabuntur, . . . imputentur.*

99 **Chapter 12**: 'If nevertheless matter is evil by nature, it must always be evil, for the nature of matter must be something certain and fixed (§1). Passages from Holy Scripture which mention a change in the nature of other things do not contradict this statement, for such passages refer to things which have a beginning and, therefore, also an end (§2). But according to Hermogenes, matter is eternal, and so it cannot be subject to change; this conclusion is also in accordance with the doctrine of Hermogenes, for he says that the reason why God cannot create out of Himself is that God, being eternal, is immutable (§3). But if we adopt this argument, it becomes impossible that good things should have been created out of evil matter (§4).'

The contents of this chapter can be summarized in three syllogisms:

I. a. What is eternal is immutable.
   b. (According to Hermogenes) matter is eternal.
   c. So matter is immutable.

II. a. (According to Hermogenes) matter is evil.
    b. (=I. c) Matter is immutable.
    c. So matter must always be evil.

III. a. Good things have been created out of matter (according to Hermogenes).
     b. (=II. c) But matter is always evil (according to H.).
     c. So matter must have experienced a change—but this is impossible because of its eternity (=I. a) ⟨, and so good things cannot have been created out of matter⟩.

[100] I adopt the distinction by Kroymann: *tam in malo perseverantem apud materiam quam et in bono apud deum, inconvertibilem et indemutabilem scilicet, quia, etc.* Most editors place a full stop after *indemutabilem*.

[101] Cf. Matt. 3.7–9. The same passage is used in *De an.* 21.4 to prove the mutability of the human soul. Further, cf. 37.4; *De pud.* 10 (240.24 f. R.-W.) and 20 (268.12 f. R.-W.); Aalders, *op. cit.* 27 f.

[102] Cf. Eph. 2.3 (also used in *De an.* 21.4—cf. the preceding note; also *ibid.* 16.7; *Adv. Marc.* 5.17 [635.12 ff. Kr.]; *De pud.* 17 [257.30 R.-W.]) and Luke 10.6.

[103] That is, by Hermogenes. Tertullian does not attack now the statement itself but rather its consequence.

[104] This very common definition of change (*locus classicus*: Aristotle, *Phys.* 191 a 6–8) is frequently adduced by Tertullian—cf. my note on *De an.* 32.7 (p. 390); cf. also below, 34.2 (n. 298).

[105] Gen. 1.21: *Et vidit deus quia bona* (*bona, bona sunt, bonum, bonum est* the *Vetus Latina*).

[106] *Ibid.* 1.22: *Et benedixit ea dominus* (the *Vetus Latina*: *et benedixit illa* [*eas, ea, eis*] *deus*).

[107] *mortua est denique sua forma.* Holmes: 'in short, its beauty is decayed in death,' with the note: 'That is, of course, by its own natural law.' If I am not mistaken, in the translation he regards *sua forma* as a nominative, in his comment as an ablative. Kellner translates: 'Denn ihre eigentliche Form ist ihr dadurch verloren gegangen.' As I see it, *sua forma* should be understood as an *ablativus limitativus*: matter has died *as regards* its 'exact form,' which, following Hermogenes, is eternity. One may doubt, however, whether the meaning is not—'it has formally died' (almost: 'it has died its natural death'—cf. Holmes' explanation), since *ex forma* is occasionally found with this meaning, e.g., in Fronto, *Ad M. Caes.* 5.37 (52): *petit nunc procurationem ex forma* ('in due form,' C. R. Haines); cf. my note on *De an.* 44.2 (p. 479). Moreover, the similar expression, *sua morte mori*, means 'to die a natural death' (cf. the epitaph of a gladiator, Dessau 5106: *sua morte obit*, and

the full treatment of this subject in Wilhelm Schulze's famous paper, 'Der Tod des Kambyses,' *Sitzungsber. d. preuss. Akad. d. Wiss.* [1912] 685–703).

[108] **Chapter 13**: 'But let us assume for the moment that good things were made out of evil matter without any change in matter—how are we to calculate this? (§1). We may seek a solution in the presence of a good element in matter, but then matter will no longer possess a uniform nature (§2). But if we accept this too and so assume matter to have been good and evil at the same time, then God is not even the creator of good things, and so He becomes still more subservient to matter (§3).'

[109] Kroymann thinks it a mistake to begin a new chapter at this point. It is true that Tertullian continues his discussion of the supposition of eternal matter as evil, but he now begins to treat it in a different manner: after refuting it in ch. 12, he now accepts it for a moment to show up its impossible consequences.

[110] Matt. 7.18, a passage of particular importance to Tertullian— cf. *De carn. Chr.* 8; *De an.* 21.5 (probably repeating the present argument—cf. my note, p. 294); *Adv. Marc.* 1.2 (292.17 ff. Kr.); 4.17 (476.7 ff. Kr.); cf. Aalders, *op. cit.* 93; A. Harnack, *Marcion. Das Evangelium vom fremden Gott* (2 ed. Leipzig 1924) 194* f. (cf. Luke 6.43).

[111] *Aut si dabimus illi aliquid etiam boni germinis.* Holmes: 'Or if we were to grant him that there is some germ of good (in it).' But *illi* =*materiae*, not =*Hermogeni*; in the beginning of the chapter Tertullian has said that he will assume Hermogenes to be right, so that there is no need now to grant something again to him. At the end of the sentence I read with Kroymann *an in ⟨eadem⟩ bono et malo potuerit convenire, luci et tenebris*, etc.

[112] *: iam nec bona ipsa deo deputabuntur, ut nec mala illi imputentur*— Holmes: 'then no longer will absolutely good things be imputed to God, just as evil things are not ascribed to Him.' The translation of *ipsa* by 'absolutely' is not correct: Tertullian means to say that in that case *even* the creation of good things will be removed from God, so that then nothing will be left to Him. Holmes' translation of the clause *ut . . . imputentur* renders the meaning correctly. Formally it is also possible to translate: 'then no longer will even good things be imputable to Him without also imputing evil things to Him,' but this would be meaningless, for Tertullian says that in that case God will lose the creation of good things, too, not that if we ascribe the creation of good things to God, we must then also necessarily ascribe to Him the creation of evil things. Therefore *ut* must indeed mean 'just as'; the subjunctive

imputentur may have potential force—unless we should substitute for it the indicative.

[113] *proprietate*. On this word, cf. the excellent note by Evans, *op. cit.* 257 f.

[114] **Chapter 14**: 'In order to avoid this conclusion, it may be said that God, though drawing indeed on matter for the creation of good things, yet produced them of His own will, and that on that account He did not become subservient to matter. But to this we may reply that at all events He also produced evil things from matter, which He can by no means have done of His own will, and that therefore, if He produced from matter both good and evil things, He still remains subservient to matter (§1). (But God must not be subservient to matter in any way:) It is more worthy of God that He created evil things from nothing than that He produced them from matter, for it is more worthy that God, even as the creator of evil, is free than that He is the servant of some other power (§2). Now if we suppose that matter did not contain anything good (return to ch. 12) and that God created the good by His own power, He can only have created it from nothing (§3).'

This chapter, concluding the discussion of the origin of good things, consists of three parts. First, Tertullian refutes a possible objection against the conclusion of the end of chapter 13—that if matter were both good and evil, God would be entirely dependent on it (§1). In addition he argues that God must have created evil things out of nothing, not out of matter (§2). Returning then to the subject of the origin of good things, he concludes that if matter did not contain any good, the good can only have been created either out of God (which, however—according to Hermogenes—is impossible), or out of nothing.

[115] *Nam*: Holmes renders 'Now,' which is inexact, since Tertullian does not add a new argument but defends his conclusion in 13.4 (13.4 *materiae deservisse*~14.1 *deservisse*) against a possible refutation; the argument thus shows that the conclusion was correct—hence the insertion of the words 'this conclusion is irrefutable' before 'for.'

[116] *proinde quatenus* (PX; *quantus* Nγ) *fecit*; Holmes: 'just because He made them,' but *quatenus* does not have a causal sense here (though this is frequent in Tertullian—cf. my note on *De an.* 1.1—p. 83). Tertullian means to say that if God made evil things out of matter, He may be to a lesser degree the author of evil than He would have been if He had made them out of nothing, but that nevertheless His authorship goes exactly (*proinde*) as far as His activity in making them out of matter. There is no need to follow Kroymann in reading *quatenus proinde*.

117 In this sentence I translate 'them' four times when Holmes translates 'all things': Tertullian is still speaking about the creation of evil, not of all things; it is only at the end of §2 that he changes the subject.

118 *Plane sic interest unde fecerit ac si de nihilo fecisset. Sic . . . ac si = aeque . . . ac si, non magis . . . quam si* (for *sic atque,* cf. Thes. L. L. 2.1080.10 ff.). The literal translation is: 'Plainly it makes no more difference whence He made them (=if He made them from something) than if He had made them from nothing'—for in both cases He would be regarded as their Creator. Tertullian then continues: *nec interest unde ecerit, ut inde fecerit unde eum magis decuit.* It should be noted that the first *unde* refers to a creation out of something, whereas the second also implies a creation out of nothing. Kroymann thoroughly alters the text: *quatenus proinde fecit* (=the end of the preceding sentence), *acsi de nihilo fecisset nec interest unde fecerit. plane sic interest, unde . . . decuit.*

119 The argument runs as follows:

I. a. If matter contained some good element, God would become subservient to matter (13.3–14.1).
   b. But God cannot be subservient to matter (14.2).
   ⟨c. Therefore matter cannot contain a good element.⟩

II. a. (=I. c). Matter did not contain a good element.
   b. God created good things.
   c. Therefore God did not create good things from matter. We may say that He created them by virtue of His own power; and from this it may again be deduced that God created good things out of nothing (14.3).

Now Tertullian does not give this argument in its strict form: he enumerates both premises and part of the conclusion of II in a *si*-clause ('if matter did not contain anything good, *and* (instead of *so*) God, if He made good things—as He did indeed—did so by His own virtue'). He then presents the correct conclusion as an immediate consequence of II. a.

120 That is, according to Hermogenes; cf. the argument in 2.2 f.

121 Cf. 2.1.

122 **Chapter 15:** 'Consequently, if the good was made neither out of matter nor out of God, it must have been created out of nothing (=the conclusion of 14.3); but if God could make one thing out of nothing, He could make all things, evil included, out of nothing (§1). If good had indeed proceeded from evil matter, matter must have experienced a change which we found (12.3) to be impossible; and so, unless we accept a creation out of nothing, all three possibilities

mentioned by Hermogenes (ch. 2) have been eliminated (§2). If evil had sprung from matter, God would still remain the author of evil, as we have already seen (9.3 ; 10.2) ; moreover, this is an extremely improbable hypothesis (§3). The argument that evil must exist as a background of the good in the world has already been refuted by Hermogenes himself (§4). So nothing opposes the supposition that evil, too, was created out of nothing (§5).'

After demonstrating by means of a long (12.4–14) and laborious argument that good things must have been created by God out of nothing, Tertullian has no difficulty in proving that the same must hold of evil things (§1). Repeating the conclusion of ch. 12 that good things cannot have been created from evil matter, he infers that thus of the three possibilities mentioned by Hermogenes (ch. 2) the only one admitted by the heretic has been eliminated; but one of the three must be true, wherefore good things must either have proceeded from God or from nothing (§2). Returning, then, to his main subject in this chapter—the origin of evil things—Tertullian again (cf. 10.2 f. and 14.1) observes that a supposition that God created evil things out of matter, does not protect Him against the accusation of being the author of evil; for if evil proceeded from matter, God was either willing that there should be evil things, or He was incapable of making only good things; and so the endeavour to exculpate God does not furnish a reason for deriving evil things from matter. Nor is it possible to refute this argument, that we cannot think of any other reason than that God wished this or could not prevent it, both of which make Him the author of evil. The strange supposition that thus God, after making good things made evil things from matter as well and thereby shielded matter from being known as evil, is not worth considering. There can be no other reason than this authorship of God, for it would have been better that the good existed alone without evil (§3). Some people say that evil was necessary as a background for the good, an assertion which has already been refuted by Hermogenes (§4). If some other reason could be found for a creation of evil out of matter—two reasons just mentioned having been refuted—evil can still have been created out of nothing: for the same argument by which the Lord is excused (by Hermogenes) when He is said to have created evil out of matter, can be used with equal right when He is thought of as having created evil out of nothing (i.e. by saying that He is not the author of evil when in fact He is). Conclusion: there is no reason why matter should not have been created out of nothing—a conclusion which is quite disagreeable to all those who do not understand the essence of evil, and who therefore are most anxious to say that God is not the author of evil; and this

they hope to prove by saying that He created evil out of matter
(§5).

There is no reason to emphasize continuity of the present chapter
with the preceding, as does Kroymann ('*male hoc loco distinguuntur
capita*'): after proving in ch. 14 that good things must have been
created by God out of nothing, Tertullian now goes on to demonstrate
that the same holds of evil things. From this it follows that there is no
reason to wonder with Kroymann that Tertullian repeats himself in
this chapter: in 15.1 he explicitly mentions the conclusion of chapter 14
as the premise of a new argument and in 15.2 this conclusion is again
inserted into the syllogism; this is quite in accordance with Tertullian's
habit of repeating conclusions of precedent arguments in his syllogisms
—cf. n. 38, my reply to Kr.'s second objection.

123 *quae aliquid protulerit ex nihilo.* Holmes: 'though it produced,'
etc.; but the clause clearly has a causal sense.

124 *Ita unde bonum constitit, iam negabit Hermogenes inde illud constare
potuisse.* Kellner puts a question-mark after *constitit*; I regard this
distinction as contrary to Tertullian's idiom. Oehler in his apparatus
writes, '*velim undeunde*' (which is accepted by Kroymann), and deletes
inde. In my opinion, *unde bonum constitit* means 'the origin of matter'
(= one of the three possibilities mentioned by Hermogenes, that is to
say, the right one): Hermogenes had already said himself (ch. 2) that
the good cannot have been created out of God or out of nothing, so he
is now obliged to say, since it has just been proved that neither can it
have proceeded from matter, that all three possibilities are out of the
question; but this is impossible, and he must therefore choose between the two which he has just rejected.

125 *eadem virtute et voluntate.*

126 Here Kroymann proposes to insert *turpiter utrumque*, which is
quite unnecessary, since before *nihil interest* or *dum nihil intersit* such
ellipses are quite frequent in Tertullian: cf. Thörnell, *Stud. Tert.* 1.30.

127 We do not know to whom Tertullian refers here. The idea itself
is not rarely found in ancient theodicies, but probably Hermogenes or
his followers are meant. It is also possible that the idea is due to Tertullian himself, and that it is an inference drawn by him from 1 Cor. 11.19
which verse he frequently quotes (cf. my note on *De an.* 3.1—pp. 114 f.).

128 *quae nunc, cum de materia operatur, mala excusat? Si excusat, adeo
ubique et undique,* etc. Kroymann and earlier editors put the question-
mark after the second *excusat*, but Tertullian often repeats a conclusion
in a *si*-clause in the course of an argument.

129 That is to say, the conclusion that God created both good and evil
things out of nothing.

[130] *destructionibus*. Kellner proposes to read *deductionibus* or *distinctionibus*, but these words are never used by Tertullian in connection with arguments; further, *destruere* frequently denotes a refutation in his works—cf. *De an.* 2.2 (with my comment, p. 101) and 3.3; cf. also *Adv. Marc.* 2.26 (372.21–23 Kr.): *quaecumque . . . colligitis ad destructionem creatoris.*

[131] **Chapter 16**: 'If God made good and evil things out of matter, it is impossible to say with Hermogenes that God is not the author of evil (§1). And if matter was the associate of God in the creation of evil, God, who actually made it, still remains its creator—so why introduce matter at all? We conclude, therefore, that God made all things out of nothing (§2). As regards the creation of evil things by God, we still have to inquire into the nature of evil. At all events, it is more worthy of God freely to have created evil out of nothing than to have done so out of matter (§3).'

In this chapter, which concludes the first part of the refutation of Hermogenes (4–15), Tertullian once more points out that it is impossible to free God from the charge of being the author of evil by introducing the notion of matter and that, therefore, there is no reason to prefer the conception of a creation from matter to that of a creation from nothing (§1 f.). A further investigation of the origin of evil is announced, but once more it is asserted that a creation of evil out of nothing is a more worthy conception of God.

[132] *articuli*: cf. below, n. 288.

[133] Cf. especially *Adv. Marc.* 2.14 (based on the interpretation of Isa. 45.7: *Ego sum qui condo mala*).

[134] Which is the very conclusion that Hermogenes means to avoid. Tertullian here also rejects it ('but God cannot be the author of evil') because he is arguing on the base of Hermogenes' argument.

[135] As discussed (on Hermogenes' premises) in ch. 12.

[136] As discussed in chs. 6–9.

[137] Wherefore we cannot make this distinction, ascribing only good to God and only evil to matter, as was required by the argument.

[138] *excusas iam causam (causa* β*) materiae* (MSS R[1] Oehler; *excludas* R[1] in marg.; *excussas* Iunius; *excludis* R[3]; *exclusa iam causa materiae* Kroymann). The argument is a repetition of 15.3. The reading *excusas* is defended by the fact that there too we find this verb: *ipsa ratione excusatura dominum.* Here, however, the meaning of *excusare* is slightly different ('*causam ex-causas*,' 'you undo the cause'). Similar alterations of the meaning of a word occur in *De an.* 2.2: *eas* (= *res*) *nunc privat* (=*privas reddit*, 'treats them as special things'), *nunc peraequat* (cf. my note

ad loc. p. 101); *ibid.* 43.7: *somnum . . . probatorem valetudinum* (= *qui valetudines probas reddit, restituit*); cf. also below, n. 231.

139 Repetition of the argument in 14.2.

140 **Chapter 17**: 'That all things were created out of nothing can also be concluded from the fact that God is the One-only God and the first, and from Scripture (Rom. 11.34 ff.) (§1). Further, if God had created all things out of some substance, that substance would have influenced His creation and so have shown Him *the way of wisdom and knowledge*—which is in flat contradiction with the passage just quoted (§2).'

This chapter constitutes a transition from the discussion by means of logical arguments to the treatment based on Scripture.

141 *Unici dei status*: 'God's condition of being the Only God'; perhaps it is best to say that the genitive has both possessive and definitive force (for the latter sense, cf. above, n. 98).

142 *ut illi quoque scripturae ratio constet*, rendered by Holmes: 'so that reason coincides with the Scripture, which says . . . . ' This translation of *constet* is erroneous (*ratio constat* means 'the account is correct'). Much better Kellner: 'So gelangt auch jene Schriftstelle zu ihrer Berechtigung.'

143 According to Oehler, this is a quotation of Rom. 11.34 f.; Kroymann refers to both Rom. 11.34,35 and Isa. 40.13,14. Since Isa. 40.13 is quoted in Rom. 11.34 (with the exception of the words ὃς συμβιβᾷ αὐτόν LXX), we may indeed with Kroymann refer to both passages, but as a quotation of Isa. 40.14 comes first (*aut quem consultatus est? aut viam intellegentiae et scientiae quis demonstravit illi?*), it seems preferable to assume here a quotation of Isa. 40.13 f. followed by one of Rom. 11.35. The first verse is explicitly quoted from Isaias in *Adv. Prax.* 19 (261.10 f. Kr.): *et Esaias dixit: quis cognovit sensum domini et quis illi consilio fuit?* The same holds of *Scorp.* 7 (159. 28 ff. R.-W.) and *Adv. Marc.* 2.2 (335. 1–4 Kr.), since also in both these passages a quotation of Isa. 40.14 follows immediately (in the MSS the sentence introducing the quotation in the latter passage reads as follows: *ipse iam apostolus tunc prospiciens haeretica corda*; Kroymann is undoubtedly right in deleting *apostolus*—after this quotation we read *cui et apostolus condicet* [Rom. 11.33], so that in the passage under discussion *apostolus* cannot possibly be the correct reading—and in adding *Esaias* after *ipse*). On the other hand, Rom. 11.34 f. is certainly quoted in *Adv. Marc.* 5.14 (625.16–18 Kr.; in this chapter Tertullian discusses Marcion's treatment of the Epistle to the Romans) and in 45.4 of the present treatise (cf. the context). We may be in doubt about the quotations occurring in *Adv. Marc.* 5.6 (590.25–591.1 Kr.) and 5.18 (638.23 f. Kr.): the fact that the

enim which is found in both passages (printed by Kroymann as forming part of the quotation in the latter case, as not belonging to it in the former) has a correspondence in Rom. 11.34 only (γάρ), is not yet sufficient reason to find in them quotations of this verse, for the same *enim* is found in *Scorp.* 7 (cf. above).

[144] *aliqua* (Iunius Kroymann; *aliquo* MSS Oehler) must be the correct reading, since *ab ea ipsa* follows.

[145] *et consilium et tractatum dispositionis*: Kroymann, referring to *De carn. res.* 6 (33.24 f. Kr.): *qui illam* (i.e. *materiam*) *et eligendo dignam iudicasset et tractando fecisset*, considers the possibility of reading *et consilium et dispositionem tractatus*. But *dispositio* is the technical term for the arranging or regulation of chaotic matter—cf. 18.2: *ad opera mundi disponenda*. The *consilium* is the general plan, the *tractatus* the correct method for the execution of that plan—their mutual relation is like that between *inventio* and *tractatio* in the handbooks on rhetoric.

[146] **Chapter 18**: 'A much worthier material for the creation of the world is mentioned by Sacred Scripture—the Wisdom of God, generated by Him as soon as He felt its necessity for the creation (§1). Now, if even God's Wisdom was born and created, we cannot possibly believe that anything exists unborn and uncreated save God (§2). Moreover, Wisdom is identical with the Word of God, and, therefore, with the Son of God; and it is impossible that anything should be anterior to the Son of God. Further, if there existed some unborn power, it would be more august than the Son of God, and then, if this power were evil, it would be impossible that evil should have been created by the Son of God (§3). Thus Hermogenes once again (cf. ch. 8) makes matter superior to God, for he makes it superior to the Word, and *the Word is God* (§4).' In his comment on the *Timaeus*, ch. 276 (pp. 307.8 ff. Wrobel), Chalcidius, in a discussion of the doctrine on matter of the *Hebraei*, quotes Proverbs 8.22–25 in proof of the assertion that the *divina sapientia* was *rerum omnium initium*, since it was created by God before the beginning of time, and that in Gen. 1.1 *initium* refers to matter.

[147] *ut Hermogenes existimavit*. Tertullian frequently uses *existimare* and *aestimare* as a designation of 'mere suppositions' (mostly of philosophers and their 'patriarchs,' the heretics) as opposed to the Truth revealed by Scripture; cf. the end of the present sentence: *non apud philosophos aestimandam, sed apud prophetas intellegendam*. Cf. nn. 31 and 166, and my comment on *De an.* 9.3: *per aestimationem . . . per revelationem*.

[148] By 'the books of the prophets' Tertullian means the entire Old Testament, for, like Philo, he regards Moses as the first prophet. For further details, see my note on *De an.* 28.1 (p. 355 f.).

¹⁴⁹ I Cor. 2.11: *Quis enim scit quae sunt dei, et quae in ipso, nisi spiritus, qui in ipso?* The same inaccurate quotation occurs in *Adv. Prax.* 8 (238.10 f. Kr.) and 19 (261.15–17 Kr.; cf. also *Adv. Marc.* 2.2: 335.10 Kr.)—see Evans 241: 'Tertullian transfers τὸ ἐν αὐτῷ from the spirit of man to the Spirit of God, and proceeds to interpret the apostle's words as referring to the Son: there are indications that his Montanism led him to think that the Paraclete was not operating until the rise of the prophetic movement, and that consequently all apostolic references to the Spirit (other than promises of future operation) must be interpreted of the Son.' See also H. Rönsch, *Das Neue Testament Tertullians* (Leipzig 1871) 670. In the next sentence (*Sophia autem spiritus*) the nominal predicate is put at the beginning as in the famous statement, *Semen est sanguis Christianorum* (*Apol.* 50.13).

¹⁵⁰ Prov. 8.27 ff.; cf. n. 157.

¹⁵¹ *materiam vere materiarum: vere* is a conjecture by Iunius (*vero* MSS, 'in vero fort.' Kroymann).

¹⁵² *non fini subditam* (*fini* Oehler, *sit* β *sibi* P [*alias: non sic* R¹ *in marg. in* P] and N, *situ* Kroymann on account of 38.1: *De situ materiae*).

¹⁵³ *non statu diversam* (corresponding with *propriam*).

¹⁵⁴ *insitam* (corresponding with *non fini subditam*).

¹⁵⁵ *propriam* (cf. n. 153).

¹⁵⁶ A reminiscence of 14.2.

¹⁵⁷ Together with the preceding quotation (cf. n. 150), this is a selection from Proverbs 8.22–25 and 27–31, probably translated from the LXX by Tertullian himself. Almost the same selection (lacking only 8.24, *prior autem abysso genita sum*, and 8.31) occurs, with slight variations, in *Adv. Prax.* 6 (cf. the very detailed comment by Evans 220–23). The order of the sentences of LXX has been disturbed in the translation. The LXX reads (I quote from the translation by Charles Thomson, edited, revised, and enlarged by C. A. Muses (Indian Hills, Col. 1954): '(22) The Lord created me, the beginning of His ways, for His works. (23) Before this age He founded me; in the beginning, (24) before He made the earth and before He made the deeps: before the fountains of water issued forth—(25) before the mountains were established and before all the hills, He bringeth me forth.' Tertullian, *Adv. Herm.* 18 (the variants found in *Adv. Prax.* 6 are added between parenth.): *Dominus* (*primo dominus*) *condidit* (*creavit*; but *condidit* again in *Adv. Prax.* 7: 235.17 f. and 236.2 Kr.; *ibid.* 11: 243.10 Kr.; *Adv. Herm.* 20.1) *me initium viarum suarum* (*suarum* om.) *in opera sua: ante saecula fundavit me* (*ante . . . me* om.) *priusquam faceret terram* (*terram faceret*), *priusquam montes collocarentur, ante omnes autem colles generavit me, prior autem abysso genita sum* (*prior . . . sum* om.; this sentence is also quoted in

Adv. Herm. 32.2). Equally curious is the translation of vv. 27–31, in which Tertullian has omitted the second part of v. 27 ('and when He set apart His own throne on the winds'), but has inserted *super ventos* in the translation of the first half of v. 28 ('when He strengthened the clouds above'). Further, the latter half of v. 28 ('and when He secured the fountains of the earth below,' τῆς ὑπ᾽ οὐρανόν), which is correctly translated in *Adv. Prax.* 6, is rendered in the present passage by *et quomodo firmos ponebat fontes eius quae sub caelo est* (likewise in 32.3 where, however, *eius* and *est* have been omitted): *firmos* comes, of course, from v. 29 ('and when He made the foundations of the earth strong'), which has been left untranslated both in the present passage and in *Adv. Prax.* 6. Finally, the words 'on all occasions' of v. 30 have been omitted.

In his comment on *Adv. Prax.* 6 Evans rightly observes that in the present chapter Tertullian declares Wisdom to have been created and generated within God for the sake of his argument, that is to say, in order to prove that nothing unborn and ungenerated exists except God alone, but that this assertion leads up to the conclusion that God was originally ἄλογος—a statement to which Tertullian would not have subscribed under any condition. On the other hand, in *Adv. Prax.* 6 and *Adv. Herm.* 20 he interprets the generation described in Prov. 8.22 ff. as a generation, not of Wisdom itself (which is coeternal with God), but of the world projected *in dei sensu*; in *Adv. Herm.* 20 he returns to the present interpretation.

[158] After the words, *si uero sophia eadem dei sermo est*, the MSS read *sensu sophia et*, for which Iunius substitutes *sensus sophiae*, Kellner *sensus est sophia*, and Oehler *sensu sophiae, et*; Kroymann enters a *crux* before the reading of the MSS and observes: 'nescio, an lateat in his verbis interpretamentum: *Iesus* (=*iħs, iens*) sive *sensus*(=λόγος Eng) *sophia est.*' In my opinion, *sensu sophia* may have originated from a marginal or interlinear note *sermo sensu sophia(e)*='N.B.! Here *sermo* is equivalent to *sophia!*' Moreover, the argument is complete without these words: *si uero sophia eadem dei sermo est, sine quo factum est nihil, sicut et dispositum* (i.e. *nihil*; in *Vig. Chr.* 9 [1955] 143 f. I have, with great hesitation, proposed to insert *est nihil in dei sensu* after *dispositum*). The syllogism runs as follows:

   a. *sine dei sermone factum est nihil.*
   b. *sine sophia dei dispositum est nihil.*
   c. *ergo sophia dei eadem dei sermo est.*

From this it follows that Engelbrecht is wrong in assuming that the words *sine sophia* should be deleted: they are essential to the argument.

159 Allusion to John 1.3, one of the Scriptural passages most quoted by Tertullian—cf. Rönsch, *op. cit.* 251 f. and 653 f.

160 Ps. 44.2. The MSS read: *eructavit enim, inquit, sermonem optimum.* Kroymann inserts *cor meum* before *sermonem.* These words occur indeed in all other quotations of this passage by Tertullian (*Adv. Marc.* 2.4: 337.20 f. Kr.; *ibid.* 4.14: 459.7 f.; *Adv. Prax.* 7: 235.23 f. Kr.; *ibid.* 11: 243.1 f.; cf. the discussion of its interpretation by Evans 226–28), but it should be kept in mind that Tertullian frequently has abbreviated quotations (cf. e.g. the omission of *feminam* in Matt. 5.28 in *De an.* 40.4 and 58.6); hence the insertion appears unnecessary.

161 *adduci* (MSS) is, in my opinion, equivalent here to *induci* (Kellner: 'herangezogen werden'). Kroymann reads *abduci* (found in δ) and explains this as equivalent to *vinci*, quoting Rom. 12.21: *noli vinci a malo, sed vince in bono malum.* Cf. my discussion of the passage in *Vig. Chr.* 9 (1955) 145.

162 John 1.1 (cf. Rönsch, *op. cit.* 250 f.).

163 John 10.30 (quoted four times in the *Adv. Prax.*: cf. Rönsch, *op. cit.* 273).

164 **Chapter 19:** 'According to the heretics, the "beginning" in which God made heaven and earth was something substantial and corporeal, which may be understood to be matter (§1). But the word *principium,* as also *initium,* certainly designates the *action* of beginning and is not the name of a substance (§2). Further, heaven and earth were actually made before all other things (§3). Moreover, a substantial thing from which another thing originates can, it is true, be called the "beginning" of that second thing, but in such cases the thing which is the "beginning" is always explicitly mentioned; therefore, if we read only the words, "In the beginning," it is clear that this refers to order in time, not to the origin of things created (§4). We can also give a different interpretation of the words, "In the beginning": the Greek word ἀρχή, of which *principium* is the Latin translation, has a secondary meaning, namely, "power," and so *In principio* may mean "In power" (§5).' A similar discussion of the various meanings of *initium* is found in the chapter of Chalcidius quoted in n. 146 above.

165 *originale instrumentum Moysei.* Holmes translates: 'the original document of Moses,' observing, however, in a note: 'which may mean "the document which treats of the origin of all things."' In my opinion, the latter interpretation is the correct one. In *De an.* 3.3, *originalis* is equivalent to *patriarchalis*—cf. my note, p. 119 f.

166 *suspiciones* (Pβ and most editions; *sumptiones* N; *praesumptiones* Kroymann) is certainly correct, for *suspicio* has the same meaning as *aestimatio,* for which cf. n. 147, also n. 31.

167 *quod in materiam interpretari possit.* We do not know who these heretics were.

168 *quae ante omnia deus fecit suorum esse proprie principium, quae (qua* Iunius Kroymann, but cf. Thörnell, *Stud. Tert.* 2.70) *priora sunt facta.* Kroymann marks a lacuna before *fecit* and observes: '*faciendo operum* velim suppleri.' But the infinitive *esse* clearly has a final sense.

169 Tertullian now instances a different case in which *principium* does not mean 'beginning' in the sense of 'origin.' The argument may be summarized by the following syllogism: 'If *principium* means "origin," the substance which is the origin of another substance is expressly mentioned. If, for instance, we say: "In the beginning the potter made a basin or a jar," the clay from which these vessels are made is not mentioned; and "beginning" in this case does not designate the substance from which other substances draw their origin, but simply refers to the order in time.'

170 Kroymann proposes to delete the last sentence which he regards as a useless repetition; however, we may interpret it as the 'official' conclusion of the argument, inserting 'so' before 'it is.'

171 *Possum et aliter 'principium' interpretari, non ab re tamen.* Kellner wrongly translates: 'Man kann Prinzip auch noch anders erklären, nicht von der Sache' (Holmes correctly: 'I might also explain this word *beginning* in another way, which would not, however, be inapposite').

172 *secundum hanc quoque significationem.* In the translation, 'second' is meant to render *quoque* ('according to this sense which ἀρχή *also* has ⟨besides the meaning "beginning"⟩').

173 One may be tempted here to leave *principium* untranslated, but, after all, for Tertullian *principium* meant 'beginning.' Here the meaning, of course, is: 'beginning,' employed as a translation of ἀρχή in John 1.3.

174 **Chapter 20:** 'It is clear, however, that ἀρχή must be equivalent to *principium* in the sense of "beginning," for God made all things in His Wisdom which, according to Scripture (Prov. 8.22), was "the beginning of His ways" (§1). Further, if "beginning" were a designation of the material of the creation, Scripture would not have said "*In* the beginning," but "*From* the beginning." But the words as we have them, "In the beginning," are particularly appropriate to the Wisdom of God since, by first inventing and arranging the creation in His mind, He actually first created the world in His Wisdom (§2). Moreover, Scripture does mention the Maker and the things made, but it does not say anything about a material from which these things were made— whence it is evident that they were made from nothing (§3). This is again shown by the Gospel (John 1.3) in which even the intermediary

of the creation is mentioned besides the Creator and the things created, but which again does not make mention of any material (§4).'

175 Here Tertullian's argument is not quite logical. He has just observed (19.5) that ἀρχή can always be translated by *principium*, but that according to the double sense of ἀρχή this *principium* can either mean 'beginning' or 'sovereignty, power.' He now wishes to prove that the meaning must be 'beginning' indeed, wherefore he has to say that ἀρχή here means nothing else than 'principium' *in its primary sense*—but instead he says that it means *principium* (which, according to 19.5, is also the case when the sense is 'power'), *and* that here *principium* really does mean 'beginning.'

176 *habemus etiam illam initium agnoscere*: Holmes' translation is completely erroneous—'we have that (Being) even acknowledging such a beginning.' The kernel of the argument is that *sophia=initium*; cf. n. 178.

177 *Dominus condidit me in opera sua* (Prov. 8.22). Pamelius, followed by Rigaltius and Kroymann, inserts *initium viarum suarum* before *in*. These words are indeed essential to the argument, but yet it is quite possible that Tertullian left them out: first, he omits parts of quotations now and then (cf. n. 160), again, this verse had just been quoted (18.1).

178 One more confused argument which may be summarized as follows:

I. a. *Deus omnia per sophiam fecit.*
    b. *Sophia initium est* (Prov. 8.22).
    c. *Ergo deus omnia per initium fecit.*

II. a. *Deus omnia in principio fecit* (Gen. 1.1).
    b. *Deus omnia per initium fecit* (=I. c).
    c. *Ergo 'in principio'='per initium'* (='in initio').

The logical form of the conclusion (which now reads: *et caelum ergo et terram deus faciens in principio, id est initio, in sophia sua fecit*) would have been: *et caelum ergo et terram deus faciens in principio, in initio, quippe in sophia, fecit.*

179 *non ita scriptura instruxisset*. Holmes: 'The Scripture would not have informed us'; but in my opinion *instruo* is here equivalent to *struo* ('*argumentationem struxisset*')—cf. *De an.* 5.3: *Zeno . . . hoc modo instruit* (follows a syllogism). On *instruo* used for *struo*, cf. my note to *ibid.* (p. 128) and to 10.3 (p. 184 f.).

180 *in qua cogitando et disponendo iam fecerat*. Holmes: 'because by meditating and arranging His plans therein, He had already done (the work of creation).' However, *in qua* should be connected with *fecerat*,

not with *cogitando et disponendo*, for a proof must be furnished for the statement, *In sophia . . . primo fecit*, which is done by means of the following syllogism:

   a. *Cogitatio et dispositio est prima sophiae operatio* (in other words: *qui cogitat et disponit, in sophia operatur*).
   b. *Deus ante opus creandi cogitavit et disposuit.*
   c. *Ergo deus in sophia primo operatus est (fecit).*

The same idea is expressed more clearly in *Adv. Prax.* 5 (233.19–22 Kr.): *nam etsi deus nondum sermonem suum miserat, proinde eum cum ipsa et in ipsa ratione intra semetipsum habebat, tacite cogitando et dispondendo secum quae per sermonem mox erat dicturus.*

[181] *sit* (NXF Kroymann; *fit* P Oehler; *sic* δ) *operatio de cogitatu viam operibus instituens* (*instituentis* Kroymann, but such personifications are quite frequent in Tertullian—cf. Thörnell, *Stud. Tert.* 1.38 ff., and my nn. 72 and 308).

[182] Gen. 1.1.

[183] *quod et deum* (Kroymann; *deus* MSS) *qui fecit et ea quae fecit ostendens unde fecerit non proinde testatur.*

[184] In this and the next sentence Holmes translates 'He,' but Tertullian is still speaking about work in general.

[185] The Old Testament mentions two things, the Maker and the things made; the New Testament adds to these two the Intermediary for the Creation: so the New Testament had still more reason to be complete and to mention also the material, if it had existed.

[186] John 1.1.

[187] John 1.1 and 3.

[188] **Chapter 21**: 'It may be countered that if a creation out of nothing is concluded from the fact that Holy Scripture does not mention a creation out of matter, a creation out of matter may with equal right be concluded from the circumstance that Scripture does not mention a creation out of nothing (§1). But in the present case it is not admissible thus to convert the argument because a creation out of matter would be less self-evident than a creation out of nothing (§2). Therefore, Scripture could quite normally omit to add that all things were made out of nothing, whereas in the case of creation out of matter it could not have omitted to mention matter (§3).'

[189] *quid*: Holmes wrongly translates (*ali*)-*quid* (not *quicquam*!) by 'anything' throughout this chapter.

[190] *diversa pars* frequently means 'the opposite party,' 'the opposition,' or simply 'my opponent(s)' in Tertullian—cf. e.g. *De carn. res.* 19 (51.8 Kr.) and Evans 244 and 281.

191 Holmes: 'Some arguments may, of course, be thus retorted easily enough; but it does not follow that they are on that account fairly admissible, where there is a diversity in the cause.' This translation does not bring out that, according to Tertullian, the argument itself is perfectly admissible, its 'converted form' only being rejected.

192 *nisi hoc ipsum aperte declaratur ex aliquo factum illud, dum ex quo factum sit ostenditur.* Oehler gives a different punctuation: . . . *factum, illud dum.* . . . Holmes translates: 'there will be danger, until it is shown of what it was made, first of its appearing to be made of nothing'; in a note he observes: 'Dum ostenditur: which Oehler and Rigalt. construe as "donec ostendatur." One reading has "dum *non* ostenditur," "so long as it is not shown."' In my opinion, it is evident that the clause *dum . . . ostenditur* should not be connected with the words coming after it, as is done by Holmes, but with the preceding clause: by showing *from which* the thing in question has been made, it is at the same time proved *that* it has been made out of something; *dum* has a causal sense which is quite common in Tertullian.

193 *ut non possit ⟨non factum⟩ videri ex aliquo* (Kroymann; *u. n. p. videri ex aliquo* MSS; *ut nunc possit videri ex aliquo* Iunius; *ut non possit videri ⟨non⟩ ex aliquo* Rigaltius; *ut omnino possit videri ex aliquo* Oehler). The addition of *factum* (and therefore of *non*) is necessary—cf. in this same chapter: *periclitabitur primo videri ex nihilo factum* and *proinde periclitabitur ex alio longe factum videri.*

194 I read *fecisse potuit, ⟨potuit⟩ scriptura non adiecisse* (*fecisse non potuit scriptura non adiecisset* α and Oehler, who places a comma after *potuit; fecisse potuit scriptura non adiecisse* β; *fecit, potuit scriptura non adiecisse* Kroymann; *fecit, non potuit scriptura non adiecisse . . .?* Engelbrecht): *potuit* must be connected with *scriptura non adiecisse*, as is evident from the words immediately following, ⟨*scriptura*⟩ *debuit edixisse.*

195 With Engelbrecht and Kroymann I read ⟨*si sci*⟩*licet ex materia fecisset.* The manuscripts have *licet* which is defended by Kellner (81 n. 1), though he translates *si*: 'wenn er wirklich aus der Materie geschaffen hatte.' Oehler follows Ursinus in reading *si et*, but in this case a pleonastic *et* is difficult to explain.

196 **Chapter 22**: 'In general, whenever something has been made out of another thing, the Scriptures always mention that second thing (§1). Therefore, if heaven and earth had been made out of something, that thing would have been mentioned—the more so in the present case, because here the conclusion that they had been made out of nothing was obvious (§2). But neither the Old nor the New Testament speak about a material serving the composition of heaven and earth (§3).'

[197] Gen. 1.11 f. (I give only the main tradition of C, the African, and E, the European text): *Fructificet (Germinet, producat, educat, fructificet, fruticet* L) *terra herbam foeni (pabuli* or *pabulum* C) *seminantem (ferentem* or *habentem* C) *semen secundum genus (suum genus* or *genus suum* C) *et secundum* (om. C) *similitudinem, et lignum fructuosum (fructiferum* E) *faciens fructum, cuius semen in ipso (in ipso sit) in se* C) *in (secundum suam* C) *similitudinem. Et factum est sic (sic est factum* C). *Et produxit (eiecit* C) *terra herbam foeni (pabuli* C) *seminantem (ferentem* C) *semen secundum genus (suum genus* or *genus suum* C; *et secundum similitudinem* add. E), *et lignum fructuosum (fructiferum* E and part of C) *faciens fructum, cuius semen (semen est* C) *in ipso (se* C) *in similitudinem (secundum suam similitudinem* C *ad genus super terram* E).

[198] Gen. 1. 20–21a (here again I add only the variants from the main tradition of the *Vetus Latina*): *Et dixit deus, Producant (eiciant* L) *aquae repentia (reptilia) animarum vivarum, et volatilia volantia super terram per firmamentum (sub firmamento* L) *caeli. Et factum est sic (sic est factum* L). *Et fecit deus cetos magnos, et omnem animam animalium repentium, quae produxerunt (eiecerunt* C, *eduxerunt* the main branch of I, a European type of the text) *aquae secundum genus ipsorum (uniuscuiusque genus* C *genus suum* [*ipsorum, eorum*] I).

[199] Gen. 1.24: *Et dixit deus: Producat (eiciat* C) *terra animam vivam (viventem* part of E; reading of P in the present passage) *secundum genus (unumquodque genus* C), *quadrupedia (et qu.* T. *Adv. Herm.* 29, *quadrupedum* C, *quadrupedes* M, a branch of the European tradition), *et repentia (serpentium* C, *serpentes* M) *et bestias (bestiarum* C) *terrae secundum genus ipsorum (ipsorum* om. T. *Adv. Herm.* 29 and the main part of E, *secundum . . . ipsorum* om. C and M).

[200] *si tantam curam instructionis nostrae insumpsit*: Kroymann reads *instructioni*, but the genitive is in complete accordance with Tertullian's idiom—cf. Thörnell, *Stud. Tert.* 1.32.

[201] *ne* β Kroymann (*ut* α *vulgo*). From the context it is evident that *ne* is the correct reading: If God had created heaven and earth out of some material, Scripture should have mentioned this material by all means, for else the conclusion that they had been created from nothing would be obvious (when the heaven and the earth were created, no other thing as yet existed from which they could seem to have sprung).— The last sentence of the chapter contains an allusion to Apoc. 22.18 f.

[202] **Chapter 23**: 'In Gen. 1.2, *And the earth was invisible and unfinished,* "earth," according to Hermogenes, designates matter; "was," moreover, indicates an eternal existence of matter in the past, and "invisible and unfinished," the amorphous state of matter (§1). Now, even if this passage should actually refer to matter, it was still quite possible that

God did not create anything out of it—indeed, it is unsuitable that God should have been in need of matter, and, moreover, Scripture does not say a word about such a creation (§2). Still this does not mean that matter was completely useless— at least it has produced a heretic! (§3).'

In this chapter Tertullian quotes the first part of Gen. 1.2 with the same text as occurs in the main strain of the *Vetus Latina* and in his own *De baptismo* (3.2): *Terra autem erat invisibilis et incomposita*. In ch. 25 he substitutes *rudis* for *incomposita*; on this *rudis* he comments in ch. 29.

That in Gen. 1.1 *terra* denotes matter, is mentioned as the view of some *Hebraei* by Chalcidius, *Comm. in Tim.* 278 (309. 4–6 Wrobel): *caelum quidem incorpoream naturam, terram vero, quae substantia est corporum, quam Graeci hylen vocant*. This view is contrasted with the—correctly recorded—theory of Philo, who regarded the heaven and earth mentioned in Gen. 1.1 as *carentes corpore et intelligibiles essentias*; cf. the full treatment of this subject by H. A. Wolfson, *Philo. Foundations of Religious Philosophy in Judaism, Christianity and Islam* (Cambridge, Mass. 1947) 1.300–309.

[203] *et 'Erat' in hoc dirigit, quasi*, etc. For this meaning of *dirigere*, cf. my note on *De an.* 1.6 (p. 96).

[204] *Putemus* (N Kroymann; *putamus* the remaining MSS Oehler).

[205] That is, like the earth. I follow α and Oehler in reading *et tale aliquid esse ex ea factum* (*et talis id sed* [*se* δ] *ex ea factum aliquid* β, hence Kroymann: *et talis, et ex ea factum aliquid*).

[206] **Chapter 24**: 'Further, Scripture does not mention any term for "matter." Therefore, if the word "earth" is to designate matter as well, two errors at once become apparent: for one, "earth" still is considered to designate this our earth only; again, if this word be used to denote something besides our earth, it will be referred, not to matter as a whole, but rather to some species of matter other than our earth. And even if matter had a name of its own in Scripture, it yet should be proved in addition that "earth" could be an alternative name for it.'

[207] *terrena appellatio* (*terrae appellatio* R Oehler Kroymann, but cf. Thörnell, *Stud. Tert.* 2.36).

[208] Because the word 'earth' is generally known as a designation proper to this our earth.

[209] *Quo magis materiae quoque nominatio extitisse debuerat, consecuta etiam terrae appellationem.* Holmes: 'There is all the greater need why mention should also have been made of Matter, if this has acquired the further sense of Earth.' This translation spoils the sense: it is not that the *word* 'matter' acquired the *sense* of earth—matter *itself* acquired the *word* 'earth' as an appellative of itself.

²¹⁰ *nec utique omni materiae* (R¹ *vulgo; nec utique omni materia* MSS, which Kroymann prints with a *crux*, adding: 'verba *nec utique omni materia* quid sibi velint, non intellego'). In my opinion, the solution of the riddle is furnished by the words preceding, *in quamcumque aliam speciem*: if matter existed, our earth would be a *species* of it and thereby *species terrae* (for, according to Hermogenes, *terra*='matter'); now, if matter does not have a name of its own (*proprium vocabulum*), but only a name which it shares with our earth (*commune vocabulum*), that is to say, *terra*, there is danger that this name, when it does not designate this our earth, is wrongly applied, not to matter as a whole (to the genus 'matter'), but to some species of matter, and even to some species other than our earth. A Swedish translation of the passage is given by Thörnell, *Stud. Tert.* 1.7 f. Kellner is certainly wrong in translating 'bei jeder Materie.'

²¹¹ *quanto non comparet*: Kroymann follows Iunius in reading *quando*, but *quanto* is much more appropriate to Tertullian's idiom.

²¹² **Chapter 25**: 'Moreover, Hermogenes thus postulates the existence of two earths. Now the offspring normally receives its name from its source, which would mean that the earth made by God received its name from the material from which He made it (§1). But our earth was quite different from shapeless matter, implying that it cannot have shared its name (§2). One may object, though, that after undergoing the process of creation, the earth was still of the same kind as matter and therefore could share its name. But in reality the difference was too great to admit of this: for one thing, our earth was good (Gen. 1.31), whereas matter, according to Hermogenes, is the source of evil (§3). Finally, if our earth is earth because matter is also earth, our earth must also be matter because matter is also matter—nay, in that case everything created out of matter must also admit of both names, "earth" and "matter" (§4). So we must arrive at the conclusion that the word "earth" can mean only this our earth (§5).'

²¹³ *A cuius habitu quid divertit, pariter et a vocatu eius recedit, appellationis sicut et condicionis proprietate.* The last words are translated by Holmes as follows: 'with a propriety which is alike demanded by the designation and the condition.' But Tertullian means to say that just as the thing in question acquires a *condicio propria* because it *ab alterius habitu divertit*, it also receives a name of its own (cf. the importance of *vocabulum proprium* in the preceding chapter) because it *ab alterius vocatu recedit*. The ablative *proprietate* may be explained as a 'resultative' ablative ('*thus* receiving a name of its own'), for which cf. my note on *De an.* 19.5 (p. 274 f.).

²¹⁴ Gen. 1.10 (not 1.31, as Oehler says, for Tertullian is now speaking

of the earth): *Et vidit deus quia bonum (Et . . . bonum est* in *De fuga* 4, = the *Vetus Latina*).

215 Here, as in *De an.* 2.3 and in *De pall.* 2.1, Tertullian alludes to a story told by Theopompus in the eighth book of his Φιλιππικαὶ Ἱστορίαι, which book is frequently quoted under the special title Θαυμάσια. Undoubtedly Tertullian had not read this book himself: he must have found the story in one of the 'miracle books' which were so avidly read by his contemporaries. Theopompus told how Silenus, having been captured by Midas, told the king the myth of the country of Meropis (probably a parody of Plato's myth of Atlantis); the feature of a revelation received by Silenus was borrowed by Theopompus from Aristotle's *Eudemus*. For a fuller treatment of this subject, cf. my paper, 'Traces of Aristotle's Lost Dialogues in Tertullian,' *Vig. Chr.* 1 (1947) 137–49.

216 **Chapter 26**: 'It should also be noted that Scripture always mentions the name of a thing before speaking about its condition—it would indeed be absurd if Scripture all of a sudden began to speak about the condition of matter without mentioning its name first (§1). Hence it is much more credible that Scripture is speaking here about a thing whose name it has already mentioned, and so we must suppose it to be speaking about this our earth. It is in this way only that the first lines of Genesis receive their full meaning (§2). The word "but" in Gen. 1.2 closely connects the second sentence with the first, thus showing once more that in Gen. 1.1 the earth as we know it, is meant (§3).'

217 Gen. 1.7 f.: *Et separavit inter aquam, quae erat infra firmamentum, et quae erat super firmamentum, et vocavit deus firmamentum caelum.* Here again Tertullian's text favours E which reads: *Et divisit (discrevit) inter medium aquae, quae erat sub firmamento* (or *infra firmamentum*), *et inter medium aquae, quae erat super* (or *supra*) *firmamentum, et . . . caelum.* C inverts the order of the relative clauses: *Et divisit (separavit) deus inter aquam, quae est super* (or *supra*) *firmamentum, et inter aquam, quae est sub firmamento, et . . . caelum.*

218 Gen. 1.27: *et fecit deus hominem, ad imaginem dei fecit illum* (in complete accordance with the main part of the *Vetus Latina*, as also with *Adv. Prax.* 12 [245.26 f. Kr.]; in *De carn. res.* 6 [33.16 f. Kr.] and *De pud.* 16, we find *hominem deus*, and in the latter passage, moreover, *ad imaginem et similitudinem dei*).

219 Gen. 2.7, a passage of paramount importance in Tertullian's works, since it is the Scriptural foundation of his doctrine on the human soul. It is also quoted in ch. 31 (a), *Adv. Marc.* 1.24 (b), *De carn. res.* 5 (c), *De an.* 3.4 (d), and *ibid.* 26.5 (e). I quote the text of the present passage with the divergences found in the other quotations: *Et* (om. a) *finxit*

(*fecit* a) *deus hominem* (*hominem deus* b) *de limo terrae* (*de terra* a, *limum de terra* b and c, *de limo terrae* om. e; the entire first part is wanting in d), *et adflavit* (*flavit* e, *flavit deus* d, *insufflavit* c) *in faciem eius* (*in eum* e) *flatum vitae* (*in faciem hominis* added in d; the entire second part is wanting in b), *et factus est homo in animam vivam* (this last part not found in e). Further, allusions to this passage are found in *Adv. Marc.* 2.4 (338.12 f. Kr.): *bonitas inflavit in animam, non mortuam, sed vivam*; ibid. 2.9 (347.3 f. Kr.): *flasse deum in faciem hominis et factum hominem in animam vivam; De an.* 9.7: *cum flasset deus in faciem homini flatum vitae et factus esset homo in animam vivam.* The main part of the *Vetus Latina* (for the variants, cf. the Beuron edition 2.38–41) reads: *et tunc finxit deus hominem de limo terrae et insufflavit in faciem eius spiritum vitae et factus est homo in animam viventem.* For Tertullian's interpretation of this verse, cf. my edition of the *De anima* 176 f. and 195 f. In the Greek text Hermogenes had substituted 'spirit' for 'breath'—cf. the Introd. 7 f.

220 *Alioquin vanum, si eius rei, cuius nullam praemiserat mentionem, id est materiae, ne ipsum quidem nomen, subito formam et habitum promulgavit, ante enarrat* (*enarravit* Kroymann, but the present tense is certainly correct—cf. E. Löfstedt, *Kritische Bemerkungen zu Tertullians Apologeticum* [Lund-Leipzig] 104), *qualis esset, antequam an esset ostendit, figuram deformat* (Iunius; *deformati* MSS, *deformavit* Kroymann), *nomen abscondit.* Holmes translates: 'How absurd is the other view of the account, when even before he had premised any mention of his subject, *i.e.* Matter,' and in a note identifies 'he' with 'Hermogenes, whose view of the narrative is criticized.' But the subject of the sentence is undoubtedly *scriptura*, as in all the preceding sentences.

221 *Nam et 'Autem' ipsum velut fibula coniunctivae particulae ad connexum narrationi adpositum est.* Kroymann also gives this text, but in his apparatus he writes: '*nam et autem ipsum, coniunctiva particula, velut fibula* fort.' However, *coniunctivae particulae* is easily understood as an explicative genitive.

222 **Chapter 27**: 'According to Hermogenes, "was" in Gen. 1.2 refers to an eternal existence in the past, whence he concludes that here eternal matter must be meant (§1). But "was" can be said of everything which *is*. Now our earth *is* made, so that we have every right to say that it *was* (§2). There remains the question whether the words "invisible and unfinished" refer to the "earth-matter" of Hermogenes or to our earth; if we can decide this, we shall know at the same time to which of the two the word "was" refers (§3).'

223 I read with Rigaltius: *Sed tu supercilia capitis, nutu digiti accommodato, altius tollens et quasi retro iactans, 'erat' inquis.* The word *supercilia*

is a conjecture by Rigaltius (*sed tu supercilio* α, *et supercilio et* β). Kroymann reads: *Sed tu supercilia, capitis nutu digiti* ('intellege: *nutui*') *adcommodato, altius tollens,* etc.

²²⁴ *quasi semper fuerit*: here again *quasi* indicates the cause mentioned or accepted by the subject of the sentence.

²²⁵ *Cui competit prima verbi positio in definitionem, eiusdem* (*eidem* Kroymann—but cf. Thörnell, *Stud. Tert.* 1.9) *etiam declinatio verbi decurret in relationem. Est definitionis caput, Erat relationis facit.* In my opinion, the genitive *eiusdem* is to be connected with *relationem*. The sense is well rendered by Holmes' free translation: 'To whatever thing the first tense of the verb is applicable for *definition*, to the same will be suitable the later form of the verb, when it has to descend to *relation*.'

²²⁶ *Magna scilicet quaestio est, si erat terra, quae facta est.* This sentence contains the premises necessary for the conclusion. The syllogism may be reconstructed thus: a. *Quidquid est, etiam erat.* b. *Terra facta est.* c. *Ergo* '*erat*' *de terra dici potest.*

²²⁷ *ut eiusdem sit Erat cuius et quod erat,* which Holmes renders: 'so that the predicate (*was*) may appertain to the same thing to which the subject (*that which was*) also belongs.' Kellner's translation, 'Dann würde das *erat* von dem gelten, was sie war,' leaves the words *cuius et* untranslated.

²²⁸ **Chapter 28**: 'If in the beginning only God and matter existed, matter cannot possibly have been invisible to God. Further, if it had actually been invisible, nothing would have been known about it— unless God made a revelation about its condition; and then Hermogenes must furnish proof of this revelation. Thus the thing called "invisible" in Genesis cannot have been matter (§1). Nor could matter be called "unfinished," for this can be attributed only to a thing which is imperfect, and something imperfect must necessarily be a thing which has been made—whereas according to Hermogenes matter is unmade. On the other hand, the predicate "unfinished' is entirely applicable to this our earth (§2).'

²²⁹ The argument runs as follows: 'If in the beginning only God and matter existed, there was nothing between God and matter (*nullo scilicet elemento obstruente*). From this it follows that God must have been able to see matter. But then matter was not invisible and so cannot be meant in Gen. 1.2.'

²³⁰ *hoc enim ipsum, quod sunt tenebrae, videtur.* The MSS read *videntur, videtur* being a conjecture by Ursinus adopted by Oehler and Kroymann. It is not impossible to retain the reading of the MSS, since in Tertullian *ipsum quod* can mean *eo ipso quod*, for instance, in *De an.* 32.9: *Ipsum enim quod hominem similem bestiae iudicas, confiteris animam*

non eandem, similem dicendo, non ipsam (for further details, cf. my note *ad loc.* 392, and G. Thörnell, in *Strena Philologica Upsaliensis, Festskrift . . . Per Persson* [Uppsala 1922] 387). However, *videtur* offers a better sense ('for the very presense of darkness can be perceived'; with *videntur* = 'for it is seen on account of the very fact that it is darkness').

[231] *caruit et rudimento. Rudimentum* here = *status rudis*; for such alterations of the meaning of words by Tertullian, cf. above, n. 138.

[232] **Chapter 29**: 'God did not at once bring the elements to perfection (§1), wherefore the earth was *invisible and unfinished* before its completion; it was invisible because it was still covered by *the waters*, as is evident from several Scriptural passages. The words, *Let the dry land appear*, and, *And God called the dry land Earth*, prove that the earth existed already at that moment and needed no longer to be formed out of matter (§2). After attaining its perfect state, the earth is no longer called "unfinished" (§3). If the words "invisible and unfinished" do indeed refer to matter, matter must have become visible in the course of time; but actually to-day it is nowhere to be seen, whereas the earth is before our eyes (§4). Further, the earth is certainly referred to in Isa. 45.18 (§5). We may conclude, then, that it is the same that is meant in Gen. 1.2 (§6).'

[233] *incultis primo elementis depalans quodam modo mundum, dehinc exornatis velut dedicans.* Holmes: 'at first He paled them out (i.e. His works), as it were, in their unformed elements, and then He arranged them in their finished beauty.' In my opinion, *incultis . . . elementis* and *exornatis* (i.e. *elementis*) are absolute ablatives. *Dedicare* has the meaning of *initiare, inaugurare*, quite frequent in Tertullian (cf. my note on *De an.* 19.7—p. 277).

[234] *sed primo esse ei contulit, dehinc non in vacuum esse supplevit*, rendered by Holmes: 'but at first He bestowed upon it being, and then He filled it, that it might not be made in vain.' But the object of *supplevit* is not *terram*, but *in vacuum esse*.

[235] Isa. 45.18 (quoted nowhere else by Tertullian).

[236] *qua forma etiam adfinis eius caro nostra producitur.* Tertullian is thinking of Gen. 2.7, which he usually quotes in this form: *Et finxit deus hominem de limo terrae, et (ad)flavit in faciem eius flatum vitae, et factus est homo in animam vivam.* We need not speak now about his interpretation of the *flatus vitae* as the soul, which interpretation is fundamental to the doctrine of the *De anima* and the *De censu animae* (cf. Introd. 8), but only about his comments on the first part of this passage. In *De an.* 27 he asserts on the basis of his traducianism that since Adam's body was created *de limo terrae*, all human bodies draw their origin from the

earth; hence in the present passage he can say that our flesh 'is akin to the earth.' Further, the water which according to Gen. 1.9 first covered the earth, is here paralleled by the *genitalis humor*. This strongly reminds us of *De bapt.* 3, in which chapter the water of baptism is compared with the water of Gen. 1.2: *non enim ipsius quoque hominis figulandi opus sociantibus aquis absolutum est? adsumpta est de terra materia, non tamen habilis nisi humecta et succida quam scilicet ante quartum diem segregatae aquae in stationem suam superstite humore limo temperarant.* In both passages, therefore, we find an interpretation of the *limus terrae* of Gen. 2.7 as a mixture of earth and 'fertilizing water.' In the same way, in *De an.* 27 (cf. my comments on this particularly important chapter, pp. 342–353) the *limus* is qualified as a *liquor opimus* from which the human seed has proceeded (*Inde erit genitale virus*, §7).—Holmes translates, 'by which is produced our flesh, in a form allied with its own,' thus wrongly connecting with *forma* the words *adfinis eius*, which, as will be clear from the discussion of this passage, must most certainly be linked with *caro nostra*.

237 *canit*, i.e. in the Psalms.

238 Ps. 23.1 f., literally translated from the LXX; not quoted elsewhere by Tertullian.

239 I follow Rigaltius and Oehler in reading *cavationem sinuum*; Kroymann adopts the reading of the MSS, *cavatiorem sinum*. I fail to understand the comparative.

240 Gen. 1.9: *Congregetur aqua in congregatione una, et videatur arida.* The *Vetus Latina*: *C. a. quae sub caelo est (quae . . . est* is omitted in a part of the texts) *in congregatione(m) una(m) et videatur (C; pareat E) arida.*

241 Gen. 1.10: *Et vocavit deus aridam terram* (= the *Vetus Latina*).

242 The argument runs as follows: 'The words *videatur arida* (Gen. 1.9) prove that the earth had already been created at that moment, for the choice of *videatur* instead of *sit* demonstrates that something already existent is spoken of; and from Gen. 1.10 it is clear that *arida*= the earth, whence again it is clear that at that moment the earth was already in existence.' The text of the last sentences reads: *Arida autem, quod erat futura ex divortio humoris, tamen terra: 'Et vocavit deus aridam terram' non materiam.* For *tamen* Kroymann reads *iam*; this would, it is true, be more logical, but the reading of the MSS can be defended: After Tertullian had stated that evidently something already existent was spoken of, Hermogenes could still reply that it is by no means certain that *arida* denotes the earth, and so could deny the conclusion that the earth already existed at that moment. 'True,' Tertullian says, 'we read only *arida* (not *arida terra*) because the separation from the water had

to be mentioned; *but* from Gen. 1.10 it is clear that *arida*=the earth, and thus we cannot conclude that *videatur arida* refers to matter.'

243 Gen. 1.11.

244 Gen. 1.24.

245 *Non alia autem materia erat invisibilis et rudis.* Kroymann reads *alias*, but *alia* is quite sound, for we have here one more sample of an abbreviated syllogism: 'What was at first *invisible and unfinished,* later received both visibility and perfection. Now, if the words "invisible and unfinished" refer to that matter from which, according to Hermogenes, God created the world, this matter must afterwards have become visible, which, however, has never happened. ⟨Hermogenes cannot avoid this conclusion by saying that the words "invisible and unfinished" do refer to matter, though not to that matter from which the world was created, for⟩ on his premises there was only one matter.

246 Isa. 45.18 (quoted only here by Tertullian). The Latin text has . . . *iste deus, qui demonstravit terram et fecit illam,* which is a literal translation of LXX: οὗτος ὁ θεὸς ὁ καταδείξας τὴν γῆν καὶ ποιήσας αὐτήν. Holmes destroys the connection with the following argument by giving the translation of the English Bible: 'He was the God that *formed* the earth and made it.'

247 *habilem.* Kroymann follows Latinius in reading *habitabilem* which is supported by the text of Isa. 45.18, quoted in §1: *Non in vacuum fecit illam, sed inhabitari.* On the other hand, *habilem* is, in my opinion, supported by the words *hanc perfruor* in §4 (I read *hanc* with α; *hac* βR¹ Oehler).

248 *separavit* (*paravit* Kroymann). The choice of the verb is undoubtedly due to Gen. 1.7, where Tertullian reads *separavit* (26.1; *Vulg. divisit*).

249 **Chapter 30**: 'Interpreting Gen. 1.2, *And darkness was upon the deep, and the Spirit of God moved over the waters,* Hermogenes supposes that matter was blended out of the four substances mentioned in this passage. But since Scripture mentions them apart, and also assigns separate places to them, the existence of such a confused body cannot be proved (§1). Further, Hermogenes himself says that matter was without form. Now it would be absurd to seek to prove the existence of a thing without form from four terms all of which designate things possessing a form. If matter really contained these four things, it cannot have been without form, and if it did not contain them, it can in no way have become known (§2).'

250 Gen. 1.2: *Et tenebrae super abyssum, et spiritus dei super aquas ferebatur* (the same translation occurs twice in ch. 32).

251 *dispositionem,* '*positionem* fort.' Kroymann. The meaning required by the context ('separate places') is indeed unusual, but we may refer to the fairly numerous cases in which Tertullian alters the meaning of words by giving them what he may have considered their literal or original sense—e.g., *rudimentum = status rudis, probator = qui probum reddit*: cf. nn. 138 and 231. On the usual meaning of *dispositio* in Tertullian, cf. the excellent note by Evans 193. In the present passage the choice of *dispositio* is also partly due to parallelism (*dispositionem—distinctionem*).

252 This is easily the most sophistic argument of the entire treatise. Tertullian means to refute Hermogenes' thesis that the *confusae substantiae* of Gen. 1.2 ('*tenebrae super abyssum*,' '*spiritus super aquas*') furnish an argument for the existence *massalis illius molis* (= matter). He first demonstrates (§1) that these substances were not 'confused' at all, but should, on the contrary, be regarded as *certa et distincta elementa* with both a form and a place of their own. In the first part of the present sentence he concludes that matter could not possibly, as was done by Hermogenes, be called 'without form,' containing as it does these four well-formed 'elements' (that this first part is indeed an independent argument is evident from the repetition in the last but one sentence of the chapter: *Si enim habebat* [i.e. *in se species istas materia*], *quomodo inducitur non habens formas?*). He then takes a further step (*non edito quid sit illud corpus confusionis, quod unicum utique credendum est, si informe est*): It might still be possible that a confused whole should have arisen from a chaotic blending of four well-formed substances, but then this *corpus confusionis* (= *massalis illius molis* in §1) should have been accurately described (Kellner's translation, 'ohne anzugeben, was denn eigentlich das Grundwesen der Verworrenheit sei,' well renders the sense, though the translation of *corpus* is incorrect). But let us assume for a moment with Hermogenes that matter was 'without form'—then it still was a unity (*unicum*) 'with one form (*uniforme*).' This curious thesis is proved in the next sentence which, in my opinion, becomes understandable only if we adopt the punctuation of Kellner's translation: *Uniforme etenim, quod informe est, informe autem, quod ex varietate confusum est*: (Kellner puts a full stop here) *unam habeat necesse est speciem, quod non habet speciem, dum ex multis unam habet speciem.* The first sentence contains this syllogism: a. *quod ex varietate confusum est* (of which genus *illud corpus confusionis* is a specimen), *informe est*; b. *quod informe est, uniforme est.* (c. *ergo illud corpus confusionis uniforme* [= *unicum*] *est*). Since, probably, Tertullian thinks the second premise rather bold, he adds a second argument, in which—as often—he inserts the conclusion into the first premise (writing *dum ex multis unam habet speciem* instead of *dum multas habet* (*continet*) *species*). Thus in his first argument he comes

to assert that formlessness as such is a form in itself (cf. the similar reasoning in *De an.* 43.6: *dialecticos in dubium deducentes totam naturalium et extranaturalium discretionem, ut et quae putaverit citra naturam esse naturae vindicari sciat posse, a qua ita esse sortita sunt, ut citra eam haberi videantur*), in the second he introduces a modification by saying that whatever has *multas species*, is indeed without form, but without form *in a special way*, since (*dum*) its formlessness is based on its having *multas species*—whereby it automatically has *unam speciem*. Holmes adopts Oehler's punctuation which leads him to the following translation: 'For that which is without form is uniform; but even that which is without form, when it is blended together from various component parts, must necessarily have one outward appearance; and it has not any appearance, until it has the one appearance (which comes) from many parts *combined*.' I fail to understand both this translation and the establishment of the text by Kroymann: *vanissimum . . . adsereretur. Non edito, quid sit illud corpus confusionis, (quod del.) unicum utique credendum est, si informe est. Uniforme etenim, quod informe. Et informe autem, quod ex varietate confusum est, unam habeat necesse est speciem, quod non habet, (speciem del.) dum ⟨nihil⟩ ex multis unam habet speciem.*

It should be noted that Tertullian is playing with two different meanings of *species*—'outward appearance, form' and 'species' (or rather 'subordinate part'; cf. especially the beginning of the next chapter). He does so of course in order to construct a contradiction between two statements of Hermogenes, namely, that matter was 'without form' and that it was a blending of four substances and, therefore, might be said to contain subordinate parts.

²⁵³ I follow Iunius in reading *autem*; the MSS have *enim* which is deleted by Kroymann.

²⁵⁴ I read *unde agnoscitur?* with van der Vliet and Kroymann (*quomodo agnoscitur?* Ursinus).

²⁵⁵ At the end of the chapter Tertullian puts Hermogenes before a dilemma, as he frequently does (e.g. *De an.* 56.8). The first part is a repetition of the preceding argument ⟨*quomodo*⟩ *inducitur non habens formas? ∼materia quae informis inducitur*). From this it is, in my opinion, once more evident that Tertullian has all the time been thinking of matter as *multiformis*.

²⁵⁶ **Chapter 31**: 'It may further be objected that in Scripture no mention is made of a creation of the four substances mentioned in Gen. 1.2, and that therefore they must have belonged to matter (§1). But Scripture says enough if it mentions only the creation of heaven and earth. These two constitute the main parts of the universe, so that their constituent parts can be understood to be included in them (§2).

Indeed, the darkness and the deep belong to the earth, the spirit and the waters to the heaven (§3). Now it is usual to mention only that which contains the parts, not the parts themselves, as two examples will show (§4). Therefore, since all the elements are contained in the heaven and the earth, there was no reason to make express mention of the creation of these elements too (§5).'

257 *ea* (Kroymann; *eam* α, *te ab* X, *te a* γ).

258 *fuerunt* (N Kroymann; *fuerint* Pβ).

259 Gen. 2.7 (cf. n. 236).

260 **Chapter 32**: 'So it was not necessary to make further mention of the creation of these four substances. But since Scripture foresaw that there would be stupid as well as crafty men who would require explicit description of their creation, it has in several passages furnished such description (§1). Enumeration of such passages: §2. But the opposition may still counter that, though these substances were indeed made by God, they were made out of matter, thereby referring Gen. 1.2 to matter in general and those other passages to the specific parts made out of matter (§3). But then, as (according to Hermogenes) the earth was made out of the earth (=matter), so also "the depth" (Gen. 1.2) must have originated from a depth which was present in matter as a species of matter, and so on. If matter, however, was "without a form," it cannot have contained such species; and "the depth," etc., mentioned in Gen. 1.2 would be identical with that depth which was a specific part of matter—but this leads to the conclusion that thus God made things which already existed (§4). We may infer that nowhere in Scripture is matter mentioned (§5).'

261 That is, Scripture.

262 *sciit* (α, R³ from *Gorz.*, Kroymann; *sicut* X, *scit* γ R¹, *Scivit* Latinius, *Sciat* Oehler, *Sciebat* van der Vliet).

263 *dissimulato tacito intellectu.* Holmes' translation, 'after paltering with the virtual meaning,' does not bring out the meaning of *dissimulato*.

264 Prov. 8.24 (cf. n. 157).

265 Cf. *De an.* 4: *Et natam autem docemus* (i.e. *animam*) *et factam ex initii consitutione*, 'Since the soul has a beginning, it is both born and made'; cf. my comment *ad loc.*, p. 121.

266 *si materiae subiecta esset* (R²; *si materiae esset* Kroymann [who refers to 31.4: *numquid et membra hominis ad materiam pertinebunt . . .?*]; *si materiae subiciatur esset* MSS; *si materiae subiciatur necesse esset* Engelbre~ht).

267 Isa. 45.7 (literal translation of LXX). This first part of the verse is quoted nowhere else by Tertullian, whereas the second half (*I . . .*

who make peace and create evil) plays an important part in his refutation of Marcion.

[268] Amos 4.13. On this verse, cf. Evans 325. Precisely the same quotation occurs in *Adv. Prax.* 28; the verse is alluded to in *Adv. Marc.* 3.6 (384.10–12 Kr.) where it is wrongly ascribed to Joel.

[269] *eum spiritum conditum ostendens, qui in terras conditas deputabatur.* Though *deputare in* with an accusative frequently occurs in the sense of 'to reckon with, to attribute to,' one is tempted to read *conditus*: 'that spirit which was thought to be created for the benefit of the earth.' Kellner translates: 'der zur Erschaffung der Erde bestimmt wurde,' which is a rendering of *in terras condendas*. For the different meanings of *spiritus* in Tertullian, cf. my comment on *De an.* 11 (pp. 193 ff.).

[270] *non ut quidam putant ipsum deum significari spiritum* (*significans* Oehler; Kroymann supposes that after *non* the words *enim credibile* may have fallen out, Engelbrecht reads *non iure quidam putant*). There is no need to change the text: *deum significari* may depend on *ostendens* (*eum spiritum conditum ostendens qui*, etc., *non . . . ipsum deum significari spiritum*), but it is also possible to see a contamination of *ut quidam putant, significans* and *quidam putant significari*; for further details, cf. E. Löfstedt, *Philologischer Kommentar zur Peregrinatio Aetheriae* (Uppsala 1911) 250 f.; also J. Svennung, *Untersuchungen zu Palladius* (Uppsala 1935) 439 f., 646.

[271] John 4.24. Cf. *Adv. Prax.* 7 (237.11 f. Kr.): *quis enim negabit deum corpus esse, etsi deus spiritus est?* Note also the interpretation of this verse by Novatian, *De Trin.* 7 (Evans 236).

[272] Isa. 57.16: *quia spiritus a me exivit et flatum omnem ego feci.* In *De an.* 11.3 the same passage is quoted (in a slightly different form: *spiritus ex me prodivit*, etc.) as proof of the assertion that the soul as *flatus dei* is actually different from the *spiritus dei*.

[273] *quomodo* (MSS and Kroymann, *quom* R¹, *cum* R³; cf. n. 157).

[274] Prov. 8.28 (cf. n. 157).

[275] *Cum ergo . . . probamus.* Kroymann reads *vero* instead of *ergo*; there is, indeed, an antithesis, but this is not expressed: *ergo* refers to the preceding paragraph and so is quite correct.

[276] *stilus . . . Moysei.* Holmes, 'the very statement of Moses,' Kellner correctly, 'in der Stelle bei Moses': *stilus* is equivalent to *locus*—cf. Hoppe, *Syntax* 123 (for passages in which *stilus* means *liber*, cf. my note on *De an.* 52.3—p. 537).

[277] Engelbrecht inserts *ipsam* into the text which, it seems to me, is not necessary.

[278] The argument is, of course, a sophism. Hermogenes had said that our earth was created out of matter which is indicated by the word

terra in Gen. 1.2 (cf. ch. 23), and thus one could speak of '*terra* (our earth) *ex terra* (matter).' Tertullian counters that in that case the *abyssus* mentioned in Gen. 1.2 must also have proceeded *ex abysso*, the *aquae ex aquis*, etc. Obviously, the relation of the 'second' to the 'first' *abyssus* is different from that between the 'second' and the 'first' earth, for the 'first' earth is matter itself in its entirety, the 'first' *abyssus* is a *species materiae* only. The entire argument is, of course, greatly different from the theory of Philo, who regarded the four 'elements' mentioned in Gen. 1.2 as 'ideas of elements' (cf. Wolfson, *Philo* 1.306 f.).

279 A repetition of the argument in 30.2.

280 That is, the real abyss (Gen. 1.2) which, according to the preceding sentence, supposedly proceeded from an abyss which was a specific part of matter (cf. n. 278) and, therefore, still incorporated in matter.

281 *ex ea*: Kroymann reads *ex eis* which is approved by Thörnell, *Stud. Tert.* 2.66. In my opinion, this *ea* can be retained and is even to be preferred to *eis*. If the 'real' abyss (cf. n. 280) actually proceeded from matter (*ex ea*), it cannot have originated from matter as such but (according to the argument just given—cf. n. 278) it must have sprung from a specific part of matter. Therefore, if the 'real' abyss had proceeded from matter *in this way* (i.e. through the intermediary of a *species materiae*), this very process would have made it unquestionable that matter contained such *species*—which, however, considering the argument in 30.2 ('*materia, utpote informis, species habere non potest*'), would be impossible. So the sentence may be paraphrased as follows: 'And, as we said above, matter could not have been without form, if it contained specific parts, so that (through the intermediary of these specific parts) other *species* were also made out of it (that is to say, the abyss, the waters, the deep, and the darkness mentioned in Gen. 1.2)— and thus, if matter was without form, these *species* cannot have proceeded from it, since this would require the existence of specific parts in a formless substance.' Next a second refutation is added: 'The latter *species* (that is, the "real" abyss, etc., which had developed out of the specific parts of matter but which now had their own existence outside of matter) would have been identical with the specific parts incorporated *in* matter (=the *species* mentioned in 30.2), for these two groups were both called *species*, and so they could not be different. But in that case God's creation of the abyss, etc. (i.e. from that abyss, etc., which, as a specific part, was incorporated in matter) would be reduced to nothing—for He would have "made" things which existed already!' We find thus one more of those 'proceeding' arguments which are so frequent in Tertullian: 'If the real abyss, etc., had proceeded from matter, matter should have contained specific parts, which is impossible,

for—according to Hermogenes—it is formless. But let us assume for a moment that matter contained such parts: then the abyss, etc., would be identical with those parts, so that God's activity as a creator (i.e. producing the real abyss, etc., from those parts) would be reduced to nothing. And this is equally impossible.' Thus the sentence, *non potuit informis fuisse materia, si species habebat, ut et aliae ex ea sint confectae,* is quite sound (Kroymann would have a lacuna after *habebat* and supposes that the words, *exclusum igitur, si non habebat,* have fallen out). After *confectae* a new sentence begins, for Tertullian here proceeds to the *gradus secundus* of his argument; and we punctuate as follows: *Nisi quod non aliae, sed ipsae ex semetipsis, siquidem non capit diversas fuisse quae iisdem nominibus eduntur, quo,* etc.

[282] *quo* (Rigaltius and Kroymann, approved by Thörnell, *Stud. Tert.* 2.66; *quod* MSS) *iam et* (*et* del R[1] and most editions, also Oehler) *operatio divina otiosa videri possit, si quae erant fecit.*

[280] *cum generosiora essent* (R[2] and Thörnell, *loc. cit.,* and already Mesnartius and Leopold; *generosiora esset* MSS; *generosior esset* Rigaltius Kroymann; *generatio sola esset* Oehler), *quae non erant facta, quam* (*quam* del. Rigaltius Leopold Oehler, *facta, quam* del. Kroymann) *si fierent.* Thörnell translates: 'während doch die Dinge, die nicht erschaffen waren, edler waren als wenn sie erschaffen würden,' and adds the following comment: 'Addit igitur sententia illa a *cum* incipiens rationem, qua magis etiam otiosa operatio divina videri possit, quippe quae illa fecerit, quae iam ante erant, immo quae, ut infecta et aeterna, generosiora (i.e. sublimiora) erant, quam si fierent.' After this, he rightly refers to 18.3 (146.6 ff. Kr.): *quale est, ut filio dei . . . aliquid fuerit praeter patrem antiquius et hoc modo utique generosius, nedum, quod innatum, fortius et, quod infectum, facto validius? Quia quod, ut esset, nullius eguit auctoris, multo sublimius erit eo, quod, ut esset, aliquem habuit auctorem.*

[284] *at* (Pβ Kroymann; *aut* NR[3] *vulgo*) is the correct reading: by reading *aut* we would get three possibilities, whereas Tertullian clearly wants to put Hermogenes before a dilemma once more: either Moses actually designated matter in Gen. 1.2 (but then it is still to be proved from Scripture that the abyss, etc., were made by God out of matter—which, of course, is impossible) or he designated merely the abyss, etc. (and then matter is mentioned nowhere in Scripture).

[285] **Chapter 33**: 'At all events, it is certain that all things were made by God, whereas it is by no means certain that they were made out of matter. But even if matter existed, we believe that it was made by God, for the rule of faith says explicitly that nothing is unborn except God. One may still doubt whether or not matter existed (though with the

help of Scripture it can be proved that it did not exist), but the main point is clear: in the final analysis everything was made out of nothing, for if it drew its origin from some other thing, that other thing was also made (and so drew its origin from nothing). Therefore, even if God had made all things from matter, at some point He made them from nothing.'

286 *colores* here has the double sense of 'colours' and of *causae fictae*— 'pretexts,' 'suppositions,' 'constructions,' (cf. *Thes. ling. lat.* 3.1722.24–47)—a meaning frequently found in the works of jurists. Cf. also n. 31.

287 *quia nihil innatum praeter deum praescribentes obtineremus*—Holmes: 'since we maintained (no less) when we held the rule of faith to be, that nothing except God was uncreated'; Kellner: 'da wir als unanfechtbare Einrede den Satz aufrecht erhalten würden, dass nichts unerschaffen sei ausser Gott.' In my opinion, the meaning of *obtineremus* is 'we would win our case' (in this sense, *obtinere* is a legal term frequently used by Tertullian—cf. my note on *De an.* 12.6—p. 205); it is contrasted with *deficiat* in the next sentence (cf. n. 288).

288 *In hunc usque articulum locus est retractatui, donec ad scripturas provocata deficiat exhibitio materiae.* I follow Holmes in translating the words *In hunc usque articulum* by 'Up to this point' (that is, the question whether matter exists or not). Kellner gives a different translation: 'Gegen diesen Satz kann man immerhin noch so lange Bedenken haben, bis das Dasein der Materie, an der Hand der Schrift geprüft, dahin schwindet.' He interprets *usque* as an adverb (*usque . . . donec*) but Tertullian usually connects *usque* with *ad* or *in* (cf. e.g. *De an.* 56.7, *ad eam diem usque*). *Articulus* here means 'point'; usually the sense is 'text' or 'Scriptural passage'—cf. Oehler's index and Evans 280.

Kroymann has serious objections against the sentence as a whole: 'offendo in verbis *in hunc—materiae*, quippe quae intolerabilem in modum turbent nexum sententiarum. Cohaerere ea arctissime cum eis, quae in initio capitis proferuntur, in aperto est. Neque tamen quicquam praestabis transpositione. Nescio igitur, an et hic duplex agnoscenda sit recensio: *sed dum illam—potuerit* (= the first sentence, in my translation: "But until . . . he cannot find it")~*in hunc—materiae*.' To me the order of the sentences does not appear disturbed at all—as is already vouched for by the contrast between *obtineremus* ('we would win our case') and *deficiat* ('loses its case') in the next sentence. After saying that the existence of matter must be an invention of Hermogenes, since (as was concluded in ch. 32) Scripture does not say a word about it, Tertullian mentions as a point certain beyond contention that all things were made by God, and adds that it is not certain that they were made out of matter; regarding the latter point, he immediately adds that if matter existed, it too was made by God because nothing save God is uncreated. Therefore, even if we may doubt for a while about the existence or non-existence of matter (but for a while only, for from Scripture it is evident that matter did not exist), yet this does not affect the main point, that everything (with the exception of God) was made and so once did not exist, from which it follows that it was made out of nothing. Thus the main argument ('Since God alone is uncreated, all things have been made, and that by Him, and since they have been made, they have been made out of nothing') is interrupted by the consideration that all things may have been made by God out of matter ('but if that were true, matter would also have been made by God; moreover, if for the moment we doubted whether or not matter existed, there is Scripture to prove that it did not'). In fact, the words *Expedita summa est* ('The main point is clear') are the immediate continuation of the sentence 'it is enough that, first, it is certain that all things were made by God.' The trend of thought would have been clearer if the sentence under discussion (which in the translation has been put in parentheses) had found its place immediately after the words, 'But even if matter had existed'; it is quite understandable, however, that after this dangerous supposition Tertullian preferred to mention at once its harmless consequence (it would 'also have been made by God').

[289] *origines rerum ex his prolatarum*. There is no reason to follow Kroymann in deleting the words *rerum ex his prolatarum*: *his* (=*talibus*, as frequently in Tertullian) refers to the beginning of the preceding sentence: *etiamsi quid ex aliquo factum est, ex facto habet censum* (=*originem*); so *his*=*factis rebus*.

[290] **Chapter 34**: 'The assertion that all things were created out of nothing is also made plausible by the circumstance that all things will eventually be reduced to nothing (§1), as is explicitly stated in several passages of Scripture (§2), and to ignore all these statements is quite impossible (§3). Further, the perishable things made by God cannot have been made by Him from anything eternal, as matter is said to be; it is, indeed, more appropriate that God should produce something eternal from something perishable (§4). Thus our perishable flesh will some day be made eternal; and of this future act of His power God has already deposited a pledge in us, that we may believe that it is out of nothing that He created the universe (§5).'

[291] *illa postremo divina dispositio suadebit*. Holmes has: 'the belief, etc., will be impressed upon us by that ultimate dispensation of God,' thus translating *postrema* instead of *postremo*. As often, Tertullian finishes an argument by referring to Scripture (cf. e.g. *De an.* 7 and 26). He cannot

find in Genesis any explicit statement about a creation from nothing, so he quotes Scriptural passages proving that all things will eventually be reduced to nothing, in order to conclude that they must also have originated from nothing (cf. the similar argument in 11.3).

292 Isa. 34.4 (quoted only here by Tertullian).

293 Matt. 24.35: *Caelum et terra praeteribunt* (some MSS of the New Testament also have the verb in the plural instead of the more common singular; cf. Aalders, *op. cit.* 78 and 98).

294 Apoc. 21.1 (quoted only here by Tertullian).

295 Apoc. 20.11 (again quoted only here; cf. the Introd. n. 1).

296 *quia scilicet quod et finit locum amittit (et finit locum* N R²; *et finit(c)io cum* Pβ; *finit et locum* Kroymann. The reading of N is rightly defended by Thörnell, *Stud. Tert.* 2.76).

297 Ps. 101. 26 f.: *Opera manuum tuarum* (R², *suarum* MSS and R¹) *caeli et ipsi peribunt. Nam et si mutabit illos velut opertorium, et mutabuntur, sed,* etc. (the second part of the quotation has been inserted into a *si*-clause, hence *mutabit*, not *mutabis*). One may doubt whether the *et* before *ipsi* belongs to the quotation or whether it serves to connect the two parts of it. Instead of *Nam* Kroymann reads *sed*, instead of *sed et* (*sed et mutare perire est pristino statui*) only *et* (with this motivation: '*sed* ut genuinam lectionem corruptelae *nam* olim adscriptum fuisse puto; caret enim sensu illud *nam*'). However, *sed* frequently occurs at the beginning of the main sentence after a *si*-clause—cf. e.g. *De an.* 33.8: *Et si pulcherrimus pavus . . ., sed tacent pennae, sed displicet vox*; further, Tertullian often writes *nam et* where we would expect to find *iam et*; cf. the numerous instances collected by Thörnell, *Stud. Tert.* 2.87 ff. (p. 91, the present sentence).

298 Cf. n. 104.

299 Apoc. 6.13 (quoted only here by Tertullian—cf. n. 1 of the Introd.).

300 Ps. 96.5: *montes . . . tamquam cera liquescent a conspectu domini.* As in the preceding quotation, the future has been substituted for the perfect tense (the LXX has an aorist) to make the quotation fit the context; a more literal translation (*liquefacti sunt*) occurs in *De res. carn.* 26 (62.20 f. Kr.).

301 Isa. 2.19: *cum surrexerit . . . confringere terram.* Also quoted in *Adv. Marc.* 4.30 (525.20 f. Kr.): *cum surrexerit comminuere terram,* and *ibid.* 5.16 (630.25 Kr.): *(dominum) consurgentem ut comminuat terram.*

302 Isa. 42. 15 (quoted only here by Tertullian).

303 Isa. 41.17: *quaerent aquam nec invenient* (LXX: ζητήσουσιν γὰρ ὕδωρ, καὶ οὐκ ἔσται). The *et* before *quaerent* should not be added to the quotation, as is done by Kroymann.

[304] Apoc. 21.1: *mare hactenus* (καὶ ἡ θάλασσα οὐκ ἔστιν ἔτι; Vulg.: *et mare iam non est*). For the translation, cf. H. Rönsch, *Das Neue Testament Tertullians* (Leipzig 1871) 720.

[305] The MSS read: *quae omnia et si aliter putaverit spiritaliter interpretanda*. Latinius, followed by Oehler, substitutes *alter* for *aliter*; Engelbrecht and Kroymann delete *spiritaliter* which, in my opinion, is the right solution: *spiritaliter* may well be regarded as a marginal or interlinear note explaining the meaning of *aliter*. It is very improbable that *aliter* should be deleted, for *aliter interpretari* is very frequently found in Tertullian's works (cf. my note on *De an.* 46.12—p. 498).

[306] *Si quae enim figurae sunt.* Holmes translates, 'all figures of speech'; but the words clearly mean *figurae* occurring in the verses just quoted.

[307] *quia nihil potest ad similitudinem de suo praestare, nisi sit ipsum quod tali similitudin⟨i⟩ praestet.* The MSS read *similitudine* which is adopted by Oehler; Engelbrecht writes ⟨*de*⟩ *tali similitudine*, Kroymann *similitudini* which is certainly right because in the *nisi*-clause *praestare*=*se praestare* (cf. Löfstedt, *Zur Sprache Tertullians* [Lund 1920] 50; the same, *Syntactica* 1 [Lund 1928] 192 f.; W. A. Baehrens, *Mnemosyne* 38 [1910] 413). In the *quia*-clause it might be preferable, because of the addition of *de suo*, to speak of an absolute, not a reflexive use of *praestare*. Holmes translates: 'because nothing is capable of imparting anything of its own for a similitude, except it actually be that very thing which it imparts in the similitude.' But *ipsum* does not designate a part of the thing in question which it imparts in the similitude but the thing itself. Kellner writes: 'weil zu einem Vergleiche nichts brauchbar sein kann, was nicht selbst die Eigenschaft besitzt, die zu einem solchen Vergleiche dient,' which means that he translates something different—*nisi sit ipsi quod* or *nisi sit ipsum habens quod*. It is only by referring the words *ipsum . . . praestet* to the thing itself that the correct connection with the principal sentence is established.

[308] *Revertor igitur ad causam definientem*, etc.: Kroymann reads *definiens* but we have here one more of Tertullian's personifications (cf. nn. 72 and 181).

[309] **Chapter 35**: 'After the question of the existence of matter comes that of its condition. If this cannot be established either, the fact of its non-existence becomes the more certain; moreover, we may find here several contradictions in Hermogenes' statement (§1). Hermogenes says that if examined according to the right method, matter is neither corporeal nor incorporeal, which is, of course, impossible (§2). But even if there existed such a third class of things in addition to the classes of corporeal and incorporeal things, one would like to know where such can be found and what are its qualities (§3).'

310 *cuius nec reliquus status consistat*, rendered by Holmes: 'when these other points concerning it prove inconsistent with each other.' But *nec . . . consistat* denotes something more fundamental: its 'further condition' becomes impossible or even unthinkable.

311 Tertullian's real conviction is pronounced in *De carn. Chr.* 11: *omne quod est corpus est sui generis; nihil est incorporale nisi quod non est.* Cf. Evans 234–36.

312 **Chapter 36**: 'Hermogenes now adds the contrary proposition that matter is partly corporeal and partly incorporeal (§1), the corporeal part consisting in that out of which bodies are created, and the incorporeal part in the irregular motion of matter (§2). But motion cannot be regarded as part of a substance because it is not a substantial thing but an *accidens* (§3): motion is an action and actions belong to the category of *accidentia*, so that motion can never be part of a substance (§4). If Hermogenes had declared matter to be immovable, he would not have thought of calling its immobility a part of its substance; so motion cannot be a part of its substance either. But the subject of motion will be discussed later (§5).'

313 *ne neutrum sit*. Holmes translates wrongly: 'in order that it may not have either'; Tertullian refers to the statement in ch. 35, according to which matter was *neutrum* indeed.

314 *rectae rationis* (R² Kroymann; *reparationis* PR¹ *reciprocationis* β the Hirsaugiensis and Oehler *reciperōnis* N) is required by the context: if matter is 'both' (i.e. corporeal and incorporeal), this is the very opposite of the statement that it is 'neither' (*ne neutrum sit* in the preceding sentence, cf. n. 313); and this statement was, according to the discussion in ch. 35, suggested to Hermogenes by the *recta ratio*. Moreover, a few sentences later we find this new statement qualified as *rectior ratio*.

315 *sicut nec alia reddit*. Holmes: 'just as that "other reason" also was'; but *alia* is a neuter plural, cf. 35.2: *ista recta ratio, quae nihil recti renuntiat, id est nihil certi*, and especially 35.3 where Tertullian complains about the fact that the *recta ratio* only says that matter is neither corporeal nor incorporeal and refrains from any further explanation.

316 *ut actus et pulsus, ut lapsus et* (δ Kroymann; *ut* α FX) *casus*.

317 *Nam si vel a semetipso quid movetur* (*si vel* Leopold Oehler; *sive* MSS R¹; *sive ⟨ab alio sive⟩ a semetipso* Kroymann). Kroymann's conjecture is not convincing because it is only in the next sentence that motion is discussed in general: *omnia denique moventur aut a semetipsis, ut animalia, aut ab aliis, ut inanimalia*. At the end of the next sentence I read: *sicut tu motum substantiam facis ⟨faciendo partem⟩ materiae incorporalem*; cf. *Vig. Chr.* 9 (1955) 145.

[318] *quae substantiae res est.* Holmes: 'which is the essential quality of substance.' But *substantiae res* is almost equivalent to *substantia*—cf. Thörnell, *Stud. Tert.* 4 (1926) 96 f.

[319] *numquid immobilitas secunda pars formae videretur?* Kroymann explains 'forma = *massa materiae*' and refers to 40.3: *quae nec partes materiae appellari convenit, cum a forma eius, ex mutatione divisa, recesserunt.* This interpretation is, in my opinion, correct; it is also supported by the words in §4 of the present chapter: *sed unam omnibus formam solius corporalitatis* (i.e. *esse dicimus*), *quae substantiae res est*: the *forma corporalitatis* is a substance (cf. n. 318), so it must mean 'their normal corporeality.'

[320] **Chapter 37**: 'Returning to his "right method," Hermogenes contends that matter is neither good nor evil: not good because, if it were good, it would always have been good, and in that case would not have required that God set it in order; not evil because in that event it would not have admitted of a change for the better, nor would God have sought to regulate it, as He would have laboured in vain (§1). We shall now discuss only the present argument, and in doing so we shall not repeat our former statement that Hermogenes should have said something positive and not made mere negations (§2). Now the contradiction in his statement is obvious: the reason why matter cannot be good, makes it evil, and the reason why it cannot be evil, makes it good—so it is both good and evil! (§3). Further, if matter were good, it could quite well be further improved, and if it were evil, God could well improve it; and if this last assertion is denied, God becomes inferior to matter! And again, when Hermogenes asserts that matter cannot have been evil, he will deny this on some other occasion (§5).'

[321] Or, 'with regard to matter' = *super materiam*: for this meaning of *super* with an accusative, cf. Hoppe, *Syntax* . . . 41 f., and *Beiträge* . . . 30.

[322] *et argumentationem* (Nβ; *et* om. P and most editors, also Oehler) is definitely the better reading. In §3 Tertullian attacks the statement itself ('matter is neither good nor evil'), in §4 the argument supporting it; this tallies with the announcement in §2: *nunc ad praesentem et solam propositionem* (§3) *et argumentationem* (§4) *tuam respondebo.*

[323] *Quod bonum* (that is, *est*), *non desiderat aut non optat aut non capit profectum, ut fiat de bono melius?* I place a comma after *bonum*. The meaning has been well understood by Holmes: 'Does that which is good never desire, never wish, never feel able to advance, so as to change its good for a better?' Kroymann writes *bonum non desiderat quod aut non optat*, etc., which in this context is quite meaningless.—In the following there is an allusion to Matt. 3.9.

³²⁴ *Sed et quam hic non vis natura malam, ⟨malam⟩* (add. van der Vliet) *alibi te confessum negabis.* Perhaps Kellner is right in putting a question mark after *negabis* (as is also done by van der Vliet): 'Hier soll nun die Materie nicht von Natur schlecht sein, aber wirst du leugnen können, dass du an andern Stellen dies eingeräumt hast?'

³²⁵ **Chapter 38**: 'By declaring matter to be *subiacens deo*, Hermogenes assigns a place in space to it, which implies that it has an outline and is not infinite (§1), but on the other hand he declares it to be infinite for the reason that it has always existed (§2). If one of his pupils should say that this refers to infinity in time only, this assertion is contradicted by Hermogenes' further statement that matter was not modelled by God as a whole but in parts. So Hermogenes means infinity in space; and this is contradicted by the fact that he assigns a place in space to matter (§3). Further, one fails to see why God could not model matter as a whole, unless He was either unable or unwilling to do so; and one would also like to know about the unformed part of matter (§4).'

³²⁶ *De situ materiae id tracto quod et de modo, ut perversitatem tuam traducam.* From Kroymann's edition we should infer that since he omits *ut* in his text without saying anything in the apparatus, PNF read *modo perversitatem*; but all the MSS read *modo et perversitatem, ut* being due to a conjecture in Rhenanus' first edition. Further, Kroymann wrongly says that P has *ut de modo* instead of *et de modo*. For *traducat*, found in all the MSS, I read *traducam*: this is in complete accordance with Tertullian's style (cf. e.g. 12.4: *Hac et ego definitione merito illum repercutiam*) and, to the best of my knowledge, *traducere* always has a personal subject in Tertullian's works. Pamelius substituted *motu* for *modo* in order to find a reference to ch. 36 here, whereas Iunius, who supposed *modo* to be equivalent to *massa* or *quantitate*, saw a connection with ch. 40 f. As I see it, *modo* refers to the chapter immediately preceding in which the *quality* of matter (neither good nor evil, according to Hermogenes) is discussed. Kellner translates: 'Hinsichtlich der Lage der Materie lehre ich wie über ihre Bewegung (*motu*), um deine verkehrten Ansichten zu beschämen'—thus translating *traducam*. The traditional reading is rendered well by Holmes: 'My observations touching the *site* of Matter, as also concerning its *mode*, have one and the same object in view—to meet and refute your perverse positions.'

³²⁷ With Kroymann I read *et utique locum ⟨adsignas⟩ illi*.

³²⁸ *extremā eum lineā patitur.* According to Kroymann, PNF read *extrema cum linea patitur*, but this *cum* is found only in F. Van der Vliet proposes to read *extremam eum* or *eius lineam patitur*; the former conjecture (with *eum*) is adopted by Kroymann.

329 *obduceris*. Holmes: 'you contradict yourself' (with the comment: 'Here a verb of the middle voice'); Kellner: 'Du bist also dessen überführt....' The latter translation spoils the argument: when Hermogenes declares matter to be infinite in space, this *will* lead to his refutation, since this statement contradicts the statements discussed in §1; therefore *obduceris* is best understood as a future tense.

330 *Debuerat enim deus ut exemplarium antiquitatis ad gloriam operis palam fecisse*. I cannot agree with Kellner's translation: 'Denn Gott hätte sie entsprechend den Vorgängen in alter Zeit zur Ehre seines Wirkens offenbar machen müssen.' It is true that Tertullian frequently regards 'the original situation' (*primordia*), i.e. the events described in the first chapters of Genesis, as *exempla* of the present state of things (cf. my note on *De an.* 9.7—p. 176) and that therefore in his works *primordii exempla* may often be translated by 'events which happened in the first times of the world and which are examples of the present situation' (cf. e.g. *De an.* 27.7). Here, however, Tertullian is not thinking of events described in Genesis, as is suggested by Kellner's translation: he means to say that if the whole of matter can be known from its parts (that is, from the parts of matter which received a form from God and which constitute the world as it is now), matter can be known from our world as it is now, and so may be regarded as a model of the present world (a further elaboration of this idea is given in 39.2 and 40.1). We may be in doubt about the correct translation of the genitive *antiquitatis*; it may mean 'belonging to the first times of the world,' but from 39.2 (*utique ex pristinis*, cf. n. 332) a different interpretation seems to be more probable, 'a model of the "old things,"' i.e. of the 'elements "first created"' (= the four 'elements' discussed in ch. 30: the darkness, the deep, the spirit, and the waters).

331 **Chapter 39**: 'Further, Hermogenes says that the changes undergone by matter demonstrate that it was divisible; but this contradicts the obvious conclusion that if God, being eternal, is indivisible, then matter, possessing the same eternity, must also be indivisible (§1). Moreover, when he says that the parts of matter contain all contained in all its own constituents, so that from the parts the whole can be known, it is impossible that the parts now existing contain anything of the old constituents of matter from which they are so widely different (§2).'

331a *a lineis tuis*—another allusion to Hermogenes' profession of painting.

332 A very difficult passage of which the original text reads: *Aeque cum dicis 'Partes autem eius omnia simul ex omnibus habent, ut ex partibus totum dinoscatur,' utique eas partes intellegi vis quae ex illa prolatae sunt,*

quae hodie videntur a nobis. Quomodo ergo omnia ex omnibus habent, utique ex pristinis, quando quae hodie videntur aliter habeant quam pristina fuerunt? Holmes: 'In like manner, when you say, "All things simultaneously throughout the universe possess portions of it, that so the whole may be ascertained from its parts," you of course mean to indicate those parts which were produced out of it, and which are now visible to us. How then is this possession (of Matter) by all things throughout the universe effected—that is, of course, from the very beginning—when the things which are now visible to us are different in their condition from what they were in the beginning?' According to Holmes, the words *omnia simul ex omnibus* are the subject in the statement of Hermogenes and *partes eius* the object. To me this is highly improbable because of the clause *ut ex partibus totum dinoscatur.* If the whole (of matter) can be known from its parts, it is much more probable that this is so because these parts contain *omnia ex omnibus* than that it is due to the reason that these parts can be found in *omnia ex omnibus.* Further, in the former case the translation of *omnia ex omnibus* is much easier ('all things taken from all constituents of matter') than in the latter ('all things out of all things'; Holmes: 'All things . . . throughout the universe'). Finally, it is much more probable that in the last sentence the subject of *habent* should be *partes*, since this is the subject of the relative clause immediately preceding; and the interpretation of *ex pristinis* becomes, in my opinion, impossible, if we regard *omnia ex omnibus* as the subject of *habent* (Holmes' 'from the very beginning' is not a translation at all) : the end of the sentence shows that these *pristina* do not exist any more (*quam pristina fuerunt*), so that, if *ex pristinis* were subjoined to a subject *omnia ex omnibus*, a different refutation should have been expected, namely, that *omnia ex omnibus* cannot be accepted as a whole, since the *pristina* have disappeared from it. On the other hand, the meaning is quite clear, when it is denied that parts of matter now visible possess all elements of the constituents of matter on the ground that the 'old' constituents of matter (Tertullian is of course thinking of the four substances mentioned in Gen. 1.2 and amply discussed in ch. 30) no longer exist as independent substances, but have ceased to be in consequence of the change which they underwent when God made the world out of them. Like the former argument, this refutation, too, is based on the idea that matter, having been developed or 'worked up' by God, must have been susceptible of change. The first sentence is correctly translated by Kellner but the second contains an error in the translation of *utique ex pristinis*: 'Wie können folglich die Teile alles aus allem haben, da sie doch aus den vorigen Teilen entstanden sind, und diejenigen, welche wir jetzt vor uns sehen, anders sind als die früheren?': *utique ex pristinis* is not to be connected with the subject but with *ex omnibus*.

[333] **Chapter 40**: 'Further, Hermogenes says that matter experienced a change for the better, implying that it first had a worse condition; and this again makes it impossible that it was the model of this world, as Hermogenes says (§1). Nor can the world be called "the mirror of matter," for the world is a *cosmos*, whereas matter was completely "unadorned"; so it is impossible that the whole of matter should be known from its now visible parts (§2). This is also impossible for the following reason: According to Hermogenes, a part of matter was not worked up for the creation of the world but remained in its formless state. Now, this entirely chaotic part can most certainly not become known from the well-formed and well-ordered things created from the other part of matter, and so the *whole* of matter is not cognizable from its now visible parts. Indeed, we cannot call these things parts of matter, since they have changed radically in consequence of their *fabricatio* from matter by God (§3).'

[334] *et vis meliora deteriorum exemplarium ferre. Exemplarium* (which in 38.4 means 'example') must mean 'copy' here (cf. such expressions as *imaginem alicuius rei ferre, praeferre, prae se ferre*). This meaning is found already in Cicero—cf. *Thes. ling. lat.* 5.2.1324.26–1325.7. Thus also Kellner ('... und lehrst, das Bessere trage das Bild des Schlechtern noch an sich') and Holmes ('and (thus) you would make the better a copy of the worse'). Hermogenes had called matter the model of the world created out of it (cf. 38.4); by *meliora* Tertullian means the things created out of matter (cf. the preceding chapter), by *deteriora* matter as it was before it was 'worked up' by God. Ch. 40 is no more than a continuation of the refutation of Hermogenes' contention that 'from the parts of matter the whole of it can be known.' According to Tertullian, this is impossible because of the changes experienced by these 'parts' (39.3), and for the same reason it is impossible to regard matter as 'the model of this world' and this world as 'the image of matter' (40.1 f.); further, this is also impossible because a part of matter never received any form (40.3).

[335] *et vis ex compositis incomposita praeberi* = *imaginem incompositorum praeberi*.

[336] *nulla res speculum est rei alterius, id est non coaequalis.* Holmes: 'that is to say, it is not its co-equal'; but *coaequalis* clearly is a genitive: if things are *coaequales*, the one is indeed the image of the other. I fail to understand Kellner's translation: 'kein Ding aber bekommt im Spiegel ein anderes Aussehen, d. h. ein ungleiches.'

[337] *comptae*.

338 The change undergone by matter when it was transformed into the things which now constitute our world, was so thorough that the world cannot possibly be called the mirror of matter. This might still have been possible, if matter had contained at least something possessing a form, or if the world, as it is now, possessed something formless; but since this is not the case, matter and the world created from it remain widely different. The argument is mainly a repetition of the last paragraph of ch. 39; it is repeated again in the last sentence of the present chapter.

339 For this qualification, cf. also 42.2.

340 This refers to 38.3.

341 Tertullian means to say that since a part of matter was not modelled at all by God, it is at all events impossible to know the whole of matter from its 'parts' (i.e. the things created by God out of matter), for even if the material which had gone into these parts could be known from them, the part of matter which was not modelled at all would still remain unknown.

342 Cf. n. 338.

343 **Chapter 41**: 'Hermogenes describes the motion of matter as entirely chaotic and compares it to the motion of boiling water, while in his argument in support of the thesis that matter is neither good nor evil he says that this motion inclined neither to good nor to evil, because it was perfectly equable (§1). Further, if this motion kept itself at a distance from both good and evil, it was in action between the two, and thus it becomes evident again (as in ch. 38) that matter was determinable (§2). Moreover, if good and evil could thus determine matter, they must, since matter was local, have been local as well, and thereby corporeal. In this way good and evil would become substances, which is impossible (§3).'

344 *confusus* R³ van der Vliet, *inconfusus* MSS. It is not probable that in this case the prefix *in-* should serve no purpose, though several instances of such usage are found in Tertullian's works (cf. my note on *De an.* 19.3—p. 272).

345 I read *vergit* with R³ (*vertit* MSS), and again farther on (171.8 Kr.) *vergebat* (R³; *vertebat* MSS), for in this same chapter Tertullian uses *devergens* and *devergebat* (§3).

346 *caccabacius* (Pβ Kroymann; *caccabatus* N; *caccabacius* R¹ Oehler). *Thes. ling. lat.* 3.4.78–81 reads *caccabaceus*, but *-ius* is also found in the only other passage in which this adjective occurs—Zeno of Verona 2.44.1: *(panes azymi) certe caccabacii non sunt. Caccabus* occurs first in Varro, *De ling. lat.* 5.127: *vas ubi coquebant cibum, ab eo caccabum appellarunt.*

347 I read *mediam, quod aiunt, aginam tenens exinde librato impetu ferebatur.* Cf. my discussion of this particularly difficult passage in *Vig. Chr.* 9 (1955) 145–47.

348 *Haec inquies non est.* Kellner: 'Das, wirst du sagen, ist nicht Unruhe' (thus translating *inquies* first as a verb, then as a substantive).

349 *vergebat*: cf. n. 345.

350 *inter* (Kroymann, *intra* MSS) *utrumque ab utroque pendebat* (R³, *censebat* MSS, *censebatur* Engelbrecht Kroymann). The correct reading, *pendebat*, is indicated by the last words of the chapter: *cum materiae motum ab utraque regione suspendis.*

351 *cum corpori accedunt*: Rigaltius and Kroymann read *accidunt*, but *accedere* is frequently used by Tertullian in connection with *accidentia*— —cf. my observations on *De an.* 6.5 (p. 139), 10.7 (p. 190), and 20.4 (p. 285).

352 With Oehler I read *devergens* (*devergent* MSS R¹ Kroymann, *devergente* R²).

353 The whole sentence should, in my opinion, read as follows: *Ad* (add. R²) *bonum autem et malum non devergens* (cf. n. 352) *materia ut ad* (my conjecture; *ut aut* MSS, *ut* Iunius, *utut* Oehler) *corporalia aut localia non devergebat.* Kroymann reads: ⟨*ad*⟩ *bonum autem et malum non* † *devergent materia ut aut . . . devergebat*; in his apparatus he gives as a possible reading: *ad bonum . . . non devergens materia, ad corporalia, ut ad localia, non devergebat,* regarding this as a duplicate of the words *dans autem locum . . . corporalia sint* (171.13–15 Kr., in our translation: 'Now when you . . . must first be corporeal'). However, the sentence under discussion is not a mere repetition of the preceding sentence: Tertullian first says that from the fact that matter, which is local, does not incline towards either good or evil, it is evident that good and evil have a place in space as well (first premise). Next he observes (*Dans autem,* etc.) that things which have a place in space must necessarily be corporeal (second premise), and adds a short digression concerning incorporeal things. Returning then to his argument, he states that the fact that matter did not incline towards either good or evil, proves that good and evil are corporeal (conclusion) as well as local (he adds a datum from one of the premises to the conclusion, as he frequently does—cf. the index to my edition of the *De anima* s. v. 'syllogisms—abundant,' p. 637).

354 One may wonder whether Tertullian wrote this in serious mood —cf. n. 311 and the comment on *De an.* 6.7 (p. 142 f.).

355 **Chapter 42**: 'Two further contradictions: a) Hermogenes says, on the one hand, that the motion of matter was chaotic and that matter "aimed at formlessness," on the other hand, that it wanted to be set in

order by God (§1); b) Next he observes that God was not equal to matter, yet he subjoins that matter had something in common with God. The latter statement is based on the assertion that matter must have had something in common with God in order that it might be "adorned" by Him. Now this is quite untrue, for if it had something in common with God, it would because of such participation in Him not want to be adorned by Him; moreover, on this assumption it might as well be said that God could be adorned by matter; and, finally, if matter really contained something because of which it should be formed by God, God would in so far be made subject to necessity (§2). As for that which God and matter are said to have in common, this is their completely free and eternal motion, and the possession of such motion makes matter entirely equal to God. Indeed, even more is granted to matter than to God, since it can move itself in a way forbidden to God (§3).'

356 *non vis videri deum aequari materiae: aequari* N Oehler, *aequare* Pβ (*-ere* V) Kroymann. In my opinion, the passive infinitive is to be preferred because Tertullian generally uses the passive forms of (*ad*)*aequare* and *comparare* when he discusses the fact that Hermogenes puts matter on one level with God—cf. e.g. 5.2 (131.21 f. Kr.): *non statim materiam comparari deo, si quid dei habeat*; moreover, it is important that *aequari* is the reading of P. It should be noted, however, that the active forms of these verbs occur now and then in this context, e.g. 7.4 (8.1) (134.23 f. Kr.): *Putas* (*putans* Kroymann) *itaque materiam deo non comparasse, quam scilicet subiciat illi*?

357 I agree with Kroymann that a full stop should be put before this sentence (R² and Oehler write a comma), since it brings an entirely new argument against the statement of Hermogenes mentioned in the first sentence of §2. Further, I read *etiam* with αXF and Kroymann (*et iam* R in P and Oehler). Kroymann observes: 'offendo in verbis *etiam in hoc*; nihil enim attulit auctor, ex quo subiecisse deum necessitati intellegatur Hermogenes.' But *etiam in hoc* must not necessarily mean 'in this respect as well'; we may also translate: 'further, in this respect.'

358 With Kroymann I read: *quod a semetipsis moveantur* (*moventur* MSS) *et semper moveantur* (*moveantur* MSS, *moventur* R³).

359 *Tamen divinum proinde.* Engelbrecht adds *utrumque* after *proinde*, but we must understand: *tamen materia proinde divina res est*—cf. Hoppe, *Beitr.* 152.

360 **Chapter 43**: 'Moreover, Hermogenes in one instance ascribes to matter a vehement commotion, whereas in another he declares its motion to have been slow (§1). And again he asserts that it was not evil

by nature, since, if it were, it could not have been improved and regulated by God; and then he declares that after it had been regulated by God, it lost its evil nature. This implies two statements contradicting his former theses—that matter was evil by nature and that it was subject to change (§2).'

361 *adprehensibilem* (Kroymann; *inadprehensibilem* α, -*lis* γ).

362 *prae*. Kroymann reads *pro*, which is unnecessary since Tertullian frequently uses *prae* with a causal sense (cf. my note on *De an.* 2.2— p. 100 f.).

363 *Nam*. Kroymann reads *iam*, but cf. n. 297, and Hoppe, *Beitr.* 120.

364 I read: *et si per compositionem dei cessavit a natura mali, a natura cessavit. Ergo et mala fuit natura*, etc. The usual punctuation is: *natura cessavit ergo, et mala fuit*, etc. The trend of thought is as follows: Hermogenes has made two statements, that matter is not evil by nature, and that its nature cannot be altered by God. Now, on another occasion he says that when it had been regulated and 'adorned' by God, it lost its nature. This leads to a conclusion which contradicts the first two statements, for if matter was reformed by God for the better, it was indeed first evil by nature, and when because of its adjustment by God it lost this evil nature, it lost its former nature, and so proved itself to be susceptible of change. In order to show the contradiction with the former statements as clearly as possible, these conclusions are repeated in their most simple form in the last sentence of the chapter which, therefore, is best opened by *Ergo* ('And so we may say that . . .'). Holmes disturbs the context by opening the last sentence by 'Now.' Kroymann has the correct punctuation, but spoils the last but one sentence by reading *et si per compositionem dei cessavit a natura, ⟨a⟩ mali natura cessavit*: in this sentence, too, the conclusion must be, not that matter lost its *evil* nature, but that it lost its *nature*.

365 **Chapter** 44: 'According to Hermogenes, God did not create the world by pervading matter, as the Stoics say, but by merely showing Himself to it and coming near to it, just as beauty produces its effect by merely showing itself and a magnet by its mere proximity (§1). But these examples are not at all relevant (§2). But to assume for the moment that they are relevant: God, then, must have made the world the moment when He appeared to it and approached it, from which it follows that before that moment He did not do this. But this is incredible, for matter was consubstantial with God because of its eternity; further, God can never have been far removed from matter, since He is everywhere (§3).'

366 Cf. H. v. Arnim, *Stoicorum veterum fragmenta* 2.1031. The comparison with *mel per favos* does not occur in the other sources.

³⁶⁷ *decor*. I fail to understand why Kroymann in this and two other passages (§2) reads *acor* instead of *decor*; though *acor* occurs in *Adv. Marc.* 1.2 (293.5 f. Kr.): *modicoque . . . fermento totam fidei massam haeretico acore desipuit* (i.e. Marcion).

³⁶⁸ An allusion to Dan. 3.59 ff.

³⁶⁹ **Chapter 45**: 'Scripture does not even mention matter: it says that first Wisdom was created, and next the Word *by whom all things were made*. This is confirmed by several other passages (§1). God indeed made all things, not by a mere appearance or a mere approach, but by the exertion of His powers. Further, if God had made the world by merely appearing to it and approaching it, He would have ceased to do so after the work of creation was completed—but the very opposite is true (§2). God's invisible powers may be regarded as his *sensus*; in this context Rom. 11.33 shows that God made all things out of nothing (§3). Hermogenes' description of matter is rather to be regarded as a portrait of Hermogenes himself (§4).'

³⁷⁰ I read *initium* (Pamelius), since this is also found in the quotation of the same passage in ch. 18 (cf. n. 157). R¹, Gelenius, and Oehler read *initia*, evidently because the manuscripts read *initiarum*, but this termination is due to *viarum* which comes immediately after it.

³⁷¹ Prov. 8.22 (cf. n. 157).

³⁷² John 1.3.

³⁷³ Ps. 32.6: *Sermone eius caeli confirmati sunt et spiritu ipsius universae virtutes eorum*. Tertullian has left untranslated the genitive τοῦ στόματος which LXX has after πνεύματι. The verse is also quoted in *Adv. Prax.* 7 (236.6–8 Kr.) and 19 (261.20–22 Kr.) with several variations.

³⁷⁴ Cf. Isa. 48.13; read *dextra* (α), not *dextera* (γ).

³⁷⁵ According to Irenaeus, *Adv. haer.* 4 *praef.* 3 (H), the 'hands of God' are the Son and the Holy Spirit: *homo . . . per manus eius* (i.e. *dei*) *plasmatus est, hoc est, per Filium et Spiritum sanctum quibus et dixit: Faciamus hominem*; 5.1.3 (H): *non enim effugit aliquando Adam manus ad quas Pater loquens, dicit: Faciamus hominem ad imaginem et similitudinem nostram*. Thus also Tertullian in *Adv. Prax.* 12 (in an explanation of the words *Faciamus hominem*): *immo quia iam adhaerebat illi filius, secunda persona, sermo ipsius, et tertia, spiritus in sermone, deus pluraliter pronuntiavit Faciamus et Nostrum et Nobis*. This contradicts the statement in the same chapter that after the creation of Light *deus* (= God) *voluit fieri et deus* (= Christ) *fecit*. Cf. on this subject the excellent note by Evans (261 f.) who has also drawn attention to the passages from Irenaeus. A similar inconsistency occurs in Irenaeus, for according to 5.15.4 (H) it was the Son only who moulded Adam.

³⁷⁶ Ps. 101.26 (cf. n. 297).

377 Isa. 40.12. The MSS read *mensus est caelum et palmo terram* (LXX: . . . ἐμέτρησεν . . . τὸν οὐρανὸν σπιθαμῇ καὶ πᾶσαν τὴν γῆν δρακί; the verse is not quoted again by Tertullian). The whole sentence should be punctuated as follows: *Hic est dei dextra et manus ambae, per quas operatus est atque molitus est*—'*Opera*' enim '*manuum tuarum*,' inquit, '*caeli*'—*per quas et* '*mensus est caelum et palmo terram*.' Oehler places a full stop before *Opera*, thus spoiling the sense; the punctuation has been corrected by Kroymann. In the last part of the sentence Kroymann follows F which has the words *et mensus* (not *mensus est*) twice, and gives this text: *per quas et mensus est*: '*mensus est * * caelum et palmo terram*'; he supposes the words *inquit, manu* to have fallen out after the second *est*. However, it is far from probable that F alone should have preserved the correct text; it seems much more plausible that we have here a conjecture by a studious copyist, and so Kroymann's addition of *inquit* becomes superfluous. We find here one of the frequent cases in which Tertullian absorbs and fully incorporates Scriptural quotations in his sentences, as if they had been written by himself (cf. e.g. n. 297 and *De an.* 57.8). As to Kroymann's addition of *manu*, it is indeed curious that the σπιθαμῇ of LXX has been left untranslated. It does not seem improbable that Tertullian, who of course considered the σπιθαμή and the δράξ to be *manus ambas dei*, first thought them to be sufficiently designated by *quas*, but in the end forgot about this and thus failed to delete *palmo*. Finally, it should be noted that *enim* does not form part of the quotation of Ps. 101.26, as is supposed by Kroymann, for it does not have a correspondence in LXX, and is lacking in the quotation of the same passage in 34.2; it serves the purpose of indicating that Ps. 101.26 is the Scriptural proof for the statement that God created the world *per manus ambas*.

378 *Noli ita deo adulari, ut*, etc. So also in *Adv. Prax.* 9 (239.19–21 Kr.): *cum eundem patrem et filium et spiritum contendunt, adversus oikonomiam monarchiae adulantes.*

379 Jer. 28 (LXX; 51 Vulg.).15 (quoted only here by Tertullian).

380 *Haec (Hae R²) sunt vires eius. Haec* as a feminine plural is found as early as Plaut. *Aul.* 386—cf. A. Fleckeisen, *Rhein. Mus.* 7.271. It is also possible, however, to understand it as a neuter plural, for Tertullian often has a neuter form in the nominal predicate—cf. Thörnell, *Stud. Tert.* 3 (1922) 29 n. 1.

381 With Oehler I read: *numquid, cum facere desiit, rursus apparere et adpropinquare cessavit?* (*facere* R vulgo, *fecerit* δ, *feceret* F, *faceret* PN). Kroymann reads *fecerat* which forces him to change the punctuation: *numquid, cum fecerat, desiit rursus apparere et adpropinquare cessavit?* This has the disadvantage that *rursus*, which clearly belongs to both *apparere*

11*

and *adpropinquare*, is connected with *apparere* alone (ἀπὸ κοινοῦ—constructions are not usual at all in Tertullian's works).

382 Cf. n. 379.

383 A similar list is given in *De carn. res.* 6 (33.9–11 Kr.) : *recogita totum illi* (i.e. *carni creandae) deum occupatum ac deditum, manu sensu opere consilio sapientia providentia et ipsa inprimis adfectione.*

384 *si* (Latinius; *ut* MSS) *apparendo tantummodo et adpropinquando profectus fuisset (profectus* MSS, *perfectus* Latinius Oehler, *praefectus* Kroymann). Kellner writes: 'Mit der Lesart *perfectus fuisset* kann ich nichts anfangen, *profectus* scheint schon eher zu passen. Der Sinn erfordert *fecisset, operatus fuisset* oder dergleichen.' In my opinion, the reading of the MSS conveys sense if taken as a reference to the last sentence of ch. 44: *credo, peregrinatus est ad illam* (=matter) *de longinquo.*

385 *factis conspiciuntur.* Before *factis, de* is added by Latinius Oehler, but, as Kroymann observes, this addition is not necessary, since the Greek text has only ποιήμασιν.

386 Rom. 1.20, which is quoted in a very different form in *De an.* 18.12: *invisibilia enim eius a conditione mundi de factitamentis intellecta visuntur.* Allusions to this verse are found in *Adv. Marc.* 4.25 (504.12 and 506.6 Kr.); it is used in an argument in *Adv. Prax.* 7 (237.11–16 Kr.): *quis enim negabit deum corpus esse, etsi deus spiritus est? Spiritus enim corpus sui generis in sua effigie. Sed si et invisibilia illa, quaecumque sunt, habent apud deum et suum corpus et suam formam, per quae soli deo visibilia sunt, quanto magis quod ex ipsius substantia emissum est sine substantia non erit?* Cf. the notes *ad loc.* by Evans 234–36.

387 *non materiae nescio quae, sed sensualia ipsius.* The last two words are translated by Holmes by 'sensible evidence of Himself,' but the meaning is evident from the quotation which follows: *Quis enim cognovit sensum domini . . .?* It is for this reason that Kroymann is certainly wrong in transposing the words under discussion *(non . . . ipsius)* to the beginning of the sentence (after *haec autem*='But these' in the translation). Cf. also *Adv. Prax.* 15 (256.5 f. Kr.): *pater enim sensu agit, filius, qui in patris sensu est, videns perficit.* Kellner's translation ('sein eigenes geistiges Vermögen') hits the mark.

388 Rom. 11.34 (cf. n. 143).

389 Rom. 11.33, also quoted in *Adv. Marc.* 2.2 (335.5–7 Kr.) immediately after Isa. 40.13 f.—cf. n. 143—in slightly different form: *o profundum divitiarum et sophiae dei, ut ⟨in⟩investigabilia* (correction by Rhenanus) *iudicia eius . . . et ⟨in⟩investigabiles* (correction by the same) *viae eius,* and *ibid.* 5.14 (625.13 f. Kr.), where only the first part is given: *o profundum divitiarum et sapientiae dei!* The words καὶ γνώσεως after σοφίας have not been translated in all three quotations.

390 *quae nec inveniri nec investigari nisi soli deo possent.* Kroymann substitutes *quo* for *quae* and *possunt* for *possent.* But the relative clause clearly has a causal sense, for it furnishes the motivation for the interpretation of Rom. 11.33 as given in the preceding sentence.

391 *alioquin investigabilia et inventibilia* (added by me—cf. *Vig. Chr.* 9 [1955] 147), *si ex materia sunt.* After *sunt* I delete the words *investigata et non inventa*, which are found in all the MSS (R³ deletes *non*, Kroymann del. *sunt . . . inventa*). In my edition I have followed R³.

392 *Nisi quod Hermogenes,* etc. Kroymann thinks that a sentence must have fallen out before *Nisi*, perhaps *in vacuum ergo laboraverunt materiarii isti* 'vel simile aliquid.' The transition to the last sentence is indeed abrupt, but it should be remembered that Tertullian frequently tops off a long and laborious argument by a witty or sarcastic remark introduced by *nisi quod*; e.g. in *De an.* 34.5: *O Helenam inter poetas et haereticos laborantem, tunc adulterio, nunc stupro infamem, nisi quod de Troia gloriosius eruitur quam de lupanari.*

393 At the end of his treatise Tertullian returns to his starting point (the description of Hermogenes in ch. 1), as he does very frequently: cf. my notes on *De an.* 25.1 (p. 320) and 58.9 (p. 593).

INDEX

INDEX

Aalders, G. J. D., 121, 123, 124
abbreviation, of Scriptural quotations, 134, 136
ablative, resultative, 141
Academy, its influence on Hermogenes, 27; *see also* Platonism
accedere = accidere, 165
adducere = inducere, 134
aestimare for "mere supposition," 131
Albinus, 9
Allie, J. L., 101
Apocalypse, frequently quoted by Theophilus of Antioch and by Tert. in the *Adv. Herm.*, 3
argumentari, 67, 107
Aristotle, *De caelo* 300 b 16–19: 96; *Eudemus* (story of Silenus and Midas): 142; *Phys.* 191 a 6–8: 123
articulus, 129, 154
Atticus in Eusebius, *Praep. Evang.* 15.6.4: 9
Augustine, *De haer.* 41: 3, 96

Baehrens, W. A., 157
Baeumker, C., 96
Becker, C. H., 97
Bindley, T. H., 101
Borleffs, J. W. P., 17, 23, 98, 99, 100
Bruhn, E., 117, 118

caccabacius, 164
Caspari, C. H., *Kirchenhist. Anecd.* 229: 8
cauterium, 103
censeri, 112
census, 111
Cerda, L. la, 24
Chalcidius, *Comm. in Tim.* 276: 131, 134; 278: 140; 300: 96
changes of meaning, 129, 145, 148
Christ, taking part in the creation of the world, 104; Christ and God occasionally confused by Tert., 103 f.; identical with Wisdom (Prov.

8.22 ff.), 15, 50 f.; Hermogenes' doctrine on, 8
clausula, 122
Clement of Alexandria, *Ecl. proph.* 56.2: 96
Codex Agobardinus, 18; Ambrosianus, 18; Ioannis Clementis Angli, 19; Coloniensis, 19; Corbeiensis, 19; Florentinus (F), 21; Florentinus (N), 21; Gorziensis, 21; Hirsaugiensis, 21; Leidensis, 21; Luxemburgensis, 21; Masburensis, 19, 99; Montepessulanus, 21; Ottobonianus, 20; Paterniacensis, 20; Trecensis, 18; Vindobonensis, 21
colores = causae fictae, 154
comparare, 111
contamination of constructions, 151
convertere in with abl., 118
Ps.–Cyprian, *Quod idola* 9: 108

datation of the *Adv. Herm.*, 13
Decretum Gelasianum, 18
dedicare = initiare, 145
Dekkers, E., 19, 98, 99
destruere, "to refute," 129
Diercks, G. F., 98
dilemma, Tert. driving his opponent into a, 149, 153
dirigere, "to interpret," 140
dispositio, 131; = *positio*, 148
diversa pars, "opposition," 137
dominus, mostly a designation for Christ, 104; *cognomen* of God, 108

elements, indicated in Gen. 1.2 according to Hermogenes, 5, 92, 152
ellipsis, before *nihil interest*, 128
Eusebius, *Hist. eccl.* 4.24.1: 89
Evans, E., 96 and *passim*
evil, origin of, 4–7, 119 f., 126 ff.
excusare = ex-causare, 129
exemplarium, "copy," 163
existimare, for "mere supposition," 131

175

Filastrius, *De haer.* 44: 3; 26 (54): 96
forma, ex, 123; *mori sua forma,* 123

Gelenius, S., 19
genitive, both possessive and definitive, 130; explicative, 122, 143
Genoude, A. de, 24
Ghellinck, J. de, 98
God, according to Hermogenes: made the universe either out of Himself or out of nothing or out of something, 4, 14, 27; the first two of these possibilities excluded, 4, 14, 27 f.; superior to matter, 14, 32 ff.; needed matter in order to make the universe, 14, 36 f.; always Lord, 4 f., 14, 28; His acting on matter, 6, 94; cannot have been the creator of evil, 4, 28, 119; matter desiring to be set in order by Him, 17, 80 f.; making the universe by merely appearing to and approaching matter, 17, 82 f.
Grant, R. M., 12

haec, a feminine plural, 169
Harnack, A., 9, 97, 124
heretics, materialist, 59
Hermogenes, life, 3; personality, 26; his profession (painting), 26, 74, 77, 85, 161; authorities for the knowledge of his doctrine, 3; doctrine, 4-8 (*see under* God, Christ, matter, soul); influenced by Platonism, 8 f.
Hermogenes, St. Paul's friend (2 Tim. 1.15), 26, 103
hic = talis, 155
Hippolytus, *Elench.* 8.17: 3; 8.17.1: 91, 94; 8.17.2: 93; 10.28: 3, 91; 10.28.1: 94; 10.28.3: 95
Holmes, P., 24 and *passim*
Hoppe, H., 103, 151, 159, 166, 167

ideo, "for *such* a reason," 118
instruo = struo, 136
ipsum quod = eo ipso quod, 144
Irenaeus, *Adv. haer.,* 4 praef. 3 (H.): 168; 5.1.3: 168; 5.15.4: 168
Iunius, F., 24 and *passim*

Justin, 1 *Apol.* 10.2, 59.1, 67.7: 97

Kellner, H., 24 and *passim*
Klussmann, A., 98
Kroymann, E., 17 and *passim*

Labriolle, P. de, 101
Lactantius, *Div. inst.* 1.6.5: 108
Lieftinck, G., 19
Löfstedt, E., 111, 120, 151, 157
Lupton, J. M., 99

Maas, P., 99
Manuscripts of Tertullian's works, *see* Codex
Marcion, 119
materialist (*materiarius*), 59
matter, according to Hermogenes: unborn and eternal, 4 f., 31, 113; origin of evil: 7, 89; needed by God to create the universe, 14, 36 f; without qualities, 5; neither corporeal nor incorporeal, 5 f., 16, 73; partly corporeal and partly incorporeal, 16, 73-75; neither good nor evil, 6, 16, 75 f.; infinite, 6, 16, 76 f.; subject to change, 7, 16, 77; divisible, 7, 16, 77 f.; "model of the world," 6 f., 16, 78 f.; and the world "the image of matter," 7, 78 f., 95; motion, 6, 17, 79-82, 93; when creating the world, God merely appeared to it and approached it, 17, 82 f.
Meropis, 142
Mesnart, M., 19
Midas, 60, 142
Minucius Felix 18.10: 108
Montanism, no traces of in the *Adv. Herm.,* 13
mori sua morte (forma), 123 f.
Moses, 51, 70, 131
Mosheim, J. L., 89

nam (et), instead of *iam (et),* 156, 167
Name, of God, 108
Neander, J. A. W., 94, 95
nisi quod, introducing an ironic comment, 171
Novatian, *De Trin.* 7: 151

obducere = refutare, 161
obtinere causam, 154

occupatio, 90, 92
Oehler, F., 23 and *passim*
originalis, 134

Pamelius, J., 19
personification, 119, 137, 157
Pfaettisch, J. M., 97
Philo, 131, 152
Plato, interpretation of the *Timaeus*, 9
Platonism, its influence on Hermogenes, 9
Plutarch, *De an. procr. in Tim.* 5 (1014 B), 9
πνεῦμα, 7
prae, with a causal sense, 167
praescriptio, 101
praestare = se praestare, 157
primordia, "the original state of things" (as described in Genesis), 161
principium, meaning in Gen. 1.1: 135
Proclus, *In Tim.* 84 F: 9
prophets, "books of the" = the Old Testament, 131
proprietas, 125

Quispel, G., 9, 11, 12

Reifferscheid, A., 98
relative clause, equivalent to a *si*-clause, 115
remarriage, 102
res, with a genitive (*substantiae res = substantia*), 159
Rhenanus, B., 21
Rigaltius, N., 24, 102
Roensch, H., 132, 134, 157
rudimentum = status rudis, 145

Schulze, W., 124
Scriptural quotations: abbreviated by Tert., 134, 136; single passages (only such as are more fully discussed in the notes): Gen. 1.1: 5, 15, 53 f., 92, 134, 135, 136; 1.2: 5, 16, 57-70, 92, 139, 148; 1.7 f.: 142; 1.9: 146; 1.10: 146; 1.11 f: 139; 1.20 f.: 139; 1.24: 139; 1.27: 142; 1.28: 102; 2.7: 7, 142, 145; Exod. 20.4: 103; Ps. 32.6: 168; 44.2: 134; 96.5: 156; Prov. 8.22 ff.: 15, 49-51, 97, 132; Isa. 40.12: 169; 40.13 f.: 130; 45.17: 150; 45.18:

147; 57.16: 151; Amos 4.13: 151; John 4.24: 151; Rom. 1.20: 170; 11.33: 170; 11.34 f.: 15, 48 f., 130; Apoc. 6.13, 20.3, 20.11, 21.1, 22.18 ff.: 96
Scripture, quoted at the end of an argument, 155
sic . . . ac si = aeque . . . ac si, 126
Silenus, 60, 142
sophisms, 148, 151
soul, Hermogenes on the, 7 f.; unborn according to Hermogenes, 91
spiritus, meanings of in Tert., 151
status, essence, 111
stilus, book, 151; passage, 151
Stirnimann, J. K., 101
Stoic doctrine, source of Hermogenes according to Tert., 27
Stoic. vet. fragm. 2.1031: 167
συνακμάζειν, 97
super, with acc. = *de*, 159
Svennung, J., 151
syllogisms, abbreviated, 147; confused, 105 f., 136; illogical, 112; inverted, 115, 121; irregular, 126; abundant, 112, 128; conclusion inserted in the first premise, 148

Tatian, *Orat. ad Graec.* 12: 97
Tertullian, his reliability as an authority for the doctrine of Hermogenes, 3 f.; his refutation of Hermogenes draws upon Theophilus of Antioch, 9-12; frequently includes inferences of his own in reports of the doctrines of his adversaries, 113 f.; referring to his earlier works in the present tense, 120 f.; likes to qualify Hermogenes' assertions as mere suppositions, 108; occasionally abbreviates Scriptural quotations, 134, 136

Adv. Marc. 1.1 (292.4-10 Kr.): 102; 1.2 (292.17 ff.): 124; 1.7 (298.20): 114; 1.10 (303.9): 108; 1.15: 97; 1.29: 13; 2.1 (333.9 f.): 104; 2.2 (335.1-4): 130; 2.14: 129; 2.22 (364.23 f.): 103; 2.26 (372.21-23): 129; 4.17 (476.7 ff.): 124; 5.6 (590.25-591.1): 130; 5.9 (602.21 f.): 122; 5.14 (625.16-18): 130; 5.18

Tertullian—*continued*.
(638.23 f.): 130; *Adv. Prax.* 1: 102;
2 (229.17–20 Kr.): 102; 4 (232.10 ff.):
121; 5: 96, 137; 5 (233.3 f.): 108;
6: 133; 7 (235.19–21): 107; 7
(237.11–16): 170; 8 (238.10 f.): 132;
9 (239.19–21): 169; 10 (240.23 f.):
107; 12: 104, 168; 13 (248.3 ff.):
114; 13 (249.18–21): 104; 15
(256.5 f.): 170; 19 (261.10 f.): 130;
26 (278.25): 112; *Adv. Valent.*
1: 102; 16: 3; *Apol.* 17.4: 108; 50.13:
132; *De an.* date: 13; 2.2: 129 (*bis*);
2.3: 142; 2.5: 107; 3.3: 129; 4: 91,
150; 5.5 f.: 107; 6.1: 105, 107; 7:
116; 10: 116; 16: 97; 21: 97; 21.4:
123; 21.5: 124; 27: 146; 38.2: 103;
43.6: 149; 43.7: 130; 55: 97; *De
bapt.* 3: 146; *De carne Chr.* 8: 124;
11: 158; *De carn. res.* 6 (33.9–
11 Kr.): 170; 6 (33.24 f.): 131;
11 (40.7–9): 105; 17 (47.22 f.): 120;
19 (51.8): 137; *De idol.* 4 (33.10
R.–W.): 103; 5 (35.18): 103; *De
monog.* 16: 89, 102; *De pall.* 2.1: 142;
De praescr. haer. 21: 101; 30.12 ff.:
3; 31: 102; 33.9: 3; *De pud.* 10
(240.24 f. R.–W.): 123; 20 (268.12 f.):
123; *De spect.* 23: 103; *De test.
anim.* 2 (136.3 R.–W.): 108; *Scorp.*
2 (147.15 R.–W.): 103; 7 (159.28 ff.):
130

Theodoret, *Haer. fab. comp.* 1.19: 3, 91,
96.

Theophilus of Antioch, refuted Hermogenes, 3; probably drawn upon
by Tert. in the *Adv. Herm.*, 9–12;
Ad Autol. 2.4: 10 f.; 2.10: 10–12,
97; 2.18: 12

Theopompus, 61, 142

Thörnell, G., 111 and *passim*

tractatus, 131

traducere = *refutare*, 160

traducianism, Tertullian's, 145

transition, from *oratio obliqua* to *oratio
recta* and vice versa, 106 f.

Uhlhorn, G., 7, 89, 94, 95

Walch, C. W. F., 89

Wisdom, assisting God in the creation
of the world, 53 f.; identified with
Christ, 54

Wolfson, H., 140, 152

ANCIENT CHRISTIAN WRITERS

The Works of the Fathers in Translation

Edited by

J. QUASTEN, S.T.D., and J. C. PLUMPE, Ph.D.

1. THE EPISTLES OF ST. CLEMENT OF ROME AND ST. IGNATIUS OF ANTIOCH. Trans. by James A. Kleist, S.J., Ph.D. Pages x + 162. 1946.
2. ST. AUGUSTINE, THE FIRST CATECHETICAL INSTRUCTION. Trans. by Joseph P. Christopher, Ph.D. Pages vi + 176. 1946.
3. ST. AUGUSTINE, FAITH, HOPE, AND CHARITY. Trans. by Louis A. Arand, S.S., S.T.D. Pages vi + 165. 1947.
4. JULIANUS POMPERIUS, THE CONTEMPLATIVE LIFE. Trans. by Sr. Mary Josephine Suelzer, Ph.D. Pages vi + 220. 1947.
5. ST. AUGUSTINE, THE LORD'S SERMON ON THE MOUNT. Trans. by John J. Jepson, S.S., Ph.D. Pages vi + 227. 1948.
6. THE DIDACHE, THE EPISTLE OF BARNABAS, THE EPISTLES AND THE MARTYRDOM OF ST. POLYCARP, THE FRAGMENTS OF PAPIAS, THE EPISTLE TO DIOGNETUS. Trans. by James A. Kleist, S.J., Ph.D. Pages vi + 235. 1948.
7. ARNOBIUS, THE CASE AGAINST THE PAGANS, Vol. 1. Trans. by George E. McCracken, Ph.D. Pages vi + 372. 1949.
8. ARNOBIUS, THE CASE AGAINST THE PAGANS, Vol. 2. Trans. by George E. McCracken, Ph.D. Pages vi + 287. 1949.
9. ST. AUGUSTINE, THE GREATNESS OF THE SOUL, THE TEACHER. Trans. by Joseph M. Colleran, C.SS.R., Ph.D. Pages vi + 255. 1950.
10. ST. ATHANASIUS, THE LIFE OF SAINT ANTONY. Trans. by Robert T. Meyers, Ph.D. Pages vi + 155. 1950.
11. ST. GREGORY THE GREAT, PASTORAL CARE. Trans. by Henry Davis, S.J., B.A. Pages vi + 281. 1950.
12. ST. AUGUSTINE, AGAINST THE ACADEMICS. Trans. by John J. O'Meara, D.Phil. Pages vi + 213. 1950.
13. TERTULLIAN, TREATIES ON MARRIAGE AND REMARRIAGE: TO HIS WIFE, AN EXHORTATION TO CHASTITY, MONOGAMY. Trans. by William P. LeSaint, S.J., S.T.D. Pages viii + 194. 1951.
14. ST. PROSPER OF AQUITAINE, THE CALL OF ALL NATIONS. Trans. by P. De Letter, S.J., S.T.D. Pages vi + 234. 1952.
15. ST. AUGUSTINE, SERMONS FOR CHRISTMAS AND EPIPHANY. Trans. by Thomas C. Lawler. Pages vi + 249. 1952.
16. ST. IRENAEUS, PROOF OF THE APOSTOLIC PREACHING. Trans. by Joseph P. Smith, S.J. Pages viii + 233. 1952.
17. THE WORKS OF ST. PATRICK, ST. SECUNDINUS, HYMN ON ST. PATRICK. Trans. by Ludwig Bieler, Ph.D. Pages vi + 121. 1953.
18. ST. GREGORY OF NYSSA, THE LORD'S PRAYER, THE BEATITUDES. Trans. by Hilda C. Graef. Pages vi + 210. 1954.
19. ORIGEN, PRAYER, EXHORTATION TO MARTYRDOM. Trans. by John J. O'Meara, D.Phil. Pages viii + 253. 1954.
20. RUFINUS, A COMMENTARY ON THE APOSTLES' CREED. Trans. by J. N. D. Kelly, D.D. Pages viii + 166. 1955.
21. ST. MAXIMUS THE CONFESSOR, THE ASCETIC LIFE, THE FOUR CENTURIES ON CHARITY. Trans. by Polycarp Sherwood, O.S.B., S.T.D. Pages viii + 285. 1955.
22. ST. AUGUSTINE, THE PROBLEM OF FREE CHOICE. Trans. by Dom Mark Pontifex. Pages vi + 291. 1955.
23. ATHENAGORAS, EMBASSY FOR THE CHRISTIANS, THE RESURRECTION OF THE DEAD. Trans. by Joseph H. Crehan, S.J. Pages vi + 193. 1956.
24. TERTULLIAN, TREATISE AGAINST HERMOGENES. Trans. by J. H. Waszink. Pages vi + 178. 1956.